THE COMPLETE
ROMAN
EMPEROR

MICHAEL SOMMER

THE COMPLETE ROMAN EMPEROR

IMPERIAL LIFE AT COURT AND ON CAMPAIGN

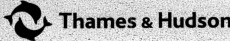

Thames & Hudson

HALF TITLE **The emperor Trajan addressing his troops. A detail from Trajan's Column, Rome, AD 113.**

TITLE PAGES **The Roman amphitheatre at Nîmes (southern France). The amphitheatre, which was capable of seating around 25,000 spectators, was built between AD 90 and 120.**

RIGHT **The Grand Camée de France, a five-layered sardonyx cameo, dating to around AD 23. In the upper panel we see the members of the Julio-Claudian family who were already deceased when the cameo was made: Augustus, with Drusus the Elder and Germanicus. In the central panel sits Tiberius, surrounded by Livia, his son Tiberius Gemellus, Drusus the Younger and Caligula. The lower panel depicts defeated barbarians.**

First published in the United Kingdom in 2010 by Thames & Hudson Ltd, 181A High Holborn, London WC1V 7QX

Copyright © 2010 Thames & Hudson Ltd, London

British Library Cataloguing-in-Publication Data
A catalogue record for this book is available from the British Library

ISBN 978-0-500-25167-6

Printed and bound in Singapore by Craft Print International Ltd.

To find out about all our publications, please visit **www.thamesandhudson.com**. There you can subscribe to our e-newsletter, browse or download our current catalogue, and buy any titles that are in print.

CONTENTS

Introduction: Imperial Lives   6

1. The Story of an Empire   12
Division into periods   12
The 1st century: in Augustus's shadow   17
The 2nd century: the apogee of power   20
The 3rd century: a kingdom of iron and rust   22
The 4th century: towards a Christian Roman empire   24
The 5th century: two Roman empires   25

2. Augustus and the Transition to Empire   26
An emperor's record   26
The assassination of Julius Caesar   28
The heir   30
Mark Antony and Octavian   31
Augustus   34
Building a dynasty   40
The principate – Augustus's legacy   42

3. Becoming Emperor   44
Educating emperors   46
Usurping power   50
AD 69   52
Senatorial careers   56
Imperial princes   58
Recusatio imperii   61
Taking office   63
An emperor's arrival   66

4. Being Emperor   70
The palace   70
Domitian's palace   75
Imperial mornings   80
At table with the emperor   82
Dinner party   85
The art of hospitality   88
The emperor and the Senate   91
The emperor as supreme judge   92
The imperial treasury   97

Managing an empire   101
Equestrian officials   105
Freedmen in the corridors of power   108
Imperial women   110
Emperors on the move   115

5. Emperors on Campaign   118
A new Alexander?   118
Trajan at Hatra   122
Commander-in-chief   124
The principate's militarization   129
Soldier emperors   131

6. Rome and Constantinople   134
Rome before the emperors   134
From brick to marble   138
Providing for the city   144
The *annona*: bread…   146
…and circuses   148
An emperor in the arena   150
Constantine and Constantinople   154
A Christian capital?   160
The second Rome   162
Emperors and bishops   165
The Apostate   167

7. Decline and Fall in the West   170
Valens at Adrianople   170
'The example of unprecedented piety'   176
Shadow emperors   178
The last emperor   180

The Roman Emperors: Brief Lives   182
Further Reading   198
Sources of Quotations   201
Sources of Illustrations   203
Index   204

IMPERIAL LIVES

What was it like to be a Roman emperor? How did the imperial system of government come into being? How was it organized, structured and maintained? Who worked for the Roman emperor and in what kinds of jobs? What did an emperor do all day long? And how did one rise to the purple in the first place? The world of the Roman empire was, in many ways, very different from our modern one, and this volume attempts to give an introduction to it from the perspective of its top representatives: the eighty-five emperors. This number includes all those who held the supreme power (and hence the title of *Augustus*) in the Roman empire, from Octavian-Augustus to Romulus Augustulus in the west and to Anastasius I – the last representative of the house of Leo – in the east. They ruled the Mediterranean world for exactly 502 years, until – in the west – imperial power finally collapsed when a sixteen-year-old emperor was deposed by one of his own generals.

From Augustus to Romulus Augustulus

The period of the emperors began with Augustus. Born Gaius Octavius, he was the adopted son of Gaius Julius Caesar, and from Caesar he inherited his name, fortune, charisma and power. Caesar was murdered in 44 BC, and Augustus learned from his mistakes. After defeating each of his rivals in turn, he created an autocracy, but a disguised one: he ruled as *princeps* ('the first one'). Nominally he was the first among equals: a senator among fellow senators. This so-called 'principate' was Augustus's legacy for future generations of emperors.

How Augustus built the empire and how he shaped the role of the Roman emperor are the topics considered in chapter 2. Each subsequent dynasty created the principate anew, but always based on the old model. The Julio-Claudians, still in the shadow of Augustus, tried to establish a working relationship with the Senate; the Flavians drew upon the military glory gained by Vespasian and Titus during the

A marble bust of Augustus wearing the civic crown (*corona civica*), a wreath of oak leaves. The civic crown was a military decoration awarded for saving a Roman citizen's life.

First Jewish Revolt; the five 'good emperors', from Nerva to Marcus Aurelius, made their credo (that the best should rule) an official policy; Septimius Severus and his house reacted to a changing environment and militarized the principate; the 'soldier emperors' from Maximinus Thrax to Carinus ruled (and almost invariably died) on campaign; Diocletian and the Tetrarchs attempted to establish a new model of joint leadership and succession; Constantine and his sons promoted Christianity; Valentinian and Theodosius tried to hold together an empire falling apart; while the nine 'shadow emperors' from Petronius Maximus to Romulus Augustulus were mere creatures of all-powerful generals, who were pulling the strings behind the scenes.

The character of each emperor's reign was itself heavily influenced by his education, upbringing and route to the top. 'Becoming emperor' (chapter 3) traces the diverse paths to power: from emperors born in the purple (Commodus and Constantius II) to those who assumed power by means of usurpation and civil war (Vespasian); from those who enjoyed a sound education in their youth (Marcus Aurelius) to those who started their careers in the army's rank and file (many of the emperors of the 3rd century).

What was 'being emperor' (chapter 4) like? Roman emperors lived in lavish palaces and enjoyed exquisite food and entertainment. Some delighted in being lords of the Roman world: they revelled in the luxury of their palaces, in the gluttony of imperial dinner parties and, above all, in the notion of unlimited power. Nero remarked that his job gave him the power to do whatever he liked; he used it to flout the unwritten behavioural code of Roman society, giving public performances as a singer, cithara player and charioteer. Commodus liked to present himself in the role of a gladiator; and, by one account, Honorius was too absorbed in his hobby of chicken farming to pay much attention to his crumbling empire.

On the other hand, many rulers regarded the imperial purple as a heavy burden and ruling the empire primarily as a service to their subjects. Marcus Aurelius was tough on himself: he allowed himself little sleep, no leisure time and hardly any food. Augustus cultivated an affable attitude towards his subjects, the senators in particular, whom he treated as equals. Many emperors, especially in the first two centuries, emulated his model and avoided airs and graces. Even a late Roman emperor like Julian, the 'Apostate', explicitly referred to Augustus when he sent home the cooks and valets of his predecessor.

How emperors performed when they were 'on campaign' was crucial to their success (chapter 5). Being emperor meant being victorious, always and without exception. For many emperors, such as Vespasian, Titus, Trajan and Septimius Severus, military glory, whether gained before accession or afterwards, formed an intrinsic part of their public image. For the soldiers, it was important that the emperor as supreme commander shared their hardship and danger. Trajan and Septimius Severus walked alongside their legionaries for hundreds of miles and many emperors did not hesitate to jump into the fray.

ABOVE **The Baths of Caracalla, built in Rome between AD 212 and 216, were designed to demonstrate the wealth and generosity of the emperor. Conceived by Septimius Severus and completed during the reign of Caracalla, the complex consisted of a public library, numerous pools and two** *palaestrae* **where wrestling was practised.**

OPPOSITE **A bust of Marcus Aurelius, the philosopher-emperor, who from his early adulthood adopted an ascetic lifestyle.**

To be sure, images of the emperor as the 'soldiers' comrade' or 'senators' friend' are exaggerations rather than accurate representations of imperial relationships. Yet projecting an image was a vital part of leadership and nowhere was this more apparent than in the two imperial capitals, Rome and Constantinople (chapter 6), which were shaped by the emperors over the course of centuries. Buildings such as the Colosseum or the lavish Baths of Caracalla and Diocletian in Rome demonstrated the rulers' generosity for all to see, while others reflected the emperors' wish to leave traces in the cityscape and to have their achievements remembered.

The protagonists of our story reveal a great deal about the empire they ruled: about its society, values and customs; about the fascinating daily life of an imperial elite and the organization of power at the empire's heart, the palace; about the ups and downs of Roman history, until its final 'decline and fall' (chapter 7); and, not least, about the power of those Romans, who, like Tacitus and Cassius Dio, wrote the history of the Roman empire for their contemporaries.

The changing face of empire

Like narratives, images have their language, too. Numerous examples of imperial imagery can be found throughout this book. Unlike the historical texts, however, the images show us how the emperors wanted to be seen. Imperial portraits, whether in sculpture, on coins or bas-relief, are in a manner of speaking official documents – paralleled in the world of texts only in Augustus's 'autobiography', the Res Gestae, and some inscriptions. Their style was often highly influential in the private sphere: Hadrian, the first emperor portrayed with a beard, turned clean-shaven men into an endangered species

and imperial women such as Agrippina and Faustina were certainly admired as fashion models and copied by the upper crust's female half.

Images reveal a lot about how an emperor saw himself. Augustus's portraits, for example the famous Prima Porta statue, generally show an ageless emperor, who emanates dignity and a quasi-religious sanctity. Images of Tiberius and Caligula are equally impersonal. Only under Claudius do individual characteristics find their way into the portrayal; the images appear less stylized and more vivid than their predecessors.

Under Nero, imperial sculpture performs a radical u-turn: it abandons Augustan classicism for good, introducing the realistic portrait of a slightly bloated young man with a sophisticated hairstyle. The realism becomes still more evident under Vespasian, who is portrayed as the personification of sobriety: unvarnished, bald and wrinkled. His bulky skull is the archetype of an Italian countryman. Under Hadrian, the realistic model is replaced with radically innovative imagery: its characteristic features are the beard and curly hair, which ever since the Hellenistic period had been the attributes not of rulers, but of philosophers. The model persisted until Septimius Severus, as a token of the emperors' philhellenism and intellectual profundity.

The busts of Caracalla mark another turning point. Short hair and a trimmed beard give the portraits a soldierly air; the inclined head is a feature copied from representations of Alexander the Great, Caracalla's great model. During the crisis-ridden 3rd century, portraits become stereotypical again, culminating in the famous group of the Tetrarchs, now in Venice: Diocletian, Maximian, Galerius and Constantius appear virtually indistinguishable from each other, the very symbol of harmony and solidarity. Under Constantine, the imperial portrait briefly returns to older styles, though with a more abstract mode of representation. The emperor's individuality further recedes during the 4th and 5th centuries: with the significant exception of Julian, the imperial portrait becomes emblematic of the ruler's divine right, not his personality. All these images of the rulers trace the development of the role of Roman emperor, showing how it evolved over the centuries.

Imperial portraiture gives us a valuable insight into the changing conceptions of what it meant to be emperor. Varying between hyper-realistic and highly stylized, each of the heads above is evidence of the way in which the emperor viewed himself, and was viewed by others.

ABOVE, FROM LEFT TO RIGHT **Hadrian, Vespasian, Caracalla and Maximian.**

OPPOSITE **The Prima Porta Augustus statue is one of the finest surviving examples of Roman sculpture. It depicts the emperor in his role as commander of the Roman army, dressed in military clothing and raising his arm as if he were addressing his troops. There are, however, elements suggesting divinity, such as his bare feet, which lead some to believe that the statue was created after the emperor's death.**

CHAPTER 1

THE STORY OF AN EMPIRE

Rome was an empire long before it was ruled by emperors. In a series of wars, the city conquered first Italy, then the entire Mediterranean. The expansion of the imperial borders in the age of the Punic Wars between Rome and Carthage (264–146 BC) prompted a severe, persistent crisis at the centre. The Roman republic and its instruments of government, which had been designed for a city-state with a limited territory, failed when faced with the task of ruling an empire.

Rome's new role as master of the Mediterranean world had social repercussions, too: the Roman republic plunged into a century of revolution (133–30 BC), from which Augustus emerged as *princeps* ('the first one'). He established the principate as a new political order, which was neither autocratic nor – overtly – monarchic, but based on a consensus between all relevant social groups. Over the centuries, however, the principate evolved into an actual monarchy, in which the old ruling class, the senators, gradually lost their importance, and new elites, mainly military professionals, ascended to power. Partly brought about by developments outside the empire, the militarization of Roman politics led to another major crisis, the 'military anarchy' of the 3rd century. The late antique empire that emerged from the crisis was, in many respects, different from the principate Augustus had established. The monarchic character of the system became fully visible, and soon Christianity became the empire's mainstream religion. In the east, the Roman empire – reduced in size, Greek in language and Orthodox in faith – survived until the conquest of Constantinople by the Ottoman Turks in 1453. In the west, it fell victim to barbarian, chiefly Germanic, invaders and a rapid process of internal decomposition.

Division into periods

Following Augustus – whose forty-year sole reign will be the subject of the next chapter – the Roman empire was ruled by eighty-five emperors, countless usurpers not included. Dividing the long history of the empire into periods is tricky.

A bronze statue of Septimius Severus in military dress. The statue was found in his home town of Lepcis Magna in the province of Africa Proconsularis (present-day Libya). Severus, a successful general and skilled administrator, emerged victorious from the crisis of AD 193.

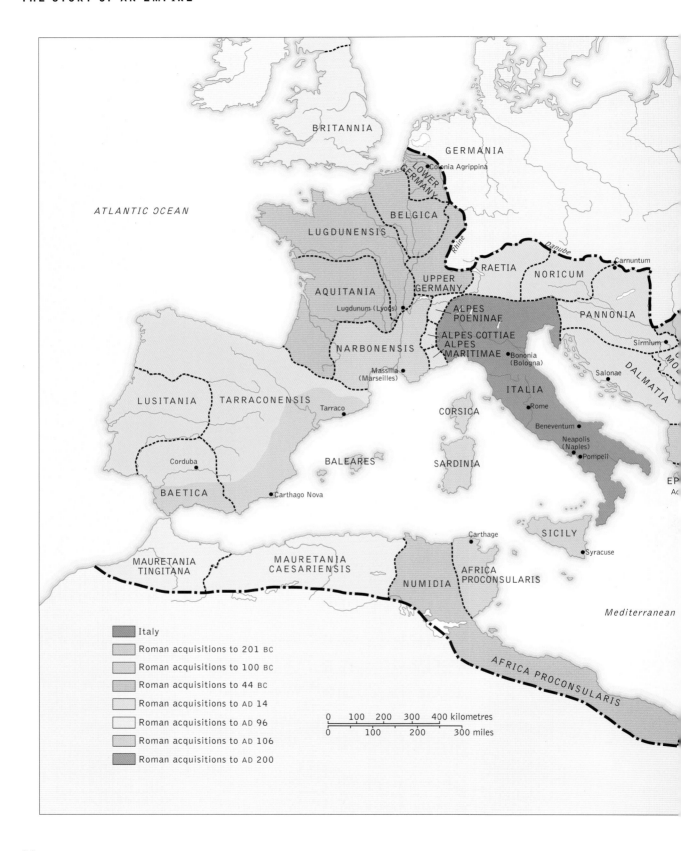

BRITANNIA

GERMANIA

ATLANTIC OCEAN

LOWER GERMANY

Colonia Agrippina

BELGICA

LUGDUNENSIS

Rhine

Danube

RAETIA

NORICUM

Carnuntum

AQUITANIA

UPPER GERMANY

ALPES POENINAE

PANNONIA

Lugdunum (Lyons)

Sirmium

ALPES COTTIAE

ALPES MARITIMAE

NARBONENSIS

Bononia (Bologna)

Salonae

DALMATIA

MO

LUSITANIA

TARRACONENSIS

Massilia (Marseilles)

ITALIA

Rome

CORSICA

Tarraco

Beneventum

Neapolis (Naples)

EP

Ac

CORDUBA

Corduba

BALEARES

SARDINIA

Pompeii

BAETICA

Carthago Nova

SICILY

Syracuse

MAURETANIA TINGITANA

MAURETANIA CAESARIENSIS

Carthage

AFRICA PROCONSULARIS

NUMIDIA

AFRICA PROCONSULARIS

Mediterranean

▨	Italy
▨	Roman acquisitions to 201 BC
▨	Roman acquisitions to 100 BC
▨	Roman acquisitions to 44 BC
▨	Roman acquisitions to AD 14
▨	Roman acquisitions to AD 96
▨	Roman acquisitions to AD 106
▨	Roman acquisitions to AD 200

```
0    100   200   300   400 kilometres
0    100       200       300 miles
```

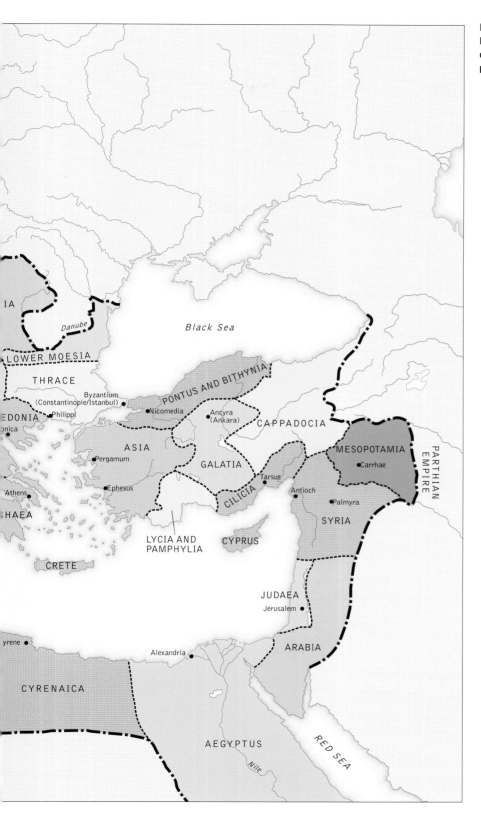

Black Sea

Danube

IA

LOWER MOESIA

THRACE

MEDONIA

onica

Philippi

Byzantium
(Constantinople/Istanbul)

Nicomedia

PONTUS AND BITHYNIA

Ancyra
(Ankara)

CAPPADOCIA

ASIA

Pergamum

GALATIA

Athens

Ephesus

HAEA

CILICIA

Tarsus

Antioch

MESOPOTAMIA

Carrhae

PARTHIAN EMPIRE

Palmyra

SYRIA

LYCIA AND
PAMPHYLIA

CYPRUS

CRETE

JUDAEA

Jerusalem

yrene

Alexandria

ARABIA

CYRENAICA

AEGYPTUS

Nile

RED SEA

Some take the dynasties as a criterion; some distinguish between a 'high' empire (roughly from Augustus to the Severans) and a 'low' empire (from AD 235 onwards); and some distinguish between the Augustan 'principate' and the much more centralized, bureaucratic and autocratic late Roman form of government, which they call 'the dominate'. Ironically, the easiest way to structure the five hundred years of the Roman empire is provided by the centuries of the common (Christian) era, even though this era was introduced only after the downfall of the Roman west (by a monk called Dionysius Exiguus, in AD 525).

The 'short' 1st century, from Tiberius to Domitian (AD 14–96), was a century of experiment: the emperors and their subjects had to find their places within the new order. Augustus was still the towering role model, emulated by most emperors of the Julio-Claudian and Flavian dynasties; but some, like Caligula and Nero, struck new paths and – disastrously – tried to revamp the job of Roman emperor.

The 2nd century, roughly from Nerva to Commodus (AD 96–192), was a period of stability and – on balance – peace. This period saw the largest territorial extension of the Roman empire and its acme of power, though the first symptoms of crisis became visible as early as the Antonine period (the reigns of Antoninus Pius and his successors, 138–192). By the 2nd century, the emperors had found their place in Roman society. A series of emperors with no sons had to adopt their successors, so adoption of the fittest became a principle of government until the century perished with Commodus, the son of Marcus Aurelius and one of the unfittest of all emperors.

The 'long' 3rd century, which began with Septimius Severus (AD 193–210) and ended with Diocletian and the first Tetrarchy (AD 284–305), was a time of crisis and transition. The Severan dynasty pushed forward the professionalization of the

Part of a relief from a triumphal arch in Lepcis Magna showing the emperor Septimius Severus, standing on a chariot and heading a triumphal procession.

Roman army, and the senators lost much of their former importance. Subsequent generations of emperors came almost exclusively from within the ranks of the army, and they had to cope with the greatest challenge the empire had faced so far: the massive onslaught of enemies on two of Rome's imperial frontiers.

During the 4th century, from Constantine to Theodosius (AD 306–395), the empire became Christian. Once again, the emperors had to find their places in a new order: they spearheaded the rise of the Christian church and became the executors of divine will on earth. After a period of regeneration, the empire witnessed a resurgence of barbarian attacks at the end of the century, and the emperors' scope of action was dramatically reduced.

The death of Theodosius in AD 395 brought about the final division of the Roman empire into two halves. The eastern empire survived the crisis, but the territorial disintegration of the Roman west was accelerated by internal rivalries and the central government's loss of authority. By 476, when the last Roman emperor in the west, Romulus Augustulus, was sent into early retirement by a Germanic general, the Roman monarchy was a mere shadow of its former self. Romulus Augustulus's departure marked (in the west) the end of an institution that had shaped the Roman world for five centuries.

The 1st century: in Augustus's shadow

Augustus had established the principate, but it was up to his successors to defend and further develop it. The inner circle of Augustus's government was represented by two families: the Julians, Augustus's own clan, and the Claudians, the family of which Livia, Augustus's wife, had become part when she married her first husband Tiberius Claudius Nero. These two families dominated Roman politics for more than half a century after Augustus's death in AD 14.

In the Julio-Claudian period, the era of Rome's great conquests had come to an end. The attempt to turn Germany into a province had failed, after three legions under the command of the general Varus were annihilated in northwestern Germany (at the battle of the Teutoburg Forest, AD 9). The subsequent campaigns of retaliation led by Germanicus, a nephew of the emperor Tiberius, turned out disastrously for Rome. Emperors after Tiberius contented themselves with marginal territorial gains in southwestern Germany: the dream of a complete annexation of Germany was over. The only major territorial acquisition Rome made in the 1st century was Britain. The island's south was conquered under Claudius in AD 43 and, in subsequent decades, the Romans subjugated the whole of England.

A Roman mask from Kalkriese, Germany. The mask was found on what was, in all likelihood, the battlefield where the Roman general Varus was defeated in AD 9. Such masks were worn by officers, on the occasion of military parades.

The empire now stretched from the Atlantic Ocean in the west to the river Euphrates in the east, from Cumbria in the northwest of Britain to the cascades of the Nile in the southwest. The 1st century was a period of consolidation. Gaul, which had been conquered by Julius Caesar, was gradually 'romanized'. So were other relatively new provinces: Spain, North Africa and the Near East. Romanization was a complex process through which the population of the Roman periphery, bit by bit, adopted Roman customs, beliefs, forms of artistic expression, technologies, styles of dress and architecture and – in the west – the Latin language. However, romanization did not result in local populations giving up their cultural identities altogether. They remained citizens of their city or members of their tribe, they continued to be Greeks or Gauls, and they became 'Roman' at the same time: loyal subjects of the emperor, who put on the toga or served in the military. A long-term consequence of romanization was that it became increasingly hard to tell what being 'Roman' actually meant.

One evidence of 'Roman-ness' was citizenship. Owing to the extension of Roman citizenship to the provincial population, more and more people were given the opportunity to shift from the camp of the defeated to that of the victors. Roman citizenship had become politically irrelevant, since the establishment of the

The Roman theatre at Lyons. The theatre in its present shape was built in the second half of the 2nd century AD. It provided seating for 10,000 people. When the theatre was originally built, around AD 15, it marked the rapid progression of romanization in Gaul after its conquest by Julius Caesar.

principate, but it was a prime means of integration in an empire becoming ever more culturally and ethnically diverse. Even so, there was anti-imperial resistance, and lots of it. Arminius, who revolted against the Roman expansion in Germany, was followed by Boudicca, a Britannic tribeswoman, who led an anti-Roman uprising in the south of England in AD 60/61. In AD 69 Gaius Julius Civilis, a Roman auxiliary commander and Batavian aristocrat (the

A relief from the Arch of Titus on the Roman Forum, built under his brother and successor Domitian in the late 1st century AD. The relief shows the triumphal procession after Titus's victory over the Jews in the First Jewish Revolt (AD 66–70). The menorah, the seven-armed candelabrum from the Temple in Jerusalem, is clearly visible.

Batavians were a tribe located in the present-day Netherlands) proclaimed a short-lived *Imperium Galliarum* and forced the legionary camp of Vetera (Xanten) to surrender.

However, all these rebellions were eclipsed by the great Jewish Revolt (AD 66–70), which was only put down after Vespasian and his son Titus marched 60,000 legionaries against Jerusalem, the capital of the insurgents. Their last stronghold, Masada, was not captured until AD 73. Palestine was a hotbed of anti-imperial resistance throughout the 1st century and well into the 2nd. Rome's troubles here were partly due to religious radicalism and sectarianism within Judaism, which made this part of the Near East virtually ungovernable. The escalation of the conflict was also undoubtedly due to chronic mismanagement on the part of the Roman governors, who were obviously ill-prepared for the job.

The Flavian dynasty that replaced the Julio-Claudians after the crisis of the year of the four emperors (AD 69, see page 52) was founded on the military success of its first two emperors, Vespasian and his son Titus, in putting down the Jewish Revolt. Despite the importance of military triumphalism in Flavian self-representation, Vespasian, Titus and his brother Domitian essentially continued the course of political consolidation: a few client kingdoms in the Near East were annexed to Roman territory, the conquest of Britain was pushed forward and the provincial elites continued to rise through the ranks of the Roman political class. By the end of the century, there were numerous Spaniards, Gauls, Africans and Greeks among the men who, at regular intervals, convened in the Senate House on the Roman Forum.

The 2nd century: the apogee of power

Once again, the failure of an emperor led to a succession crisis. Domitian was murdered in AD 96, which resulted in the short and troubled reign of Nerva. Before he died, Nerva adopted Trajan, who came from the Spanish city of Italica and was the first provincial to don the imperial purple. Trajan became the military emperor par excellence (see page 118): he conquered the kingdom of Dacia in two bloody wars, annexed the Nabataean client kingdom and launched a large-scale invasion of Parthian Mesopotamia. However, Roman rule between the Euphrates and the Tigris was soon challenged by local insurgents, and after the emperor's death in AD 117, Trajan's successor Hadrian abandoned the recently acquired territories.

Hadrian also abandoned Trajan's expansionism, switching over to a policy of containment. He fortified Rome's long frontiers on the Rhine and in Britain, where Hadrian's Wall was built. Once again, Palestine proved to be a trouble spot: the Second Jewish Revolt led by Simon Bar Kokhba (about whom we know very little)

OPPOSITE **A comparison of the average duration of emperors' reigns indicates how exceptional was the longevity of Augustus.**

BELOW **Hadrian's Wall in northern England. The wall was strengthened with forts at regular intervals. It marked the empire's northern frontier in Britain, until Antoninus Pius pushed it even further north into Scotland, where the Antonine Wall was built.**

AVERAGE DURATION OF IMPERIAL REIGNS

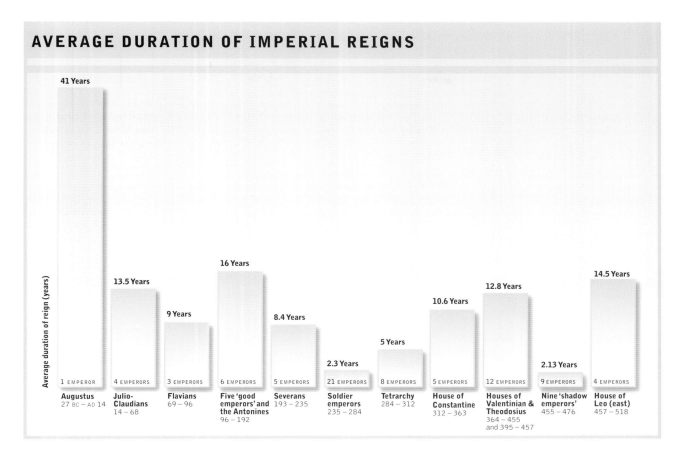

Average duration of reign (years)

41 Years	13.5 Years	9 Years	16 Years	8.4 Years	2.3 Years	5 Years	10.6 Years	12.8 Years	2.13 Years	14.5 Years
1 EMPEROR	4 EMPERORS	3 EMPERORS	6 EMPERORS	5 EMPERORS	21 EMPERORS	8 EMPERORS	5 EMPERORS	12 EMPERORS	9 EMPERORS	4 EMPERORS
Augustus 27 BC – AD 14	**Julio-Claudians** 14 – 68	**Flavians** 69 – 96	**Five 'good emperors' and the Antonines** 96 – 192	**Severans** 193 – 235	**Soldier emperors** 235 – 284	**Tetrarchy** 284 – 312	**House of Constantine** 312 – 363	**Houses of Valentinian & Theodosius** 364 – 455 and 395 – 457	**Nine 'shadow emperors'** 455 – 476	**House of Leo (east)** 457 – 518

ravaged the Levant from AD 132 to 135. Still more worrying were the incursions of several Germanic tribes, among them the Marcomanni and the Quadi, who crossed the Danube frontier into Pannonia in AD 166 and were immediately confronted by Marcus Aurelius. Fighting continued at least till 182 and cost an immense number of lives. Marcus's reign was further overshadowed by the great plague that an army had brought to the west from Mesopotamia in 165, and which killed countless people throughout the empire.

For the rest, however, the years from Hadrian's accession to the death of Marcus Aurelius were an era of peace, stability and prosperity. Early in this period, the Greek orator Dio Chrysostom ('golden mouth'), in his speech *On Wealth*, vaunted the Romans' just laws, the decency of their citizens and the moderation of their rulers. A few decades later, towards the end of the Antonine era, Dio's colleague and compatriot Aelius Aristides praised the Romans for having organized 'the whole inhabited world like a single household'.

This may be rhetorical exaggeration, but there seems to have been a universal feeling that under Hadrian, Antoninus Pius and Marcus Aurelius the Roman world was in the best of hands. From Nerva to Antoninus, no emperor had had a son, and

A *tetradrachm* coin issued by the Jewish rebels during the Bar Kokhba Revolt (AD 132–135). It shows the façade of the Temple in Jerusalem, around which the name of Bar Kokhba is written.

so adoption became, for almost ninety years, the principle of succession. Combined with an ideal of Stoicism, the rule of the wisest man, it produced an impressive series of 'good emperors' with the highest ethical standards. The period ended, however, with the reign of the erratic Commodus, whose assassination on New Year's Eve 192 prompted the third major crisis of the system of government Augustus had created.

The 3rd century: a kingdom of iron and rust

The murder of Commodus triggered a civil war, from which Septimius Severus, who was descended from a Punic family in the North African town of Lepcis Magna, emerged victorious. As emperor, he proved that he had learned the lesson of the civil war: he supported the soldiery wherever he could, giving them better pay and substantially increasing their overall numbers. Laws were designed to make a soldier's life a little more comfortable – after all, Severus owed his victory to the legions. According to Cassius Dio, Severus, on his deathbed, advised his two sons, Caracalla and Geta, to 'be at one with each other, to make the soldiers rich and not to give a damn about anybody else'. Most emperors of the 3rd century faithfully complied – at least as far as the soldiers were concerned.

The traditional elite, namely the senators, did not take to the Severan approach to politics. The historian Cassius Dio, himself a senator, complained that his own time was a 'kingdom of iron and rust' compared to the 'golden age' of Marcus Aurelius. However, the worst was still to come: in AD 224, Ardashir, a local dynast from Persia (present-day Fars, a province in southern Iran) defeated the Parthian king Artabanus IV. Two years later, he was in control of Ctesiphon, the Parthian

A scene from a Sasanian rock relief in Bishapur (Fars province in present-day Iran) that celebrates the triumph of the Sasanian king Shapur over the Roman emperors Gordian III, Philip the Arab and Valerian. Philip is kneeling before Shapur's horse; Gordian is trampled under its hooves.

Mounted Sarmatian warriors, shown on Trajan's column in Rome. The Sarmatians were a tribal confederation composed of various Iranian peoples who, in the 3rd century BC, took possession of present-day Ukraine and South Russia. Their relationship with the Roman empire was ambivalent: they repeatedly invaded Roman territory, but they were also sought-after as cavalry in the Roman auxiliary troops.

capital in Mesopotamia. A new dynasty had replaced the Arsacids, who had ruled the Parthian east for almost five hundred years, and the emerging Sasanian empire proved to be far more dynamic and expansionist than its predecessor state. Soon, Rome's eastern provinces began to feel the strain of recurrent Persian attacks, some of them advancing as far as Antioch in Syria. In 260, a Roman army commanded by the emperor Valerian was utterly routed near Carrhae in Mesopotamia, and Valerian himself was captured.

To the Persian menace was added the rising pressure from increasingly restive tribes in the *barbaricum* to the west and north of the Roman frontiers along the Rhine and the Danube. Throughout the 230s, 240s and 250s, large parts of the empire were affected by Germanic invasions. In 233 the Alamanni, a new tribal confederation in southwest Germany, crossed the Rhine and savaged Gaul and Raetia. A few years later, other tribal groups punctured the Danube frontier: the Sarmatians threatened Dacia and the Goths and Carpi invaded the provinces of Moesia on the lower Danube (present-day Bulgaria). A frontier that had previously been relatively calm – despite the odd barbarian incursion – had become a hotspot of violence and disorder.

What had happened? During the centuries after Caesar's conquest of Gaul (57–53 BC), the Germanic tribes and their leadership had undergone a series of dramatic changes. Small, ethnically compact and mostly sedentary groups had – in a long-term process – gradually evolved into large, highly mobile tribal confederations, under the strong and efficient leadership of charismatic warrior kings. These groups were held together by the fortunes of war and loyalty to the leader, rather than by ethnicity. Entire new 'tribes' – such as the 'Goths' or the 'Vandals' – could form around one leader if he was successful in winning battles and booty. These group identities, based on personal allegiance, were highly unstable and could shift within a few decades, if not years. For such groups, the Roman empire and the wealth and security it provided represented a continuous temptation. Overpopulation, a series of natural disasters and the resulting famines may also have contributed to the tense situation that replaced the century-long peace in the AD 230s.

In the subsequent decades Roman emperors confronted the same tribes over and over again. In 251, the emperor Decius was killed in an ambush, fighting Goths under their king Cniva in Lower Moesia. In 259, the year before Valerian was captured, Franks, Alamanni and other tribal groups advanced deep into Gaul, Raetia and even northern Italy. In reaction, the Gallic provinces and adjacent parts of the empire, including Britain and Spain, proclaimed their own emperor and this vast area split off from Rome for more than a decade. Postumus, the Gallic usurper, managed to stabilize the frontier and even reached a temporary settlement with Gallienus, the ruler in Rome.

Though these incursions did not result in any permanent territorial losses (the evacuation of the province of Dacia by Aurelian in 271 was a notable exception), they did inflict substantial economic damage on many provinces. Still more serious were the psychological ill effects: the Roman empire's aura of invincibility was lost for good during the troubled decades of the 3rd century. The military crisis was also interwoven with a political one, in which struggling emperors were challenged by pretenders, whom – all too often – they themselves had promoted to the highest ranks in order to fight the barbarians (see pages 131–133).

Peace and stability did not return until Diocletian came to power. He was himself a military man, but one with a vision: he formed the Tetrarchy, a council of two supreme and two subordinated rulers, thus integrating powerful allies (as well as potential rivals) into his power structure. The 'long' 3rd century ended when Diocletian, along with his colleague Maximian, abdicated of his own free will in 305.

The 4th century: towards a Christian Roman empire

Ingenious as it was, the Tetrarchy, Diocletian's creation, failed. The next generation was unwilling to give away what they regarded as their legitimate dynastic prerogatives. Once again, the empire plunged into civil war – this time for some twenty years, until Constantine the Great defeated his last rival, Licinius, at the

A marble head of the emperor Diocletian who, in AD 284, appointed his fellow-officer Maximian as co-emperor. The joint rulership was later expanded into the Tetrarchy.

battle of Chrysopolis in AD 324. By then, Constantine's legions had grown used to marching under the sign of the cross, the symbol of Christianity, of which the emperor became a fervent advocate. Under Constantine and his sons, polytheism was gradually repressed, and the Church obtained more and more privileges for itself. The empire's Christianization proved to be irreversible: an attempt to roll back history and establish a pagan 'state church' failed (see page 167). By the end of the 4th century, there were merely pockets of polytheism in an overwhelmingly Christian empire.

Under Constantine and his successors, the Roman state became not only more Christian, but also more bureaucratic and more centralized. The Tetrarchs had already begun to reform the army, the government and the system of taxation, and their successors in the 4th century continued on the same course. Provinces were split, new tiers of administration introduced and new offices, including a central court bureaucracy, established.

All this did not prevent Rome from being troubled by an increasingly competitive external environment. The emperor Julian's Persian campaign in 363 ended in catastrophic failure. Even more disastrous was Valens's defeat by the Goths at the battle of Adrianople fifteen years later (see pages 173–176). Both battles were symptomatic of the rapidly changing strategic situation. In the last quarter of the 4th century the empire, which seemed to have been restored to its old glory under Diocletian and Constantine, was under pressure once again.

TOP **The Licinius Cameo, which shows the emperor's triumph over barbarians. Licinius holds a globe in his hand, the symbol of universal power. The cameo, whose authenticity has been disputed, is now in the Louvre in Paris.**

ABOVE **Nummus coin issued by Constantine showing the Labarum, the standard with the cross.**

The 5th century: two Roman empires

In AD 395 Theodosius the Great died and the empire was, not for the first time, split in two halves, each ruled by a son of Theodosius. This time, however, the division was permanent and the two halves drifted apart at enormous speed. By the middle of the 5th century they were two loosely associated political entities, each with its own ruler, its own elite and its own political interests. Increasingly, they were also divided by religion and language.

What really distinguished them in the long term was their ultimate fate. Both empires were initially troubled by barbarian invaders and internal strife, but the east emerged stronger and more unified from the crisis, whereas the west was conquered piecemeal by the Germanic peoples who established their own kingdoms on Roman soil. The east commanded an immense economic potential, but the west was gradually deprived of its vital resources by Germanic conquest.

CHAPTER 2

AUGUSTUS AND THE TRANSITION TO EMPIRE

**When the great Julius Caesar was murdered in 44 BC, the future
emperor Augustus was just eighteen. He died at seventy-five,
which, by the standards of the time, made him as old as
Methuselah. In the roughly six decades between 44 BC and AD 14,
his career was one of the most remarkable in world history.**

His real name was Gaius Octavius, though modern scholars usually call him
Octavian. Starting as Caesar's sole heir and posthumous adoptive son, he became
a member of the second triumvirate, the military junta that ran Rome from 42 BC
onwards. After his victory over his main rival Mark Antony at the battle of Actium
in 31 BC he became sole ruler, and in 27 BC the Senate awarded him the title of
Augustus. In 2 BC he was named *pater patriae*, 'father of the country'. During his
long reign, republican Rome was gradually transformed into a monarchy, and
power was taken away from the Senate and the people and concentrated in
the hands of one man. At the same time, Rome's imperial booty – the entire
Mediterranean world stretching from the Atlantic to the river Euphrates –
evolved into an empire deserving of the name. Conquerors and conquered
alike were transformed into the emperor's subjects.

An emperor's record

In his old age, Augustus did something unprecedented: he wrote an account of the
achievements of his life (his Res Gestae). In thirty-five short chapters, the ageing
monarch painstakingly specified the ways in which Rome and its people had
benefited from his rule. Starting with the political career which had turned the
young aristocrat Octavius into, first, Julius Caesar Octavianus and then Augustus,
the sole ruler of the Roman world, the emperor goes on to describe his largesse: he
funded countless temples, public works and gladiatorial spectacles; he donated
money to all kinds of charitable purposes; he provided his soldiers and veterans
with money and land – and all out of his own pocket. Augustus then turns to his
military glory and diplomatic successes: he enumerates the far-flung countries that

he forced to accept the Roman yoke, but he wisely refrains from mentioning the disastrous battle of the Teutoburg Forest in AD 9, one of the most ignominious defeats suffered by the Roman army in its long, glorious history.

The most remarkable part of the account is the final section, which deals with the great man's role in Roman government. He describes how, on 13 January 27 BC, he abdicated from the extraordinary power he had previously held and 'handed back' the republic to the Senate and people of Rome. In return, he received various honours and the title of *Augustus*.

PREVIOUS PAGE **The Gemma Augustea, an onyx cameo of *c*. AD 9–12. The upper register shows Augustus crowned by Oikoumene, the personification of the inhabited world. Below is a Roman victory over barbarians.**

'After that time,' he concludes, 'I took precedence of all in authority, but of power I possessed no more than those who were my colleagues in any magistracy.'

Augustus, in his Res Gestae

Romans had felt uneasy about monarchic rule since the last king, a malicious Etruscan named Tarquinius Superbus, had been expelled from their city in around 500 BC. Legend has it that Lucius Junius Brutus, who had played a leading role in Tarquinius's eviction, became the Roman republic's first consul. Those events were distant history when Augustus and other noblemen were struggling for supreme power in the Roman world, but the notion of freedom inherent in the republic's foundation myth was still vital. When Julius Caesar, Augustus's great-uncle, was believed to be reaching for kingship, it cost him his life.

The assassination of Julius Caesar

In the early morning of 15 March 44 BC, Caesar felt sick, and was not inclined to attend the Senate meeting that was scheduled in the Theatre of Pompey that very morning. In addition, his wife Calpurnia had dreamed of him bleeding to death in her arms. However, when Decimus Brutus, one of the conspirators, came to Caesar's home urging him not to disappoint the senators waiting for him, he changed his mind. Towards midday he entered the meeting. The biographer Suetonius reports:

'As he took his seat, the conspirators gathered about him as if to pay their respects, and straightway Tillius Cimber, who had assumed the lead, came nearer as though to ask something; and when Caesar with a gesture put him off to another time, Cimber caught his toga by both shoulders; then as Caesar cried, "Why, this is violence!" one of the Cascas stabbed him from one side just below the throat.'

Suetonius

Stabbed twenty-three times, the dictator died. Caesar left an immense power vacuum, which resulted in immediate chaos. It soon became apparent that the conspirators had failed to make adequate plans for what should happen after the assassination. Their leaders – Marcus Junius Brutus and Gaius Cassius Longinus, two distinguished senators – had counted on the dictator's death to release the spirit of freedom on which the republic was founded, and inspire a popular uprising. Instead, the capital was paralysed with shock. The plotters' rhetoric failed to spark the broad popular movement they had hoped for; the Roman crowds remained hostile, indifferent at best. The senators, most of whom had been totally unsuspecting, rushed home, and so did Mark Antony, Caesar's colleague in the consulship and his most loyal henchman. A formidable adversary had escaped, and the conspirators had no plan, no money and – above all – no army.

Mark Antony had all three. He energetically forged an ad hoc coalition of Caesar's former followers, seized the dictator's money and mobilized an army that was encamped near Rome. Two days after the murder, he convoked the Senate and negotiated a compromise: the assassins were given amnesty, but Caesar's laws and provisions, his *acta*, continued to be effective. Caesar had bequeathed every Roman citizen the sum of 300 *sestertii*, half the annual pay of a legionary. When Mark Antony publicly announced the will, tumult broke out. The crowd seized Caesar's corpse and burned it on a pyre while lamenting and cursing the murderers. Brutus, Cassius and their co-conspirators had to flee Rome and took refuge in Italian towns.

ABOVE *Morte di Cesare* ('Death of Caesar'), an oil painting by Vincenzo Camuccini (1771–1844). Caesar (in the yellow tunic), is stabbed by the conspirators led by Cassius and Brutus.

OPPOSITE A marble bust of the young Octavian, now in the Capitoline Museum in Rome.

BELOW A carnelian gem depicting Mark Antony.

The heir

Mark Antony's position in Rome was unchallengeable – or so it seemed. In April 44 BC, he left the capital to supervise the assignment of land to Caesar's veterans in the region of Campania. A smooth settlement of this delicate issue would undoubtedly improve his standing with the military, an important asset in the struggle that was looming.

Meanwhile, a young man landed near the small Apulian town of Lupiae (Lecce). His name was Gaius Octavius (Octavian), and he was the great-nephew of Julius Caesar. The eighteen-year-old had spent some time in Apollonia, in present-day Albania, where he was supposed to meet the army Caesar had assembled for his Parthian war – a campaign in the east the dictator was preparing when he was murdered. Instead of Octavian joining the army, the army joined him as soon as he reached Italian soil. Furthermore, the youth received Caesar's war chest. When he marched northward through Italy, towards Rome, Caesar's veterans hailed him, urging him to take revenge for their leader's death.

Why was this? Caesar, in his will, had posthumously adopted his great-nephew. This made the youth his heir to the full extent: he not only inherited the dictator's substantial financial means, but also came into his social relationships. Like any Roman senator, Caesar had left his network of friends (*amici*) and clients (*clientes*) to his heir. In Rome, friendship (*amicitia*) and *patrocinium*, the relationship between a client and his patron (*patronus*), implied more than emotional ties. They were bonds of mutual solidarity, which had a very practical force. A *patronus* was required to help his *clientes* under all circumstances; and in turn, the clients had to support their patron when necessary. So it was only natural that the soldiers and veterans who had gone through thick and thin with the great Caesar should now project all their hopes onto his adoptive son.

The young man was entirely aware of the power that control of a large army gave him. However, he also made overtures to the representatives of the old senatorial elite: when he reached Naples, he met Cicero, one of the leading figures in the Senate. In early May he reached Rome, where the crowds of veterans and Caesar's former supporters received him enthusiastically. A clash with Mark Antony was now inevitable: the first

Fragment of an equestrian bronze statue of Augustus, from *c.* 10 BC. It once had inlaid eyes, made of a white stone or ivory. The statue was recovered from an underwater site in Greece.

Aureus coin with a portrait of Marcus Lepidus, the triumvir. It was issued by the mint master Mussidius Longus in 42 BC. The reverse shows a cornucopia, the symbol of wealth.

issue between them was Caesar's will. When Mark Antony refused to hand over the money that Caesar had bequeathed to the citizens, Octavian started to pay it himself. In July he also sponsored lavish games in the deceased's honour. By October 44 BC the Caesarian party was divided, with open hostility between Octavian, who now called himself Gaius Julius Caesar after his adoptive father, and Mark Antony.

Mark Antony and Octavian

Mark Antony and Octavian were not foes for long. After Caesar's adoptive son had won a victory over Antony at Modena (March 43 BC), both sides returned to the negotiating table. There, Lepidus, one of Caesar's most fervent former supporters, mediated a new settlement. The three of them struck a deal to divide the Roman empire among themselves: a new alliance, the so-called Second Triumvirate, was forged in early November 43 BC. Lepidus received the west, Mark Antony the east, and what remained – Italy – was young Octavian's prize. They had divided up the Roman world, but first they had to conquer it.

Now was the time to settle old scores. The triumvirs had 300 senators and 2,000 members of the equestrian order proscribed. Among the first victims was Cicero, whose escape ended near his estate at Formiae on the coast of Latium. The great orator and distinguished senator was captured and beheaded by Antony's men before he could embark for Greece, where Brutus and Cassius, the murderers of Caesar, had assembled a large army. At their command were the substantial economic resources of the Roman empire's eastern half. The triumvirs landed their army in Dyrrhachium, in present-day Albania, from where they proceeded eastward, into Macedonia. There, near the town of Philippi, Brutus and Cassius were defeated in two battles.

On the battlefield, Brutus and Cassius committed suicide. The almost century-long struggle between supporters of the old republic, and those who had denounced the consensus upon which it had once rested, had come to an end. Some enemies were still fighting in various parts of the Mediterranean – most notably Sextus Pompey, Gnaeus Pompey's son – but on the whole the triumvirs were the Roman world's undisputed lords. Octavian had the most delicate task of the three: he had to settle nearly 100,000 veterans on Italian soil, a job that inevitably cost him the sympathies of those who lost their landed property to the veterans. No fewer than eighteen Italian towns were dispossessed of their territories. At the same time, some of the veterans (especially those who had previously served under Caesar) fretted about being deprived of their fair share. Lucius Antonius, Mark Antony's brother and the consul of the year 41 BC, stirred up their rage against Octavian: Italy plunged into new civil war.

The situation soon escalated. Lucius Antonius courted the old senatorial elite and openly declared Octavian and Lepidus *hostes* (enemies) of the state. Octavian surrounded and besieged the consul and his army in the town of Perusia (Perugia). In the unfolding Perusian War, Mark Antony remained neutral, even though he was Lucius's brother. In February 40 BC, Lucius Antonius had to surrender. Octavian spared Lucius and his soldiers, but he had Perusia razed and executed its dignitaries, along with hundreds of his enemies who had taken refuge in the town.

The veterans and Lucius Antonius were not Octavian's only concerns. Sextus Pompey, who had escaped to Sicily after his defeat in the battle at Munda in 45 BC, had converted the island into a stronghold and now controlled the Tyrrhenian Sea with his powerful navy. He threatened to cut off Rome from the North African grain supply that was so vital to feed the capital's growing population. Now, in the crisis resulting from the Perusian War, an alliance between Pompey's son and Mark Antony seemed imminent. The eastern triumvir adjourned his campaign against the Parthians and had his troops landed near Octavian's naval base Brundisium, which he besieged. However, the soldiers refused to fight each other, and Octavian and Mark Antony were forced to settle their differences. The triumvirate was revived, but now Lepidus, who was paid off with North Africa, was clearly the weakest of the three.

The Roman world remained divided for one more turbulent decade. Lepidus was soon to be pushed aside altogether, the relationship between Octavian and Mark Antony worsened gradually and the war against Sextus Pompey gained momentum. Octavian, in return for protection of the grain supply, had ceded Sicily, Corsica and Sardinia to Sextus Pompey in the Pact of Misenum (39 BC), but the peace was short-lived. The naval battle of Cumae (38 BC) ended inconclusively, but in the next year Antony made his fleet available to Octavian, whose admiral Marcus Agrippa won two decisive victories over Pompey at Mylae and Naulochus (36 BC). Only a few months later, Mark Antony had Pompey executed at Miletus (35 BC). Lepidus, whom

OPPOSITE **Queen Cleopatra VII. She is depicted in reliefs as a traditional Egyptian queen, but she was Greek: her dynasty was descended from Ptolemy, one of Alexander the Great's generals.**

BELOW **Plan of the naval battle of Actium, which took place on 2 September 31 BC off the coast of northwestern Greece. Antony and Cleopatra's fleet was decisively defeated.**

Octavian accused of collaboration with Pompey, was now ousted for good.

Meanwhile, the triumvir of the east had opened his campaign against the Parthians. Though he won a number of battles and advanced into the Parthian territories of Armenia and Media, he finally had to withdraw after heavy losses (38–32 BC). Despite his marriage to Octavia, Octavian's sister, in 36 BC Antony married the Ptolemaic queen of Egypt, Cleopatra, to whom he ceded Roman territories in Cyprus, Syria, Phoenicia and Asia Minor. Shortly after, he sent his divorce letter to Rome, where Octavia had remained with her brother.

Open conflict between the two triumvirs was now inevitable and Octavian soon declared war, blaming Mark Antony for surrendering the eastern provinces to his wife, an oriental queen. Both rulers made the populations of their respective spheres of power swear oaths of loyalty, and Octavian expelled Antony's substantial number of remaining followers in the Senate. On 2 September 31 BC, two Roman fleets clashed off the mainland of western Greece, near Actium: Agrippa won a decisive victory over Antony and Cleopatra, who escaped to Alexandria. Octavian conquered the Egyptian capital a year later. Antony and Cleopatra both committed suicide, and Egypt was annexed as a province of the Roman empire, whose sole ruler was now Octavian.

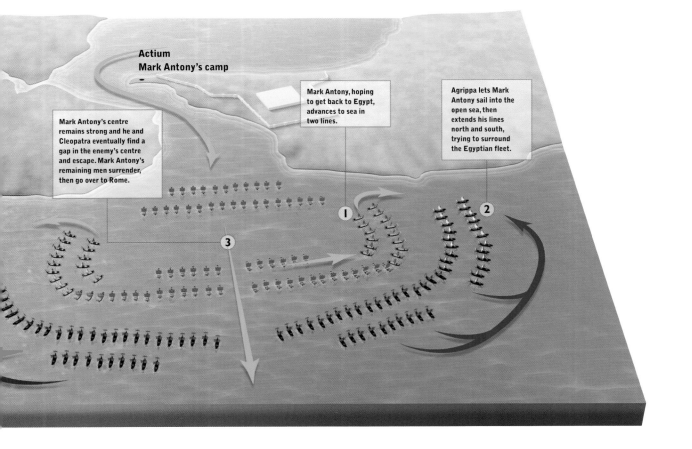

Actium
Mark Antony's camp

Mark Antony, hoping to get back to Egypt, advances to sea in two lines.

Agrippa lets Mark Antony sail into the open sea, then extends his lines north and south, trying to surround the Egyptian fleet.

Mark Antony's centre remains strong and he and Cleopatra eventually find a gap in the enemy's centre and escape. Mark Antony's remaining men surrender, then go over to Rome.

AUGUSTUS **AND OTHER IMPERIAL TITLES**

The Latin word augustus, **meaning 'the illustrious one', 'the sublime one', shares the same root as the Latin verb** augere: **'to enhance', 'to increase'. The Senate awarded the honorific title to Octavian on 16 January 27 BC. Lucius Munacius Plancus, a distinguished senator, who had been an ally of first Caesar, then Mark Antony and finally Octavian, made the proposal. Octavian made 'Augustus' a part of his name: henceforth he called himself** Imperator Caesar Augustus. **The title was the true split between the republic and the new model of government: it encompassed the principate's charismatic and quasi-sacred character, which was based on Augustus's personal authority.**

Augustus also made *Imperator* an integral part of the emperor's name. In the republic, an *Imperator* had been the holder of a military command (an *imperium*). Augustus's successor Tiberius did not accept the name from the Senate, nor did he inherit it from his predecessor. Yet he used it on coins. From Caligula onwards, all emperors used *Augustus* as a title, usually in combination with *Imperator*. Galba was the first emperor who awarded the title of *Caesar* to his designated successor. From the 2nd century onward *Caesar* became the title of the heirs apparent only.

Until AD 161, there was only one *Augustus* in the empire. Marcus Aurelius, upon his own accession, appointed his cousin Lucius Verus *Augustus*. Formally, therefore, the younger man became almost equal; in fact, Verus remained a junior partner throughout the reign, partly owing to his lack of qualifications, but also because he had received the purple from the hands of his cousin. Valerian appointed his son Gallienus *Augustus* in 253; his sphere of action was the west, whereas Valerian operated in the east. Again, Gallienus was clearly junior: only his father held the title *pontifex maximus*, the supreme priesthood.

In AD 285 Diocletian appointed Maximian first *Caesar* and, a year later, *Augustus*. Maximian was the first to be provided with his own palace and staff. Though Diocletian remained the senior *Augustus* (as is confirmed by his epithet *Iovius*, 'Jupiter-like', whereas Maximian was only *Herculius*), this model came closer to a joint rulership than any of the preceding arrangements. When Galerius and Constantius I were appointed as sub-emperors, they each received the title of *Caesar*. After this, for much of the period until the reign of Julian (361–363) there was more

Augustus

Having outcompeted his rivals one by one, Octavian was now by far the most powerful man in the Roman empire, but his position rested on arms. He was basically a military dictator with almost unlimited power. Yet Caesar's example had shown where this could lead: Rome's senatorial class might have been battered by civil war, but it was still determined not to allow monarchy to gain a foothold in Rome. Following his victory at Actium, Octavian served as consul year by year, but this was only an interim solution.

What Octavian needed was a lasting arrangement with Rome's senatorial aristocracy. In order to achieve it, he made a surprising move: on 13 January 27 BC, he appeared before the Senate and announced his immediate abdication of all the extraordinary powers the triumvirs had accumulated. In turn for having thus 'restored' the republic, he received from the Senate the *imperium proconsulare* – the authority of those former supreme magistrates who had commanded the armies in than one *Augustus*, but usually one of them claimed primacy: Galerius (305–311), Maximinus Daia (311–312), Constantine (312–325), Constantine II (337–340), Constantius II (340–350). After having been appointed *Augustus* by his brother Valentinian I (364–375), Valens (364–378), became the first truly equal co-emperor. From this time onwards, the presence in the empire of two equal *Augusti* became normal – the final division of 395 was thus anticipated.

On inscriptions and coins, emperors appear keen to list their numerous titles, of which *Augustus* is only one component. Usually, the full name begins with IMP(erator) CAES(ar); it continues with the emperor's personal names, for instance T(itus). If the emperor was adopted, the first name was followed by the family names of the adoptive father: AELIVS HARDRIANVS – ANTONINVS PIVS. Then come magistracies and offices: PROCONSVL, PONT(ifex) MAX(imus), the number of consulships (e.g. CO(n)S(ul) IV) and awards of the powers of a plebeian tribune (TRIB(unicia) POT(estas) III. The list ends with various triumphal and honorific acclamations: GERMANICVS DACICVS.

This, then, was the full name and titles of the emperor Antoninus Pius in AD 158: IMPERATOR CAESAR TITUS AELIUS HADRIANUS ANTONINUS PIUS PROCONSUL PONTIFEX MAXIMUS CONSUL IV TRIBUNICIA POTESTAS III GERMANICUS DACICUS.

An inscription of AD 160 honouring the emperor Marcus Aurelius and listing his full names and titles.

the provinces. The highly militarized frontier provinces were no longer governed by proconsuls, but by *legati* (envoys) who were appointed by Octavian from the senatorial order. Without holding any formal office, the victor of Actium could control the army, the pivotal instrument of power in Roman politics.

Three days after this act of state, the Senate conferred the title of *Augustus* on Octavian. As visible expressions of the honour he received two laurel trees, which flanked the gates of his house, and a 'shield of virtue' (*clipeus virtutis*), which was fixed above his door. His full title was now *Imperator Caesar divi filius Augustus*. Augustus preferred the term *princeps* ('the first one') to describe his position, in order to express his precedence over his – in principle equal – fellow senators. The system that the ceremony inaugurated deliberately avoided any appearance of monarchy. It was based on the senators' acceptance of the *princeps*, which in turn was due to his termination of a civil war that had lasted, with interruptions, for more than a century.

Silver *denarius* of Augustus. The reverse shows the two laurel trees honouring the emperor.

The energies and resources previously absorbed by civil war were soon to be redirected to the fringes of the Roman world. Roman legions overpowered rebellions in Gaul (29 BC) and Thrace (29–28 BC). They completed, under the command of Agrippa, the so far inchoate conquest of the Iberian Peninsula (from 27 BC onwards), annexed the North African kingdom of Numidia (26 BC) and reached the southern tip of the Arabian Peninsula, modern Yemen (24 BC). Finally, they forced into submission the rebellious tribes inhabiting the Alps (15 BC) and the plains of present-day Hungary (13 BC). In response to incursions by Germanic tribes into the provinces of Gaul, a Roman army, led by Augustus's stepson Drusus, invaded Germany (12 BC), thus preparing the vast area between the Rhine and the Elbe for annexation as a new province. The peoples living at the empire's edge discovered that 'peace' with the Romans meant submission. In his biography of Agricola, Tacitus records a British chief's complaint:

> To ravage, to slaughter, to usurp under false titles, they call empire; and where they make a desert, they call it peace.

Detail from the Tropaeum Alpium, built in 7/6 BC to commemorate the victories of Tiberius and Drusus over the tribes of the Alps in 15 BC. Weapons hanging from a tree trunk are arranged to form a *tropaeum*, a temporary victory monument put up by Greeks and Romans after a successful battle. At its foot are the (female and male) personifications of conquered tribes.

The twofold peace that Augustus brought to Rome's empire and its foes became the focal point of his self-representation as a ruler. Following the battle of Actium, the gates of the Temple of Janus were closed for the first time since the end of the First Punic War (241 BC). This rare ritual symbolically marked the complete silence of arms in the Roman world. In 17 BC, the emperor inaugurated a new age (*saeculum*) of peace and prosperity. In the republic, Saecular Games had been a religious ritual held at intervals of roughly 100 years, but now they received a completely different meaning. When the Pax Augusta ('Augustan Peace') was announced in 17 BC, it meant that an unhappy past of civil strife and exterior threat had finally come to an end.

‘Faith, Honour, ancient Modesty, And Peace, and Virtue, spite of scorn, Come back to earth; and Plenty, see, With teeming horn’

Horace (Augustus's favourite poet)

EMPEROR WORSHIP

After Julius Caesar's final victory over the allies of Pompey at Thapsus (6 April 46 BC), Cassius Dio states that the Senate decreed, among other honours, 'that his statue in bronze should be mounted upon a likeness of the inhabited world, with an inscription to the effect that he was a demigod'. Two years later, the dictator was dead, murdered by members of the very Senate that had declared him a 'demigod'.

The incident taught Octavian, Caesar's adoptive son, that divine honours for a living ruler were a delicate matter. Caesar, the demigod, became a fully fledged god after his death: in 42 BC the Senate decreed his deification, thus making Octavian *Divi filius* ('the son of the deified'). Octavian-Augustus and all his successors abstained from being worshipped as Roman state gods – as long as they were alive. After their deaths, 'good' emperors were deified. Usually, rulers who had been able to arrange for their succession in their lifetime had a realistic chance of becoming Roman state gods once they had passed away. Augustus, Claudius, Vespasian, Titus, Trajan, Hadrian, Antoninus Pius, Marcus Aurelius and Septimius Severus were all deified after their deaths. Deceased emperors had their own cults, sanctuaries and priests, the *Sodales Augustales*.

Though living emperors were not worshipped as state gods, they could be the objects of private worship. In Rome, the *Lares Augusti*, Augustus's ancestral gods, had their cults along with the *Genius Augusti*, the divine nature manifest in his person. In the provinces, especially in the Greek-speaking east, where ruler worship had a long-standing tradition, ruling emperors were publicly worshipped, in cults organized on a provincial level. Nothing like this ever happened in Italy.

Did the worshippers genuinely believe in the emperor's divinity? Evidently, he was human; but the concept of divinity in Roman religion differed sharply from those of the modern, mostly monotheistic world religions. For a Roman, it was perfectly legitimate to credit with divine honours someone who stood socially above himself: the master for the slave; the commander for the soldiers; the emperor for his subjects. Divinity was a relative, not an absolute, category.

In the 3rd century AD, the worship of the deceased emperors rapidly declined. The living rulers, however, began to associate themselves with particular deities: Elagabalus styled himself as emperor-priest of the sun god from Emesa in Syria; later, Aurelian propagated the cult of Sol Invictus, another sun deity, who was declared *conservator Augusti* ('preserver of the emperor'); and Diocletian and Maximian attached themselves to Jupiter and Hercules respectively. This did not make the emperor himself a divine being, but his rule was now closely associated with a specific deity. In visual representations, emperors now appeared adorned with a nimbus. With the empire's Christianization, divinity was replaced by divine right: emperor worship ceased for good in the 4th century, but the Christian emperors inherited their pagan predecessors' divine aura.

Detail from an agate and sardonyx cameo, probably depicting the apotheosis of the emperor Claudius.

Four years later, in 13 BC, the Senate promised to build an altar for the goddess of peace (Ara Pacis), which was completed in 9 BC. The reliefs of its main frieze show a procession of Roman dignitaries led by Augustus and Agrippa. The themes of the frieze include not only *pax* (peace) but *concordia* ('harmony'), *pietas* ('sense of duty'), *humanitas* ('decency'), and *copia* ('wealth'). Built in the Campus Martius, the capital's northern neighbourhood, the Ara Pacis became the epicentre of a whole new urban topography entirely dedicated to Augustus and his glory. At noon on 23 September, the *princeps*'s birthday, the shadow cast by a large obelisk, carried to Rome from the Egyptian city of Heliopolis and still to be seen in Piazza Colonna in front of the Italian Parliament, pointed to the altar's centre. The obelisk was the hand of a colossal sundial. In the evening of the same day in September, the shadow reached another pivotal building: the ruler's mausoleum, built in 29 BC as a massive rotunda with a diameter of 90 m (295 ft), crowned by a tumulus. Rome could rest easy; the *princeps*, who at the moment of his death in AD 9 became the god *divus Augustus*, was watching over his city and her empire.

The Ara Pacis Augustae, viewed from the southeast. The panels to either side of the main entrance depict Roma (left) and another female personification, probably Tellus, mother earth (right).

ABOVE **A detail of the southern frieze of the Ara Pacis Augustae. The frieze depicts a religious procession, in which the entire imperial family takes part. In the foreground is Agrippa (with veiled head, left), followed by his son Gaius Caesar, his wife Julia (Augustus's daughter), Tiberius, Antonia the Younger (Drusus's wife), young Germanicus and Drusus.**

RIGHT **Panel from the Ara Pacis showing Tellus, embodying wealth and abundance.**

Building a dynasty

When Augustus became sole ruler, he was just over thirty years old. Nonetheless, he began to plan for the time after his death, building his mausoleum in 29 BC. At about the same time, the *princeps* was beginning to ponder who should be his heir. That there should be a successor was, at least in the early days of his rule, by no means taken for granted. Augustus's rule was based on his personal authority, which was derived largely from the peace he had brought to a war-stricken empire. His powers consisted in a package of republican authorities, conferred on him by the Senate. The principate was not an 'office', certainly not that of a monarch who could simply hand down his royal prerogatives to the next in line.

And yet Augustus began to build a dynasty almost from the moment he achieved sole power. His only daughter, Julia, born in 39 BC, was destined to become the lynchpin of his dynastic planning. In 25 BC, Julia was married to Gaius Claudius Marcellus, Augustus's seventeen-year-old nephew. Soon, Marcellus began to climb the *cursus honorum*, the hierarchy of senatorial magistracies. However, in 23 BC, the *princeps* fell seriously ill and the man to whom he handed over his signet ring was not Marcellus, but Agrippa, his brother-in-arms since the early days. Augustus recovered, but Marcellus unexpectedly died a few months later. Julia, his widow, was now married to Agrippa, whose position as second-in-command was thus confirmed. In the next few years, Julia gave birth to five children: Gaius, Julia, Lucius, Agrippina and Agrippa, who was born after his father's sudden death in 12 BC and therefore called Postumus.

Augustus's hopes for dynastic continuity now rested on Gaius and Lucius. He adopted his two grandsons in 17 BC, the year of the Saecular Games. By then his reign had lasted long enough to make a return to republican government impossible. Everybody, even his former opponents in the Senate, had got used to the rule of one man, and the peace and stability it meant for Rome. However, Gaius and Lucius, who henceforth bore the name 'Caesar', were still too young to rule should Augustus unexpectedly die. An interim candidate was needed, a role for which Tiberius, Augustus's stepson from his third wife Livia, seemed the perfect candidate.

Tiberius, born in 42 BC, was the son of Livia's first husband Tiberius Claudius Nero, an old ally of the murderers of Caesar. Livia had divorced him in order to marry Augustus in 38 BC. Tiberius and his younger brother, Drusus, both became acclaimed military commanders who won victories in Germany, the Alps and Pannonia. Drusus died in 9 BC, but Tiberius gradually ascended to the role of emperor-in-waiting. He assumed his first consulship in 13 BC, was married to the barely widowed Julia (12 BC) and received the *tribunicia potestas* (6 BC), which gave him the power to intervene against any magistrate's decision. In 7 BC, Tiberius celebrated a magnificent triumph for his victory over the Germanic tribes.

Still, Augustus made it clear to his stepson that he was no more than a placeholder for Gaius and Lucius Caesar. Gaius was declared *princeps iuventutis* ('the first of the young') and designated for the consulship of the year AD 1 in 4 BC. He also married Livilla, Drusus's daughter. Tiberius was unable to bear the affront: in the year before Gaius reached adulthood and put on the *toga virilis*, the white garment worn by Roman men, he left Rome and took refuge on the island of Rhodes, in the Aegean. There, he dedicated himself to philosophical studies. Tiberius's departure triggered a major crisis of the principate. In 2 BC, Augustus forced his daughter Julia, Tiberius's wife, into exile on the tiny island of Pandateria, off the coast of Latium. We can only speculate as to his reasons – the official version was Julia's alleged promiscuity – but the incident made clear Tiberius's complete loss of power at court. Though he repeatedly intervened on his wife's behalf, Augustus was relentless: Julia, whom Tiberius later divorced, spent the rest of her miserable life on the island.

Meanwhile, in 2 BC, Gaius Caesar received a supreme command in the oriental provinces, where he displayed some diplomatic skill and negotiated a peace with the Parthians. In AD 1, he became consul. However, Augustus's plan to prepare Gaius and Lucius for succession was doomed to failure. Lucius died in AD 2 at the age of nineteen, and Gaius just eighteen months later, at twenty-four. Augustus was sixty-five years old and desperately needed an heir. The only remaining candidate was Tiberius, whose return to Rome Augustus had permitted, at Livia's request, in AD 1, after seven years of exile. Now, after the death of

LEFT **A marble bust of Julia, daughter of Augustus. It was her fate to be a pawn in her father's dynastic planning.**

BELOW **This marble portrait of Augustus's friend Marcus Agrippa (*c.* 25 BC) was found at Gabii near Rome and is now in the Louvre.**

Gaius Caesar, Augustus adopted his forty-five-year-old stepson, who in turn adopted Germanicus, the son of his brother Drusus. A dynasty was created at last: when Augustus died, in AD 14, Tiberius's succession was undisputed. His own offspring, the Julians, and Livia's descendants, the Claudians, were to rule Rome till AD 68, when Nero, Augustus's great-grandson, was forced to stab himself.

The principate – Augustus's legacy

Augustus provided the, in a sense unequalled, role model for all future emperors. The form of government he created, the principate, was customized for him, his personal authority and the specific historical circumstances in which he had assumed power. When Octavian 'restored' the republic in 27 BC and was subsequently invested as *Augustus* by the senators, the time was ripe for a new consensus: everybody agreed that the traditional elite, Rome's senatorial aristocracy, was incapable of governing the empire. There was no alternative to Augustus and to monarchic government, but nobody wanted to admit that the republic had ceased to exist and that the new order was in fact a monarchy.

Sardonyx cameo of the emperor Tiberius, who eventually succeeded Augustus.

The principate might have been only a short episode, had it not been for Augustus's exceptional longevity. When he died, the system he had established had firmly taken root. However, the fact that the principate was tailored for Augustus put a considerable strain on his successors. Unlike any other monarchy, the Roman emperorship was not an office that could be held and passed on to a successor. What could be handed down were titles, powers (such as the *imperium proconsulare*) and assets. To a certain degree, the soldiers' and the people's loyalty was hereditary, too; but authority, charisma and the acceptance that Augustus's personal qualities had commanded had to be achieved by every emperor anew.

In the eyes of a critical observer like Tacitus, Augustus's shoes were too big for any of his successors to fill. Invariably, the historian describes Tiberius, Caligula, Claudius and Nero as bloodthirsty tyrants, degenerate morons and inept weaklings, hypocritical and morally corrupt. Judged impartially, some of these emperors performed better, some worse. The architecture of the principate provided only a framework, which had to be filled by each individual emperor's personality and skills. This was, as Aloys Winterling put it in his recent biography of Caligula, 'an unsecured exchange note on the future'. Half a century after Augustus's death, the crisis of the 'year of the four emperors' (AD 69) revealed the structural flaws within his design (see page 52).

On the other hand, the principate's vague outlines prevented it from fossilizing. As a form of government, it could easily keep up with social change: when, from the 2nd century onwards, the military replaced the senatorial aristocracy as the political order's main pillar, the principate automatically assumed a more warlike and more autocratic aspect. The charade that had distinguished the first two centuries of Roman imperial history was now over.

'You will enjoy fully the reality of the kingship without the odium which attaches to the name of "king"', says Maecenas, Augustus's old friend, in a speech Cassius Dio has him give before the emperor, who has recently assumed office.

> **'You should yourself, in consultation with the best men, enact all the appropriate laws, without the possibility of any opposition or remonstrance to these laws on the part of any one from the masses.'**
>
> Maecenas addresses Augustus
> (reported by Cassius Dio)

Quite obviously, Maecenas's words are an anachronism: they reflect the Roman monarchy of the 3rd century AD rather than that of the 1st century BC, the Severan rather than the Augustan principate. They also reflect the system's mutability, which enabled it to survive several centuries and countless historical vicissitudes.

CHAPTER 3

BECOMING EMPEROR

There was no single career path leading to imperial power. Normally, an emperor's son was expected to succeed his father. The dynastic principle was weak, however, and there were stronger factors: Nero was preferred to Claudius's son Britannicus because his mother intervened for him. Very few emperors inherited power from their fathers and the first one who did – Commodus, the son of Marcus Aurelius – was a miserable failure. Emperors took possession of the purple in diverse ways: as rightful heirs, as legacy hunters or as usurpers.

In order to succeed, would-be emperors needed distinct qualities. In the first place, they had to be of noble birth, senators. The first Roman emperor to come from the second class of the Roman imperial elite, the equestrian order, was Macrinus in AD 217, and he ruled for only fourteen months. For a long time, emperors came from Italy; Augustus's family originated from Velitrae in the capital's immediate hinterland. The Flavians had their origins in Sabina in Latium. Claudius was the first emperor to be born in a province, at Lugdunum (Lyons) in Gaul. Trajan was the first Roman ruler whose family had been resident outside Italy for several generations; they came from the Spanish town Italica, a colony of Roman veterans. All these emperors spoke Latin as their mother tongue. The first to grow up speaking another language was Septimius Severus, at the end of the 2nd century, who as a child had spoken Punic, the language of ancient Carthage. Still more exotic was Philip the Arab, who came from the province of Arabia, present-day Jordan.

Good leadership and the ability to communicate with the main social pressure groups of Rome – the Senate, the army and the urban *plebs* – were absolute requirements. Military skills were important, but not indispensable: Augustus was not much of a general and Claudius never personally led an army. Education was useful, though too much focus on the arts was not. The emperor who, like Nero, wanted chiefly to be a poet and a musician could not fulfil his imperial role.

Head of a bronze statue of Macrinus, the first emperor to come from the equestrian order. The statue dates from *c.* AD 217 and its realism marks the renunciation of the idealized sculptural depictions of the Antonine and Severan periods.

PLACES OF BIRTH OF THE EMPERORS

Dynasty	Rome	Italy outside Rome	Gaul/ Germany	Britain	Spain	Balkans	North Africa	Egypt	Asia Minor	Near East	Unknown	Total
The Julio-Claudians and the civil war 27 BC – AD 68	2	5	1									8
The Flavians 69 – 96	2	1										3
The five 'good emperors' and the Antonines 69 – 192	1	4			2							7
Crisis of 193 and Severan dynasty 193 – 235		2	1				2			2		7
Soldier emperors 235 – 284	1	2	1			6	1		2	1	7	21
Tetrarchs 284 – 312						7				1		8
House of Constantine 312 – 363		1				4					1	6
Houses of Valentinian and Theodosius 364 – 455/364 – 457		1	1		2	6					2	12
Nine 'shadow emperors' 455 – 476	3	1	1			2					2	9
House of Leo 457 – 518					3		1					4

Educating emperors

Hardly any Roman emperors were born in the purple. Before Constantius II (337–361), the son of Constantine the Great, only two were born to ruling emperors: Vespasian's son Titus (79–81) and Commodus (180–192), son of Marcus Aurelius. Even in longer-ruling dynasties, such as the Julio-Claudian family, succession often took unexpected turns. Claudius was a surprise candidate proclaimed in the chaos following Caligula's death, and Nero owed his succession to the insatiable ambition of his mother Agrippina, whom Claudius had married five years before his death.

Even so, emperors had to be prepared for ruling. Greeks and Romans alike were convinced that education was crucial for a good ruler. In the 4th century BC, the Greek historian Xenophon had written his *Cyropaedia* ('the education of Cyrus'). The work presents Cyrus, the founder of the ancient Persian empire of the Achaemenids, as the prototype of a virtuous king, an example for others to emulate. According to Xenophon, the key to good, just rule was education, *paideia* in Greek: the excellent *paideia* enjoyed by the young Cyrus yielded rich fruit when he was king. With his *Cyropaedia*, Xenophon created a whole new literary genre, which remained popular throughout antiquity, the Middle Ages and the Renaissance: the *speculum principum* or 'mirror for princes'.

When Nero became emperor designate after Agrippina's marriage to Claudius, his mother was anxious to give her twelve-year-old son the best possible education. The child was given into the custody of Lucius Annaeus Seneca, a Spanish-born

ABOVE AND OPPOSITE TOP
The birthplaces of the Roman emperors, from Augustus to the House of Leo in the east. From the 3rd century onwards, an increasing number of rulers came from the Balkan provinces.

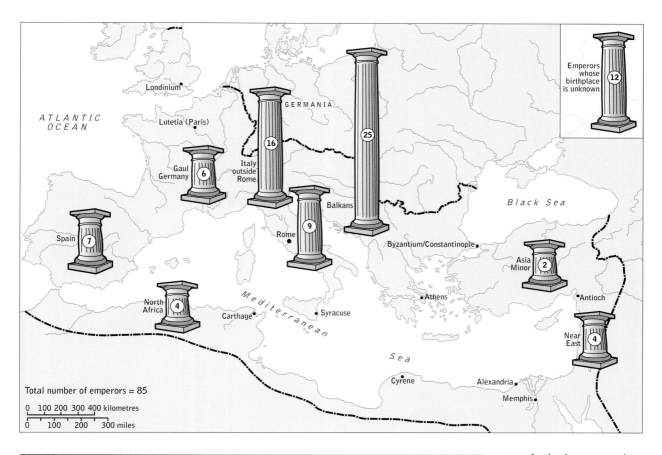

Emperors whose birthplace is unknown — 12

GERMANIA — 25

Italy outside Rome — 16

Gaul Germany — 6

Balkans — 9

Rome

Spain — 7

North Africa — 4

Asia Minor — 2

Near East — 4

Londinium

Lutetia (Paris)

ATLANTIC OCEAN

Byzantium/Constantinople

Black Sea

Antioch

Athens

Carthage

Syracuse

Mediterranean Sea

Cyrene

Alexandria

Memphis

Total number of emperors = 85

0 100 200 300 400 kilometres

0 100 200 300 miles

LEFT **A school scene carved on a sandstone tombstone from Neumagen, Germany, around AD 180–185. The teacher (on the left), probably a Greek, is instructing his pupil, who holds a scroll. A second pupil, making a gesture of greeting, is approaching from the right.**

senator, Stoic philosopher and writer of numerous essays, dialogues and tragedies. Seneca was an excellent choice: an all-round intellectual, he trained Nero in philosophy, literature and statecraft. It is possible that he used his own tragedies as illustrative material for ethical instruction. It may have been Seneca who aroused or fostered the youth's passion for theatre and music.

A manifesto of Seneca's educational ideals is his paper *De clementia* ('On mercy'), written in AD 55/56, shortly after Nero's accession to the throne. In this

A GOOD EMPEROR'S EDUCATION

A 'good' emperor needed many qualities, of which education was arguably the most important. When Hadrian adopted Antoninus Pius, he decreed that Antoninus in turn had to adopt Marcus Annius Verus, the future Marcus Aurelius. When he thus entered the inner circle of power, Marcus was sixteen years old. By then, he had passed through the usual stages of a young Roman aristocrat's education: he had started with Latin grammar and then proceeded to Greek language and literature. In both fields he had benefited from the instruction of leading experts.

When he was about eighteen, he also received tuition in law, rhetoric and philosophy. The last had a rather marginal place in the aristocratic curriculum, but Marcus was soon hooked on it. In his philosophical studies, in which he received guidance from the senator Marcus Junius Rusticus, a famous Stoic, the prospective emperor sought answers to the many questions that were on his mind. Stoicism, with its rigid emphasis on duty and virtue, suited the future ruler best. In later years, while he fought his wars against the Marcomanni and Quadi, he wrote down his *Meditations* ('To himself'), a set of guidelines for his own actions, in which he summarized the philosophy of the Stoics: 'Death, like birth, is a revelation of nature [...]. There is nothing in it to put us out of countenance' and: 'Live not one's life as though one had a thousand years, but live each day as the last.'

Marcus's favourite teacher was not a philosopher, however, but his tutor in Latin rhetoric and literature, Marcus Cornelius Fronto. Fronto's canon was archaic, according to the taste prevailing in his time: he preferred

Sallust to Tacitus and Ennius and Plautus to Horace, Virgil and Ovid, the famous poets of the Augustan age. Intellectually, Marcus increasingly turned away from such models, but he developed a lasting affection for Fronto, documented in their surviving correspondence. Initially, his enthusiasm for Fronto may even have had a homoerotic component. When the beloved teacher fell ill, a desperate Marcus wrote: 'but I do not know where my courage has gone; I only know that it is on the way to you'. When Marcus became emperor, the letters grew more formal, but the friendship survived.

A bust of the young Marcus Aurelius, *c.* AD 140, found in the villa of Antoninus Pius at Lanuvium, near Rome.

short essay, in which he directly addresses the emperor, the instructor – very much in the manner of Xenophon's *Cyropaedia* – paints a portrait of the good ruler. Seneca praises Nero's virtue, and in particular his mercy, as – unlike all his predecessors – the then eighteen-year-old had never shed any blood. It is mercy and the ability to forgive that sets apart the good ruler from the ordinary man:

> Cruel and inexorable anger is not seemly for a king, for thus he does not rise much above the other man, toward whose own level he descends by being angry at him. But if he grants life, if he grants position to those who have imperilled and deserve to lose them, he does what none but a sovereign may.

Seneca then explains to Nero the difference between a 'king' – i.e. a good emperor – and a tyrant: while the tyrant sows fear everywhere, the good king is the one:

> Whose care embraces all, who, while guarding here with greater vigilance, there with less, yet fosters each and every part of the state as a portion of himself; who is inclined to the milder course even if it would profit him to punish.

For Seneca, mildness, a sense of justice, moderation and accessibility are the indispensable principles of good rule. In this manifesto, the perspective of a Roman senator merges with the intellectual credo of the Stoic philosopher. The Stoa, the leading philosophical school in the early imperial period, believed in self-conquest and in overcoming emotional drives, above all rage. An ethical life implied consideration of others and public spirit. The senator in Seneca reminded Nero to respect the political and social sensibilities of the Roman aristocracy. The good emperor styled himself as a fellow senator, not as a master; virtuous rule demanded modesty and affability instead of affectations and demonstrations of power.

The education of Nero was a success story – at least in the beginning. The emperor Trajan, who was born under Claudius, later remarked that the first five years of Nero's rule were the happiest ones Rome had ever experienced. The happiness Trajan recalls was largely owing to the fact that Seneca and Burrus, the prefect of the Praetorian Guard, were jointly running the state with Nero as a dormant partner. The experiment got out of hand when the young emperor finally discovered how much power he had. His first victim was

A marble statue of Nero as a child, wearing a toga, *c.* AD 48–50. Around his neck hangs the *bulla*, a golden amulet worn by male children. In his left hand, he holds a scroll. The statue may have been commissioned after Agrippina's marriage to Claudius.

Britannicus, his adoptive brother (AD 55), then he killed Agrippina (59), and later his wife Octavia, Claudius's daughter (62). Finally, Seneca himself, who had been involved in a plot against his old pupil, was forced to commit suicide in 65. Burrus had already died of cancer in 62. Despite all Seneca's efforts to make Nero an ideal emperor, the last Julio-Claudian became famous as a tyrant, not as a king of mercy. Not surprisingly, people of influence started trying to get rid of him.

Usurping power

Few Roman emperors died peacefully. Some were murdered, a few lost their lives on the battlefield and one – Valerian in 260 – was taken prisoner by the enemy and died in captivity. Most of those who were ousted by force succumbed to usurpers: generals who, supported by the armies they commanded, claimed power for themselves.

FAMOUS USURPERS

Usurper's name	The emperor he tried to usurp	Year	City/region	The usurper's fate
Lucius Antonius Saturninus	Domitian	89	Mainz, Upper Germany	Defeated by the army of Lower Germany, and killed in battle (89).
Avidius Cassius	Marcus Aurelius	175	Near East	Murdered (175).
Pescennius Niger	Septimius Severus	193	Antioch, Syria	Defeated by Septimius Severus at Issus (194), captured and executed.
Postumus	Gallienus	260	Cologne, Lower Germany	Established a regional empire in Gaul; killed by his own soldiers at Mainz (269).
Zenobia	Aurelian	272	Palmyra, Syria	Defeated and captured by Aurelian (272).
Carausius	Maximian	286	Gesoriacum, Gaul	Established a regional empire in Britain and northern Gaul; murdered by his own official Allectus (293).
Magnentius	Constantius II	350	Autun, Gaul	Killed the emperor Constans; defeated by Constantius II and committed suicide.
Procopius	Valens	365	Constantinople	Defeated by Valens at Thyatira; captured and executed (366).
Eugenius	Theodosius I	392	Lyons, Gaul	Defeated by Theodosius and executed (394).
Priscus Attalus	Honorius	409 and 411	Rome and Bordeaux, Gaul	Usurped twice, backed by the Visigoths; captured by Honorius and exiled.

OPPOSITE *The Dying Seneca*, painted by Peter Paul Rubens in 1612/1613. Rubens shows Seneca's suicide in his bath, assisted by a doctor (right). The painter modelled his portrait of the philosopher after a famous ancient statue of a fisherman, which was then believed to represent Seneca.

LEFT Many who tried to usurp imperial power were unsuccessful. The chart lists some of the pretenders who failed to obtain the purple.

Tacitus alluded to such senatorial pretenders in his *Histories* when he stated that – following the death of Nero – emperors could be created outside the capital city.

> '**The secret of empire was now disclosed, that an emperor could be made elsewhere than at Rome.**'
>
> Tacitus, Histories

The scenario for a Roman usurpation remained basically unaltered over the centuries. Emperors who failed to communicate with the groups constituting the principate – the Senate, the military and the urban *plebs* of Rome – lost acceptance. Once an emperor had lost the support of one or more of these groups, his rule was on the verge of failure. All of a sudden, it became obvious that the emperor was not the only one 'capable of ruling' – *capax imperii*, in Tacitus's words. The senatorial officials who were in command of the armies garrisoned along the empire's long frontiers were tempted to have themselves proclaimed by their legions. Once a pretender was declared, a clash with the incumbent emperor was unavoidable.

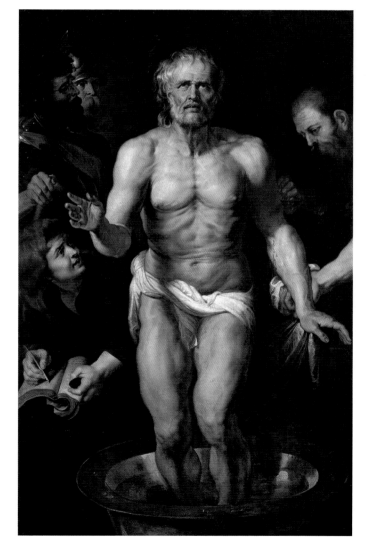

In AD 68, Nero's reign, marked by an impressive series of disasters, was on the brink of collapse. An atrocious war between Parthia and Rome had ravaged the east for more than a decade (54–66) and cost countless Roman soldiers their lives; in 64, Rome had fallen victim to a blaze that had burned to ashes two-thirds of the capital; in 65, a plot of leading senators against Nero had been discovered, and many, including the distinguished senator Piso and the philosopher Seneca, had been executed or forced to commit suicide; in the following year another conspiracy had been uncovered, this time involving Gnaeus Domitius Corbulo, Nero's most able general, who was forced to kill himself; and finally the outbreak of the First Jewish Revolt (AD 66–70) had turned an important part of the Roman Near East once again into a slaughterhouse.

In the midst of such crisis and catastrophe, the art-obsessed emperor sought distraction in a tour through Greece (AD 66–68), where the crowds cheered the cithara-playing emperor's performances. No wonder: the philhellene emperor had declared Greece 'free' and exempt from taxation. Indulging his own artistic obsessions, he had lost touch with reality. To make matters worse, an emperor in the role of an artist did not appeal to the senators. Roman aristocrats, who held their traditions in high esteem, might write history or, perhaps, dabble in poetry, but performing as an actor or musician did not befit their rank. An emperor who stepped onto the stage, such as Nero, stepped out of his imperial character.

By 68, when Nero returned to Rome, the discontent with his reign had reached alarming proportions. However, going back to the republican form of government that some senators may still have favoured was, by now, out of the question. The aftermath of Caligula's assassination had proved this sufficiently clearly: in AD 41, the Senate had briefly discussed the republic's restoration, but had soon discovered that the military would not tolerate a power vacuum.

Not surprisingly, it was the military that took the initiative in 68. In Gaul, the governor of the province of Lugdunensis, Gaius Julius Vindex, revolted against the emperor. He received support from local tribes and persuaded his colleague Servius Sulpicius Galba, the governor of Tarraconensis in Spain, to claim the purple for himself. On 3 April, Galba was proclaimed emperor in Carthago Nova, modern Cartagena. Though Vindex was finally defeated by the powerful Rhine army, whose commander Lucius Verginius Rufus had delayed his decision for several months, Galba's proclamation was confirmed by the Senate in Rome. At the head of his army, the usurper set off for Rome on 8 June. The day after, Nero, who had lost any support, committed suicide.

Galba was now emperor, unchallenged at first. Tacitus's *Histories* gives us a vivid description of his personality and the circumstances of his accession:

> Galba was weak and old. …Galba's approach to Rome had been slow and bloody. …Galba's entrance into Rome was ill-omened, because so many thousands of unarmed soldiers had been massacred, and this inspired fear in the very men who had been their murderers. …Here was abundant fuel for a revolution; while the soldiers' favour did not incline to any individual, they were ready for the use of anyone who had the courage.

AD 69

Brutal purges were Galba's first mistake. His second was that he dismissed what the soldiers believed to be their legitimate entitlement: on the accession of a new emperor, the soldiers were used to receiving a payment in money, the *donativum*.

Map of the empire in AD 68/69, showing the deployment of the legions and the locations of the four usurpers.

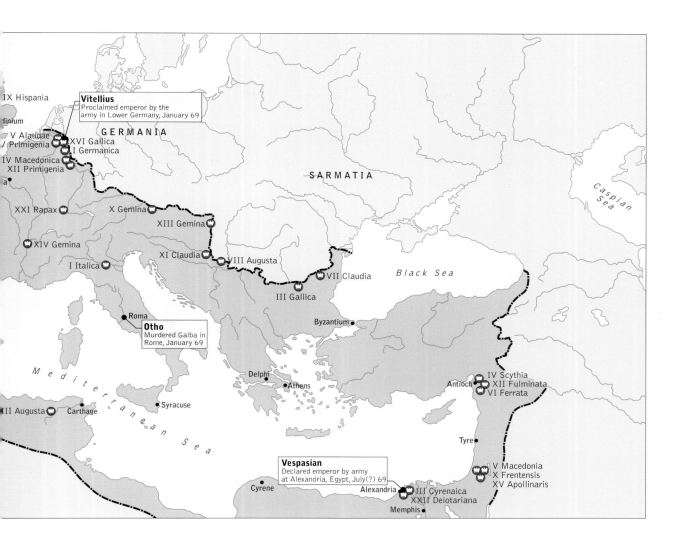

The soldiers who had supported Galba and those of the Praetorian Guard, which had deserted Nero, now claimed what they regarded as their just deserts. Galba, however, was minded 'to recruit his soldiers, not to buy them', as he publicly declared. He refused to pay the *donativum*. Honourable as such a bold gesture may have been, it cost him the sympathy of the soldiers. On 2 January 69, Aulus Vitellius, the commander of the army in Lower Germany, took advantage of the soldiers' unhappiness and had himself declared emperor at Cologne. Without hesitation, he marched the bulk of the German army – consisting of his own two legions and two more from Upper Germany – off to Rome.

However, the soldiers were not Galba's only concern. When he became emperor, he was over seventy years old. His two sons had already died. The problem of the succession was urgent, and the only way to solve it was to adopt a young aristocrat. On 10 January 69, he presented to the public Lucius Calpurnius Piso, the thirty-

Copper *sestertius* coin issued by the short-lived emperor Vitellius in AD 69.

year-old son of a consul whom Nero had forced into exile. In spite of his impeccable biography, Piso lacked any support from the powerful aristocratic networks to which Galba owed his accession. One member of such a network was Marcus Salvius Otho, the governor of the province of Lusitania (present-day Portugal), who had backed Galba's usurpation from the beginning and, quite understandably, expected to be designated Galba's heir. Otho felt ignored and disappointed: choosing Piso was Galba's third and final mistake.

Five days later, Galba was dead. Otho had agitated against Galba and incited the Praetorian Guard to desert the emperor. On the Roman Forum, some soldiers acclaimed Otho as the new emperor, and Galba and Piso were murdered by their own escort. Otho was now emperor and received the Senate's confirmation, but in the meantime Vitellius was still marching on the capital. By March 69, his huge army had crossed the Alps and entered Italy. Otho had no choice but to fight: at Bedriacum, near Cremona, his army was defeated and Otho took his own life (16 April 69).

However, Vitellius's reign was also short-lived. On 1 July, Titus Flavius Vespasian was proclaimed emperor in Alexandria. The legions of the east and of the Danube army declared for Vespasian, and by October the usurper's force had reached Italy. Again, two Roman armies clashed at Bedriacum. This time, Vespasian's soldiers left the battlefield as victors. The remainder of Vitellius's army switched sides shortly after, and Rome, where street fighting had already set in, was defenceless. The Flavian troops marched into the capital in December. Vitellius made a futile attempt to disguise himself and hide, but was discovered and killed. The year AD 69, which had seen three emperors perish in quick succession, finally brought peace to Rome and the empire.

The year of the four emperors marks the first serious crisis of the principate. For scholars, AD 69 is instructive because it reveals some essential truths about how power was won and lost in Rome. First, it proves how much the emperor depended on the consent of the main social groups. Second, the legions were crucial in the making of a new emperor: if they were unhappy with the ruler, they could proclaim their senatorial commander emperor and march behind him to Rome, as they did with Vitellius. Third, aristocratic networking was important: whether a usurper got the backing of fellow commanders and was able to forge a coalition with them depended largely on the reputation he had with his fellow senators. Respected men, such as Vespasian, could convince other influential men to support their struggle for

This bronze portrait bust may depict Otho, who was acclaimed emperor after the murder of Galba, but whose own reign lasted barely a few months. The bust was cut from a statuette, presumably in modern times.

power. A successful military commander with authority and credit with the army was, per se, *capax imperii*. Fourth, any usurpation soon gained momentum: once a pretender had been acclaimed, civil war, with the clash of the two rival armies and the death of one of the leaders, was inevitable. Battle could only be avoided if one army defected from its champion.

The events of AD 69 revealed that Augustus's creation, the principate, successful as it had been so far, was not flawless. In principle, the emperor was still the military dictator that Augustus had been at the start of his career. There was no strong dynastic principle, nor indeed any other rule for succession, that effectively shielded ruling emperors from the threat of usurpation. They were not legitimate, inasmuch as their authority was neither inalienable nor subject to an institution's formal approval or denial. As a consequence, the individual ruler relied on acceptance, which could be lost.

The crisis of AD 69 was the pattern for all the civil wars that shook the empire in the centuries to come. After the murder of Commodus, the 'year of the six emperors' (AD 193), from which Septimius Severus emerged victorious, followed roughly the same screenplay, with a rush of usurpations, and one very peculiar episode in which the emperorship was auctioned to the highest bidder (see page 106).

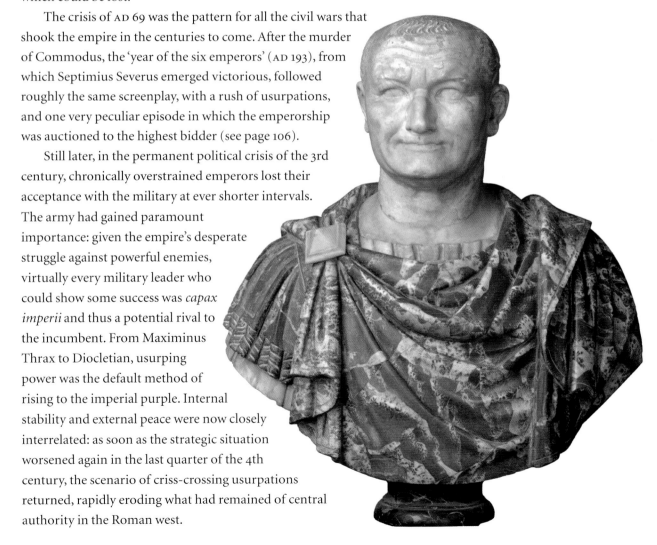

A marble bust of the emperor Vespasian, the ultimate victor of the conflicts of AD 69. The head's realism is striking and contrasts sharply with the idealized sculpture of the Julio-Claudian period. The unglamorized nature of the portrait reflects Vespasian's down-to-earth approach to government.

Still later, in the permanent political crisis of the 3rd century, chronically overstrained emperors lost their acceptance with the military at ever shorter intervals. The army had gained paramount importance: given the empire's desperate struggle against powerful enemies, virtually every military leader who could show some success was *capax imperii* and thus a potential rival to the incumbent. From Maximinus Thrax to Diocletian, usurping power was the default method of rising to the imperial purple. Internal stability and external peace were now closely interrelated: as soon as the strategic situation worsened again in the last quarter of the 4th century, the scenario of criss-crossing usurpations returned, rapidly eroding what had remained of central authority in the Roman west.

Senatorial careers

When Nero ascended the throne, he was exceptionally young: just sixteen years old.
Most emperors were much older when they assumed office: Galba was seventy-one,
Nerva sixty-five and Vespasian almost sixty. All these men had been distinguished
senators, experienced magistrates and formidable military commanders long before
they put on the imperial purple. In Roman politics, status was of paramount
importance. In such a society, it was unthinkable that a non-senator could rise to
the top position, that of emperor. For more than two centuries, until the praetorian
prefect Macrinus usurped power, all emperors were rooted in the senatorial order;
and the careers that led them into the imperial palace were senatorial.

In the republic, Rome's senatorial aristocracy, the nobility, had been a *noblesse
de robe*, an aristocracy that owed its position to its role in government. Men achieved
a seat in the Senate by rising through the *cursus honorum*, a ladder of hierarchic
offices, each of which could be held at a given age. Each post was subject to election
in the people's assembly and was held for one year

A group of senators, shown
in a marble relief from a
sarcophagus. The young man
(left) is probably Gordian III.
The sarcophagus, from
Acilia, near Ostia, dates
to *c*. AD 240.

only, and the offices were strictly collegial
(nobody held sole office). Each office
on the 'ladder' had clearly defined
competences. The first one was
quaestor (in charge of the finances),
followed by either aedile (responsible
for public order, public buildings
and the games) or plebeian
tribune (*tribunus plebis*, the
representatives of the *plebs*).
The second highest magistracy
was that of praetor, responsible
largely for legal business. On top
of the hierarchy were the two
consuls who held supreme
command in times of war and
the presidency in the Senate.
For centuries, Rome's political
elite was recruited from a
narrow inner circle of a few
clans and – to a lesser extent –
a wider band of politically
successful individuals, from the
same social background. These

groups had de facto monopolized access to the consulship and the high senatorial magistracies. Only exceptionally did outsiders succeed.

Not much of this changed in the imperial period, though the republican offices were now politically irrelevant. The *cursus honorum* essentially became a machine whose most significant purpose was to produce the empire's administrative elite – future emperors included. Though Augustus himself never slogged his way up the steps of the *cursus* (in 43 BC, he became a senator without having ever served in one of the magistracies, and in the same year, he was elected consul), many of his successors did. If they were members of the ruling dynasty, aspirants to the imperial purple completed the *cursus honorum* on the fast track, usually reaching consular rank at a very young age. In such a way they qualified for the highest ranks in the provincial administration. Tiberius became praetor when he was twenty-five (in the republic, the minimum age had been forty); Hadrian, who had been a military tribune at the age of eighteen, held the quaestorship at the age of twenty-five, served as plebeian tribune when he was twenty-six, became praetor at the age of twenty-nine and finally, when he was just thirty-two, consul. Gaius Caesar, Augustus's grandson and designated successor, even skipped the *cursus* altogether: he was appointed consul *designatus* as a boy of fourteen and took office as a consul at the age of twenty, though he died a few years later.

Gaius Caesar, Augustus's designated heir, who did not live to inherit the imperial purple. This marble bust is now in the British Museum.

Emperors who came to power as usurpers had all – until Macrinus – completed the *cursus honorum* in the normal way and served as consuls. Galba, Otho and Vitellius were sons of distinguished consuls and, as a matter of course, they too pursued senatorial careers. Vespasian, whose father, Flavius Sabinus, had been of equestrian rank, served as a military tribune in Thrace and as quaestor (about AD 26) in Crete, before he ran for the aedileship, which – as his biographer Suetonius informs us – 'he did not get until he had failed once, and just barely, as the last of six [candidates]'. After his praetorship, in AD 39 or 40, he became, under Claudius, a legionary commander in Germany and Britain (42–47), where he excelled. He was rewarded, in 44, with the *ornamenta triumphalia* (the regalia of a triumph; after the principate had been established, only members of the *princeps*'s family were awarded with an actual triumph) and, in 51, the consulship. Vespasian now belonged to the imperial establishment's inner circle: under Nero, he served as a proconsul in Africa (63–64) and later joined the emperor on his tour through Greece (66–67). In

AD 67, he was appointed supreme commander of the task force deployed against the Jewish Revolt, which comprised three legions, 60,000 men altogether. Less than three years later, he was emperor himself.

Septimius Severus and his fellow usurper Pescennius Niger were of equestrian descent, but had both reached the consulship under Commodus. Severus benefited from the protection of his uncle Gaius, a consul of the year 160. Pertinax, Commodus's immediate successor, also reached the consulship, despite his humble background as the son of a freedman. Pertinax was the representative of a new type of career officer, whose skills and accomplishments enabled him to rise rapidly through the military ranks. Later, he held high offices in the imperial administration and was appointed praetorian senator and then consul. The three months of his emperorship were the apex of a career that would have been unthinkable in previous times.

Pertinax was the prototype of a professional. Before him, virtually all emperors had been amateurs in the business of military leadership. Usually, like any young man at the beginning of his senatorial career, a future emperor could look back on an endless line of ancestors who had all distinguished themselves in their service to the Roman state. At the age of eighteen, a senator's son would usually join the college of the *vigintisexviri* ('26 men') who were assigned to specific duties, such as issuing coins, overseeing the city cleaning, and simple judicial tasks. The next step of his career would be – before he could run for the office of quaestor – military service. The young aristocrat joined the army at twenty-two, as a military tribune. In this capacity, he was the deputy of the legionary commander, the *legatus*. This was all the military experience a Roman aristocrat acquired before he held the highest commands later in his life.

Lack of military professionalism was the major drawback of emperors trained as Roman senators. The empire's rapid militarization under the Severans and their successors – the 'soldier emperors' – made the senatorial career path obsolete for the emperorship. The 'new' emperors of the 3rd century were, almost without exception, career soldiers with no prestigious pedigree, but with plenty of military experience. Many of them came from the relatively backward Balkan provinces. They were bound to change the empire in style, but also in substance.

Imperial princes

Men like Galba, Otho and Vitellius, as well as Vespasian, Nerva and Trajan, all rose to the empire's top job because they could show extraordinary military or administrative achievements and/or had excellent political connections. A very different group were those who were, if not born in the purple, at least emperors-in-

A marble portrait bust of Germanicus in his youth, *c.* AD 14–23, from Toulouse, France.

training from a relatively young age. In AD 12, Germanicus was promoted consul at the age of twenty-six (the normal minimum age was forty-three), having served previously only as quaestor. Two years later – Augustus had just died – he became supreme commander of the Roman forces in Germany.

When Augustus's grandson Gaius Caesar put on the *toga virilis* of an adult man, the Roman *plebs* demanded that he be promoted to consul at once, at the age of just fourteen. Augustus denied him the consulship, but granted Gaius the right to attend the sessions of the Senate and designated him for a consulship when he reached the age of twenty. He received an *imperium proconsulare* on his departure to the east and took office as consul in AD 1.

From Augustus onwards, most emperors shared their imperial authority – namely the *imperium* of the proconsul in the provinces and the *tribunicia potestas*, the plebeian tribune's authority in Rome – with their designated successors and made them consuls or at least consul-designates at the earliest opportunity. Nero was designated consul shortly after his adoption by Claudius (AD 50); Titus, Vespasian's oldest son, held his first consulship jointly with his father in AD 70. He received his first *imperium* in the same year and the *tribunicia potestas* in the year after.

The transfer of the imperial power's core elements to the designated heir during the incumbent's lifetime was designed to smooth the process of succession, which in Rome was – due to the lack of a properly working dynastic principle – particularly hazardous. Making the successor a joint partner in rule gave him a realistic chance to gain popularity and to establish a relationship with his future subjects. The actual moment of succession would then appear as a continuation of the previous regime.

In this statue, made in AD 80, Titus is shown giving a speech, with his right arm outstretched and a scroll in his left hand. His facial features are softer than those of his father Vespasian, but the Flavian family resemblance is unmistakable.

ADOPTION

In republican Rome, the continuity of a family clan (gens) was of prime importance. If a family was on the verge of dying out for lack of a male heir, its members could usually hope for help from other aristocratic families: a father with more than one son might give up one of his own sons for adoption. Adoption in Rome could take various legal forms, but most commonly an adult male was transferred from the paternal power (patria potestas) of one father of the family (pater familias) into that of another. This was achieved through three consecutive symbolic acts of sale.

Adopted sons changed their names to reflect their new status. Until the 3rd century AD, Roman citizens had three names, the *tria nomina*: a personal first name (*praenomen*); a clan name (*gentilnomen*), and a third name (*cognomen*) which was originally a personal nickname, but later became hereditary within families. After an adoption, the adoptive son added his biological father's clan name, expanded to include the suffix *-ianus*, to his adoptive father's *gentilnomen* and *cognomen*. Thus, when Publius Aemilius Paullus was adopted by Publius Cornelius Scipio Africanus the Elder, he became Publius Cornelius Scipio Aemil*ianus*. Mutatis mutandis, Gaius Octavius (the future Augustus) became Gaius Julius Caesar Octav*ianus*, after he had been posthumously adopted by Caesar – though he never used that name and preferred to be called *Divi filius*, 'the son of the deified (Julius Caesar)' instead.

In the imperial period, adoption became common in order to secure dynastic succession. Augustus adopted Marcellus, Gaius and Lucius Caesar and finally Tiberius. Claudius adopted Nero, even though he had a son of his own, Britannicus. Nerva adopted Trajan and thus established the tradition of 'adoptive emperorship': neither Nerva, Trajan, Hadrian nor Antoninus Pius had a son of his own. They were guided by the maxim that 'the best' (*optimus*) should rule, a principle derived from Stoic philosophy and put in a nutshell by Pliny the Younger in his panegyric (AD 100)

on Trajan: 'how glad are you,' he addresses the deceased Nerva, 'that the one whom you have selected so wisely for being the best, is the best both in reality and in peoples' minds.'

Marcus Aurelius had a son, Commodus, and the principle of adoption was abandoned. Later, however, Septimius Severus claimed to be the adopted son of Marcus Aurelius – a conspicuous fiction, which, however, emphasized the intention of continuity. Elagabalus was forced to adopt his cousin Alexianus and designate him as heir when his own government became unpopular. In the 3rd century, when the army was the key institution in the making of an emperor, adoption became irrelevant for securing dynastic continuity: the Tetrarchs did not adopt but co-opted their successors, and so did Gratian, when he appointed Theodosius *Augustus* of the east in 379.

The adoption of Marcus Aurelius and Lucius Verus, on a marble relief from the Library of Celsus in Ephesus, after AD 169.

Recusatio imperii

Even if a candidate had all the requirements for the purple, he was well advised not to appear too keen on it. After all, the good emperor regarded emperorship as a burden, not an enjoyment. *Recusatio imperii* – the new emperor's ostentatious reluctance to assume office – became a ritual highly significant for the relationship between the ruler and the senators. When he first appeared before the Senate, the new emperor would conventionally reject the purple and, in response, the senators would stand up as one man and plead with him to accept the responsibility. Begrudgingly, the emperor would then unwillingly yield to their persuasion and accept his powers from the Senate. The *recusatio* was a pure orchestration, of course: the emperor had no intention of refusing the powers that he, in fact, already held; nor did the senators genuinely believe in his reluctance.

Again, decorum was crucial. Suetonius blamed Tiberius for overdoing the ritual:

> Though Tiberius did not hesitate at once to assume and to exercise the imperial authority, surrounding himself with a guard of soldiers, that is, with the actual power and the outward sign of sovereignty, yet …

‘…[Tiberius] refused the title for a long time, with barefaced hypocrisy now upbraiding his friends who urged him to accept it, saying that they did not realize what a monster the empire was.’

Suetonius, describing the pretended reluctance of an emperor to take office

After much dilatoriness, he acquiesced:

> At last, as though on compulsion, and complaining that a wretched and burdensome slavery was being forced upon him, he accepted the empire, but in such fashion as to suggest the hope that he would one day lay it down. His own words are: 'Until I come to the time when it may seem right to you to grant an old man some repose.'

Though Tiberius's hesitation was probably authentic, the senators took it as hypocrisy. Conditioned by decades of tokenistic communication with Augustus, the senators were unable to believe in an emperor who sincerely hesitated to assume the burden of empire. The misunderstanding soon got worse. According to the *Annals* of Tacitus, Tiberius announced to the Senate that he intended to share his power:

> Only the mind of the deified Augustus was equal to such a burden: he himself had found, when called by the sovereign to share his anxieties, how arduous, how dependent upon fortune, was the task of ruling a world!

He thought, then, that, in a state which had the support of so many eminent men, they ought not to devolve the entire duties on any one person; the business of government would be more easily carried out by the joint efforts of a number.

In the Roman historian's eyes, this 'was more dignified than convincing'. Rather than showing the relief Tiberius may have expected, the senators were terrified: 'But the Fathers, whose one dread was that they might seem to comprehend him, melted in plaints, tears, and prayers.'

Tiberius had grossly overestimated the senator's love of freedom. For them, the emperor's *recusatio imperii* created a disturbing situation – how disturbing it was became clear when the Senate had to decide upon a case of alleged defamation of the emperor. Tacitus reports:

This incensed the emperor to such a degree that, breaking through his taciturnity, he exclaimed that, in this case, he too would vote, openly and under oath – the object being to impose a similar obligation on the rest.

The senators, however, felt uneasy about voting:

> **'There remained even yet some traces of dying liberty. Accordingly Gnaeus Piso inquired: 'In what order will you register your opinion, Caesar? If first, I shall have something to follow: if last of all, I fear I may inadvertently find myself on the other side.'**
>
> Suetonius

The words went home; and with a meekness that showed how profoundly he rued his unwary outburst, he voted for the acquittal of the defendant on the counts of treason.

Though it was misunderstood, Tiberius's *recusatio* fits neatly into the general parameters of political communication in Rome. Eagerness for power was indecent. Accordingly, all emperors – or those who aspired to become emperors – tried to avoid giving the impression that they were keen to seize power. Only after intense persuasion (and even some massive threats) did Vespasian give in and accept the army's acclamation in Alexandria in Egypt. Many of the 3rd century's numerous pretenders tried to downplay their active role in the usurpation: Macrinus, for example, waited three days before he let himself be talked round. A reluctant Probus was, according to the *Historia Augusta*, proclaimed emperor by the soldiers, who hastily threw the purple robe over him. The historiographer uses the motif of the *recusatio* in order to portray Probus in the best light: it was only his sense of responsibility that made the general yield to his soldiers' pleas. The constant use of the *recusatio* by emperors and would-be emperors made it an effective literary device, which Roman authors employed to characterize their protagonists: the bad emperor was keen to rule, while the reluctant good emperor needed persuasion.

Taking office

The emperor is dead – long live the emperor. Over the five hundred years of Roman imperial history, a new emperor took office more than eighty times – countless unsuccessful usurpers not included. Our sources – in this case Tacitus, Suetonius, Cassius Dio and the Jewish historian Flavius Josephus – give us particularly detailed information about the death of Tiberius and the succession of Gaius, Germanicus's son, who grew up in the legionary camps and whom everybody called Caligula ('little boots': *caligae* were the soldiers' footwear).

Tiberius's reign had had a rather promising start, but a frustrated and increasingly moody Tiberius soon retreated to his sumptuous palace on Capri. There he was joined, in AD 31, by Caligula, his great-nephew, who was then in his early twenties. Suetonius writes that on Capri, Caligula enjoyed attending the executions and tortures ordered by Tiberius. Nevertheless, his position was

The Villa Jovis, Tiberius's palace on Capri. The palace, built on terraces cut into the rock, overlooks the cliffs of the island's northeastern tip. The lavish palace, in its insular seclusion, became a symbol of Tiberius's misanthropy.

precarious: Tiberius suspected that Caligula, once in power, might harm his own grandson Tiberius Gemellus (the 'twin'), a suspicion not altogether misguided. Caligula, however, became the protégé of Macro, Tiberius's influential praetorian prefect, who saved his life several times and turned out to be a crucial figure in the succession crisis.

A statue of the emperor Caligula.

Until the very end, Tiberius was undecided whether to designate Gemellus or Caligula as his heir. In his will, he had made provisions for a joint rulership. After the emperor's death, on 16 March AD 37, at the naval base of Misenum near Naples, the soldiers of the Praetorian Guard who were present acclaimed Caligula. This move had been skilfully prepared by Macro, who also arranged for Tiberius's will to be declared ineffective by the Senate (18 March).

Ten days later, Caligula arrived in Rome, where he convened the Senate as well as selected representatives of the equestrian order and the populace. He delivered a speech in which he flattered the senators, vowed to share his power with them, promised to put an end to the prosecution of lese-majesty and referred to himself as the Senate's 'pupil'. Before the eyes of the public, he burned the accusations remaining from Tiberius's reign. An urgent matter was the treatment of the deceased emperor: should he be declared a state god, like Augustus twenty-three years before and Julius Caesar seventy-eight years before, as Caligula had requested in a letter to the Senate before his arrival at Rome? Or was he rather to fall prey to the *damnatio memoriae*, the ultimate memory sanction the Senate could impose on an individual by formal resolution, including the deliberate obliteration of his name and the revocation of all his laws?

Many senators inclined to the *damnatio*, such was the hatred towards Tiberius, who had ordered the execution of countless Roman aristocrats. However, Caligula had a duty of piety to the man who was his great-uncle and adoptive grandfather, and Tiberius received a lavish, honourable burial in the mausoleum of Augustus. Caligula himself delivered the funeral address, in which he looked back to the reign of Augustus and reminded his audience of his own father, Germanicus, but only casually referred to Tiberius. Also, significantly, he paid tribute to those members of his family who had died under Tiberius. Though the will had been declared ineffective, Caligula paid the deceased's bequest to the Roman *plebs* and the soldiery.

In his first weeks as Roman emperor, then, Caligula had done an excellent job. He had reconciled a previously alienated senatorial elite with Julio-Claudian rule; he had drawn a clear line between himself and his predecessor, but without offending against the rules of piety and

discrediting his great-uncle altogether; he had lived up to the expectations of the senators by presenting himself as humble and placable, and of the military and the Roman *plebs* by his generosity; he had maintained the equilibrium between continuity and change and was, in return, embraced with enthusiasm. However, a series of blows soon changed this, and Caligula went down as one of the most dreadful tyrants ever to afflict Rome. Still, for a few joyful months, as the biographer Suetonius points out, the Romans were living under the impression 'that the city had been founded a second time'.

Caligula's first days in office were typical of the rather peaceful period of the first two centuries AD. Usually, each new emperor presented himself to the Senate, to the crowds in Rome and to the Praetorian Guard; in a speech, he promised to rule in collaboration with the senators and to abstain from autocracy. Many emperors also expressed their piety towards their predecessors. Antoninus Pius was faced with a difficult situation when he brought before the Senate the request that the deceased emperor Hadrian be deified. Many senators harboured ill-feeling towards Hadrian, who, in his later years, had secluded himself from the public; the atmosphere in the curia was chilly. In the end, Antoninus had to bring his entire authority to bear, but Hadrian was deified.

The mausoleum of Augustus in Rome, seen from the east. The building was excavated in the first half of the 20th century. In antiquity, it was crowned by a cone-shaped tumulus, which was planted with cypresses.

Most emperors in the 3rd century took office far from Rome, often on the battlefield. They had little time to address the Senate with well-worded speeches, and some of them did not even enter Rome as emperors. Under the Tetrarchs (see Box, opposite), in contrast, the transfer of office from one generation of rulers to the next, which took place in 305, was a carefully staged ceremony, arranged in advance.

An emperor's arrival

The first arrival – *adventus* – of an emperor in an imperial capital or one of the other major cities was, at all times, an extraordinary event:

> All the meadows were crowded, not only with people who hastened to gaze at you, but with flocks of animals leaving their remote pastures and forests; the peasants hurried to visit each other, spreading everywhere the news of what they had seen; fires were lit on the altars, incense put on, libations poured and victims sacrificed. Everybody was enthusiastic; there was dancing and cheering everywhere, and they praised and thanked the gods. Jupiter was…invoked as a conspicuous and present god.

A section of frieze from the Arch of Constantine, west face, showing the departure (*profectio*) of Constantine and his army from Milan towards Rome, defended by Maxentius. In the circular frame above the frieze is Luna, the moon goddess, on her chariot.

THE TETRARCHY

When Diocletian came to power in AD 284, it seemed that he was just another short-lived soldier emperor struggling to hold at bay Rome's external and his own internal enemies. However, his reign turned out very differently.

The crisis of the 3rd century had shown that no single emperor could rule the entire Roman world. Diocletian followed his own path to resolve the dilemma. In autumn 285, he appointed Maximian, a fellow officer, *Caesar*; and a few months later, he promoted him to the rank of *Augustus*. Maximian, like Diocletian, came from the Balkans, but the two men were not related. Sharing power with a dynastic outsider was unprecedented, but Diocletian went one step further. In 293, the *Augusti* appointed two other officers, neither of them related, as *Caesares* or sub-emperors: Constantius and Galerius were now their designated successors. By the time the two *Augusti* met in Rome in 303, on the occasion of Diocletian's 20th anniversary, Diocletian had decided upon their joint abdication. On 1 May 305, Diocletian and Maximian stepped down and Constantius and Galerius became *Augusti*. Immediately, they appointed two new *Caesares*: Severus and Maximinus Daia.

To what extent the Tetrarchy's architecture followed an ingenious master plan, worked out in advance by Diocletian, is hard to decide. Many of our sources are hostile towards Diocletian and show little interest in his system of government. It seems likely that the integration of potential enemies into the inner circle of power and the increase in imperial manpower were outcomes intended by Diocletian. He may have improvised many of the details, but the Tetrarchy still marks a clear break with the traditions of the principate established by Augustus.

In the medium term, the Tetrarchy worked well, partly due to decreasing pressure from outside: a few usurpations were swiftly put down and a regional empire in Britain under Carausius was finally reincorporated in 297. In the long run, however, the Tetrarchy failed, because the sons of the Tetrarchs were unwilling to abandon what they perceived as their birthright: to inherit power from their fathers. The Tetrarchy perished in a new series of civil wars, from which Constantine finally emerged as Rome's sole ruler in 325.

Porphyry group of the Tetrarchs, now in St Mark's Basilica, Venice. The four emperors are represented almost identically. They embrace each other, which further emphasizes their solidarity.

The conspicuous and present Jupiter in this case was none other than Diocletian, the emperor who steered the rolling ship of the Roman state back on course in the late 3rd century. The description above comes from an unknown orator of the period, the author of a *panegyricus* – a public speech in praise of a person – for Maximian, Diocletian's colleague as emperor. He is referring to the two emperors' arrival at Milan in early 291. At this time, Diocletian and Maximian had jointly ruled the empire for more than five years, during which period they had never met. While Diocletian had been responsible for the empire's eastern half, Maximian had looked after the west. Now they convened in the north Italian city in order to decide on their future political strategy.

For Milan and the entire region, the emperors' arrival was a historical event: when the rulers approached 'the whole of Italy was filled with a brighter light'. Accordingly, the welcome was more than warm. The emperors, coming from opposite directions, met before the gates and then advanced together into the city, in a triumph-like procession: a vivid image of harmony and solidarity. Diocletian and Maximian were greeted by the peasants, and followed by the townspeople and the local dignitaries. Their procession passed images of the local deities while bands played music everywhere in the city. Having finally arrived at the palace, the two rulers received the crowd's cheers.

The panegyrist's emperors are barely human: rather, they become manifest as supernatural beings. The addressee of the panegyric descends from the Alps as once the divine hero Hercules had done – Herculius was the name Maximian had given himself. With his 'divine traces' the emperor had opened up the Alps; the rays of the sun had shown him the way. True, this is the perspective of a panegyric, and we are at the dawn of late antiquity, when the rulers begin to be transfigured into a sacred sphere, remote from their subjects, sharing in divine right. Still, the appearance of an emperor in any period always had an enormous impact on the eyewitnesses and was a carefully staged event. For the ruler, it was an opportunity to show himself to the inhabitants of the empire's towns and cities: he could prove his generosity and accessibility. In turn, the *adventus* of an emperor turned the city he visited into a stage. An emperor's visit was prestigious: it enhanced the city's status and often brought about quite material benefits, too. On the other hand, maintaining an emperor and providing board and lodging for his entourage could be costly.

The ritual of *adventus* emerged in AD 69, the 'year of the four emperors', when, as Tacitus remarked, emperors were 'made elsewhere than in Rome' for the first time. The *adventus* in the capital was a decisive moment in an emperor's political career. One emperor to be 'made elsewhere' was Vespasian. The general, who had been about to put down the Jewish Revolt (AD 66–70), was proclaimed emperor in July 69. After the defeat of his rival Vitellius, Vespasian, at the head of his army, approached Rome in the summer of the following year. Flavius Josephus, the Jewish historian whom Vespasian had taken captive, describes scenes very similar to Diocletian's and Maximian's visit to Milan:

> 'Then it was that the whole multitude that had remained in the city, with their wives and children, came into the road, and waited for him there; and for those whom he passed by, they made all sorts of acclamations, on account of the joy they had to see him, and the pleasantness of his countenance, and styled him their Benefactor and Saviour, and the only person who was worthy to be ruler of the city of Rome.'
>
> Flavius Josephus

And now the city was like a temple, full of garlands and sweet odours; nor was it easy for him to come to the imperial palace, for the multitude of the people that stood about him, where yet at last he performed his sacrifices of thanksgiving to his household gods for his safe return to the city. The multitude did also betake themselves to feasting; which feasts and drink-offerings they celebrated by their tribes, and their families, and their neighbourhoods, and still prayed God to grant that Vespasian, his sons, and all their posterity, might continue in the Roman government for a very long time, and that his dominion might be preserved from all opposition.

Josephus's narrative exposes the downright messianic expectations that the crowd rested upon the ruler. For them, Vespasian was a 'saviour', the city almost turned into a 'temple'. The religious veneration of the urban *plebs* confronted the new emperor with his first challenge: he obviously had to respond, but without alienating the senators, for whom worshipping a living emperor was hardly appropriate. The senators, highly conscious of the dignity of their class, expected privileged treatment – but so did the soldiers, whose loyalty rested solely on the emperor. In a setting in which all the groups present – the urban crowds, the Senate and the army – were latently competing for the emperor's favour, he had to balance his behaviour carefully. It was all too easy to affront somebody. Vespasian had no such difficulty: his *adventus* in Rome, happening after months of civil war, was an impressive display of harmony, celebrating the regained *consensus universorum*, the consensus of all citizens.

CHAPTER 4

BEING EMPEROR

Hadrian restlessly travelled his empire, Trajan and Septimius Severus waged war after war, Claudius was a skilled, diligent administrator, and Titus excelled in disaster management after Vesuvius overwhelmed the Campanian towns of Pompeii and Herculaneum, a fire devastated Rome and a plague killed tens of thousands. Each emperor faced different challenges and set a different course, but the concept of what an emperor's duties should be changed only very gradually.

The emperor had to keep the empire safe and prosperous, and had to prove himself a successful commander-in-chief, a fair supreme justice and an accessible, generous and merciful sovereign. An emperor's day was filled with hard work, uncomfortable decisions and arduous public performance; at the same time he could sample the pleasures of a luxurious lifestyle beyond the wildest dreams of the vast majority of his contemporaries. At his command was unprecedented wealth and power, but the imperial bureaucracy he had to rely upon was – by modern standards – minimal. The Roman emperor epitomized Rome's might, but losing power inevitably meant losing one's life.

The palace

The palace was the stage on which, for the most part, the drama of the Roman emperors unfolded. In fact, there was not one single palace, but many. Augustus resided in a *domus*, a private house, on the Palatine Hill; Tiberius and Caligula enlarged the imperial complex on the hill; Nero had the sumptuous Domus Aurea built for himself in the hollow where the Colosseum now stands; the imposing structures of the Domus Flavia and the Domus Augustana on the Palatine were commissioned by Domitian; Hadrian was the builder and owner of the Villa Hadriana, the charming rural estate near Tivoli, some 30 km (18 miles) east of Rome; later emperors had vast, fortified residences near the troubled frontiers; and Constantine's successors in the east lived in the luxurious chambers of

IMPERIAL PALACES

Palace	Emperor	Location	Date completed
'House of Augustus'/ 'House of Livia'	Augustus	Palatine Hill, Rome	36 BC
Villa Jovis	Tiberius	Capri	AD 27
Domus Aurea	Nero	Central Rome	AD 64
Domus Augustana/ Domus Flavia	Domitian	Palatine Hill	AD 92
Hadrian's Villa	Hadrian	Tivoli, Latium	AD 134
Palace of Diocletian	Diocletian	Nicomedia (Izmit), Turkey	AD 280s
Palace of Maximian	Maximian	Mediolanum (Milan), Italy	
Palace of Constantius I	Constantius I	Augusta Treverorum (Trier), Germany	AD 293
Palace of Galerius	Galerius	Thessalonica (Thessaloniki), Greece	c. AD 300
Palace of Galerius	Galerius	Romuliana (Gamzigrad), Serbia	c. AD 305
Palace of Diocletian (retirement residence)	Diocletian	Spalato (Split), Croatia	AD 305
Great Palace	Constantine the Great, Theodosius I, Justinian	Constantinople	from AD 330 onwards
Imperial Palace	Honorius/ Galla Placidia	Ravenna	AD 402

PREVIOUS PAGE **A detail from the pedestal of the obelisk of Theodosius, Constantinople. The obelisk was brought to Constantinople in AD 390 and put up in the Hippodrome. The image shows a circus scene: Theodosius, standing in the imperial lodge, holds a laurel wreath, with which he is about to crown a race winner.**

BELOW **One of a number of wall paintings, in the so-called Second Style, which have been preserved from the House of Augustus. The Second Style features relative (though no strict linear) perspective. This detail shows a small bird.**

Constantinople's imperial palace, the stage for the 6th-century historian Procopius's malicious, exceedingly entertaining *Secret History*.

Of course, great palaces existed long before the first Roman emperor took office. The rulers of the first territorial states in Mesopotamia, the pharaohs of Egypt, and later the kings of the Hittite empire and Mycenaean Greece resided in large buildings designed for both habitation and administration, and which also provided storage for the ruler's accumulated wealth. However, the Latin word *palatium* (first used by the poet Ovid) and the English word 'palace' both come from the name of

The Canopus, an artificial canal in Hadrian's Villa in Tibur (Tivoli, near Rome). The architecture is modelled on an ideal Egyptian landscape to commemorate Antinous, Hadrian's young lover, who drowned in the Nile in AD 130. The Villa was a huge complex of dozens of buildings, among them private dwellings, a basilica, several bath houses, a library and a theatre.

A detail of a wall painting
from Nero's Domus Aurea,
depicting a love scene.

the Roman hill – the Palatine – on which the mother of all imperial palaces stood. The nucleus of this palace was the *domus* that Augustus had bought for himself on the western part of the hill. This house was, according to Suetonius, 'remarkable neither for size nor elegance, having but short colonnades with columns of Alban stone, and rooms without any marble decorations or handsome pavements'. The remains of this dwelling are scant, but archaeology has revealed that the *domus* actually formed part of a much larger complex of buildings, truly 'roofs worthy of a god', as Ovid puts it.

Tiberius acquired much of the aristocratic neighbourhood adjacent to the temple of the Magna Mater; under Caligula, the houses were pooled together and the area transformed into a single residence, the so-called Domus Tiberiana. From here, Caligula's successors Claudius, Vespasian and Titus ruled the Roman world. Nero had it enlarged and partly rebuilt after the fire of AD 64. After this, the Domus Aurea was built, a villa in an artificially constructed rural estate in the middle of town covering the area from the Circus Maximus in the southwest, over the Palatine, the Caelian and the Oppian Hills to the Esquiline Hill in the northeast. With its overt architectural extravagance, it marked a turning away from the deliberate modesty of previous imperial residences. The unfinished Domus Aurea was later dismantled under Vespasian to give way to the Colosseum. Much of the conglomeration of imperial dwellings on the Palatine burned down in the disastrous fire of AD 80.

Domitian's palace

The devastation caused by the blaze of AD 80 gave Domitian the opportunity to have the emperors' residential hill – the Palatine – radically reshaped. The new complex was divided into three parts: the Domus Flavia, for official purposes; the Domus Augustana, the emperor's private residence; and the garden stadium, the so-called 'hippodrome'. Towering high above the Palatine on its huge substructures, visible even from the Circus Maximus, the new palace became one of the most imposing buildings in the Roman cityscape. The whole structure bore witness to the emperor's ability to change the world around him according to his will: rather than just inhabiting a *domus* or villa, he literally 'occupied' the Palatine itself. The new structure was a true, purpose-built palace – a *palatium*.

A reconstruction of Nero's Domus Aurea. The building of the palace, after the great fire in AD 64, had an immense impact on the Roman cityscape. It was later demolished by order of Vespasian, but some of the subterranean parts have survived and are still visible.

Private and public activities were concentrated in different wings of the palace, but the border was permeable. The Domus Flavia, Domus Augustana and stadium were designed as three axes, clearly distinct structures, but connected by two colonnaded courtyards (*peristylia*). The main entrance to the reception rooms of the Domus Flavia faced northeast, towards the Roman Forum, from where visitors had to climb a steep road, the Clivus Palatinus, in order to reach the palace. Inside the Domus Flavia was a gigantic three-storey hall with an apse, the so-called Aula Regia. It was flanked by a smaller hall (*basilica*), which also had an apse, and a room with niches for statues. Having passed through the Aula Regia, the visitor entered a colonnaded courtyard with a garden, water basin and fountain. Opposite the Aula, across the courtyard, was another very large, three-storey hall with an apse: a dining room (*triclinium*) for up to 180 guests. Either side of it were small courtyards.

The large rooms were purpose-built for two of the prime occasions when the emperor met the public: the morning reception ceremony (*salutatio*, see page 81) and the evening banquet with distinguished members of the public (*convivium*, see page 85). The apses were spaces reserved for the emperor. Here, he presented himself to the crowds in majestic exclusiveness, with them and yet aloof. In his apse, on a single couch, he dined alone, gazing at the spectacle of the eating crowd, himself the focus of their attention. This manipulation of proximity and separation was quite deliberately engineered by Domitian. An adulatory ode by the poet Statius gushes:

ABOVE **The remains of the Domus Augustana, seen from the Circus Maximus. From here, the emperors could attend the games in the Circus without leaving their palace. The vaults are not parts of the actual palace, but supporting structures.**

OPPOSITE **The so-called Garden Stadium connected the Domus Augustana and the Domus Flavia with other parts of the imperial palace, later demolished to make way for a new wing constructed under Septimius Severus. It was not a place for physical exercise, but a courtyard with a garden, featuring fountains and colonnades.**

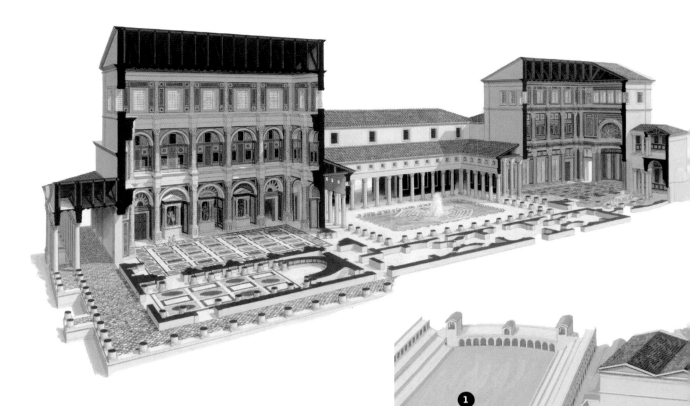

> ‘Do I see you reclining, ruler of the lands and sublime father of the world, you, hope of mankind, you, care of the gods? Am I allowed to see your face close, between the wassail and the tables, and not get up?’
>
> The poet Statius addresses Domitian

Even the private wing of the palace was a public stage. As a matter of course the emperor's friends, advisers, client kings and high officials had access to his private chambers, even to his bedroom (*cubiculum*). As we have seen, the two wings of the palace were not isolated from each other, but connected through courtyards and passages. Though the remains of the Domus Augustana are very poorly preserved, it is safe to say that its maze of differently sized rooms served a wide range of purposes, from pure leisure to official administration.

Finally, the palace's layout allowed the emperor to attend the games in the Circus Maximus without leaving

OPPOSITE **Reconstruction of a section of the Domus Flavia. Large parts of the palace were occupied by two giant halls, the Aula Regia (left) and a dining room (*triclinium*) for 180 guests (right). The two halls were connected by a colonnaded courtyard with a fountain.**

BELOW **Reconstruction of the imperial palaces on the Palatine with the Domus Augustana adjacent to the Garden Stadium and the Domus Flavia. The whole complex overlooked the Circus Maximus (left).**

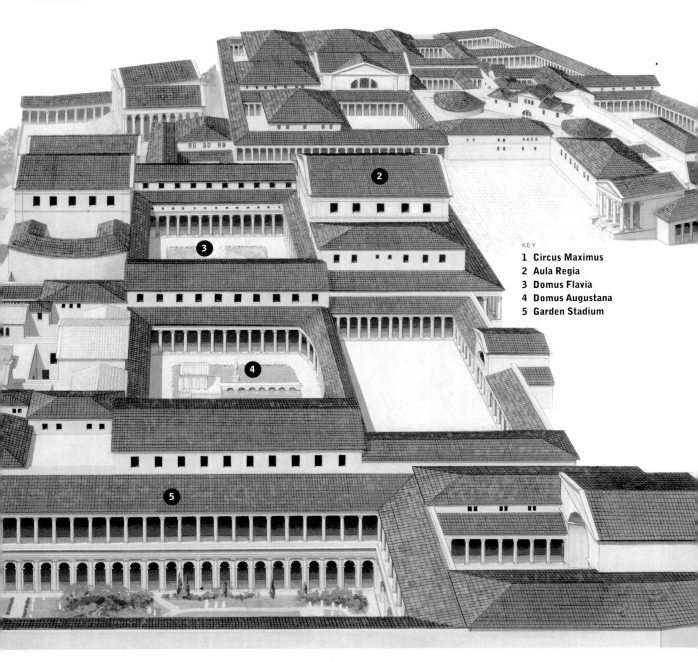

KEY

1 Circus Maximus
2 Aula Regia
3 Domus Flavia
4 Domus Augustana
5 Garden Stadium

his private chambers. The southwestern part of the Domus Augustana overlooked the Circus, with its auditorium for at least 250,000 people. The emperor could see and be seen – a public figure even in his private rooms. Both the deliberately blurred division between public and private and the palace's immediate proximity to a stadium were seminal features. Domitian's own rule ultimately failed, but his trend-setting palace was an important step in the institutionalization and solidification of the principate.

Imperial mornings

The average Roman was an early bird. In an age before electric light, the day lasted from sunrise to sunset, and day and night were each divided into twelve equal hours, so the length of one hour varied over the seasons and between day and night. People got up at cock-crow, when the first hour struck, and went to bed at sundown. Obviously, Roman emperors were no average Romans. Their sleeping habits differed, depending on their constitution and character. Suetonius recorded that Augustus habitually slept late: 'when sleep came to him he often prolonged it until after daylight'. Clearly this was sufficiently unusual to merit comment.

> **'He detested early rising and when he had to get up earlier than usual because of some official or religious duty, to avoid inconveniencing himself he spent the night in the room of one of his friends near the appointed place.'**
> Suetonius describing Augustus

Other emperors were more austere in their sleeping habits. Vespasian and Septimius Severus began to work before dawn; Marcus Aurelius rose early to dedicate some time to his philosophical studies; Constantine the Great and his son Constantius II read the Bible; Julian spent the small hours dealing with state affairs and the Muses. Julian also refused to sleep under warm downs and preferred a rugged blanket instead; on campaign, he slept on the floor like the soldiers, as did the young Marcus Aurelius. In general, Roman historians tend to praise moderate and regular sleeping habits. If, on the other hand, an emperor suffered from insomnia, this

Marcus Aurelius greeted by the Dea Roma, the personification of the city and state of Rome. Marble relief from a triumphal arch, 2nd century AD.

could well be a sign of strangeness of character, if not downright insanity: Suetonius notes that 'Caligula was tormented with sleeplessness', as he 'was terrified by strange apparitions'.

An ancient Roman breakfast (*ientaculum*) was not much of a meal: Vespasian, for example, took just a glass of water. After this the emperor got dressed, whereupon it was time for the *salutatio*. This was the morning audience in which petitioners could present their pleas to, and claimants have their lawsuits decided by, the emperor. The *salutatio* was serious business: in the age of the republic, the great senators had received their friends and clients in droves in their private houses every day. The ritual had symbolically reflected their authority: the larger the crowd, the more influential the host. It had underpinned the complex mutual relationships of loyalty, solidarity, protection and support between those with power and those without, relationships that had profoundly structured republican society.

Augustus, realizing the ritual's importance, maintained it for his emerging political system, the principate. When the emperor was in Rome, it was expected that the entire Senate and at least the upper echelons of the equestrian order would attend the *salutatio*. It was, however, open to any Roman citizen and anyone could bring a plea before the emperor. According to Aulus Gellius, who wrote in the 2nd century AD, the space in front of the imperial palace on the Palatine Hill was 'crowded with people of almost any background' every morning. Only senators with urgent commitments or health problems were excused. On the other hand, emperors could exclude individuals from the *salutatio* as a mark of disfavour: Nero once had Vespasian barred from the audience, because he had repeatedly fallen asleep during Nero's artistic performances. Some emperors, such as Hadrian, closed the palace on certain days and refused to admit petitioners, but this remained the exception.

The group of people expected at a *salutatio* varied according to the occasion. On an ordinary day, only senators, members of the

Water and fruit, depicted in a wall painting from the 'House of the Cervi' at Herculaneum, *c.* AD 45–79.

AN EMPEROR'S DAY

Before dawn	Reading letters and petitions (Vespasian, Septimius Severus)
1st hour	Morning reception of friends – short walk or swimming –
2nd	morning prayer (Severus Alexander)
3rd	Salutatio – legal hearings
4th	Hunting
5th	Ride – gymnastics – bathing
6th	Prandium (lunch) – ride
7th	Nap
8th	Office work – reading
9th	Meetings with advisory council and friends
10th	Walk
11th	
12th	Cena (dinner) – private study
After dusk	Convivium (dinner party)

equestrian order, petitioners and people requiring the emperor's service as supreme judge would have come to the palace. On special occasions, principally feast days, far larger crowds would have attended. Seneca provides us with instructions for the correct holding of a *salutatio*: the emperor was supposed to admit the whole group of visitors at once, but organized according to social rank. For the emperor, the ritual was time-consuming and sometimes tedious, but inevitable in order to make his presence felt by his subjects. For his visitors, it was a conveniently institutionalized and impersonal way to display their loyalty.

At table with the emperor

If there was some time left before lunch, the more athletic emperors might indulge in some physical exercise. The young Severus Alexander (ruled AD 222–235) enjoyed ball games, running or wrestling.

> Then, after having himself rubbed with oil, he would bathe, but rarely,
> if ever, in a hot bath, for he always used a swimming-pool, remaining in
> it about an hour; and before he took any food he would drink about a
> pint of cold water from the Claudian aqueduct,

reports the Historia Augusta, a collection of (rather unreliable) late emperors' biographies. This would be followed by a light meal, which preceded lunch (*prandium*):

> On coming out of the bath he would take a quantity of milk and bread,
> some eggs, and then a drink of mead. Thus refreshed, he would sometimes
> proceed to luncheon, sometimes put off eating until the evening meal, but
> more frequently he took luncheon.

For the ancient historians, an emperor's eating habits (like his sleeping patterns) were a mirror of his character, moral and ethical standards. Usually, a good emperor ate modestly and preferred simple dishes. Suetonius informs us that Augustus 'would eat even before dinner, wherever and whenever he felt hungry' but he was, on the other hand, 'a light eater…and as a rule ate plain food. He particularly liked coarse bread, small fishes, hand-made moist cheese, and green figs of the second crop.' Even more frugal was Tiberius, who is said to have 'often served at formal dinners meats left over from the day before and partly consumed, or the half of a boar, declaring that it had all the qualities of a whole one'. In his case, parsimony had long ago turned into avarice.

Fronto (see Box, page 48) the teacher of the philosopher-emperor Marcus Aurelius, had to persuade his student to eat. 'Have you eaten, Lord?' he used to ask Marcus, and would not leave him in peace until he had replied 'yes, I have.' Before

The emperor Vitellius, who was famed for his greed and extravagance.

Marcus Aurelius assumed power, when his adoptive father Antoninus Pius fell ill, he refused to bathe, eat and drink. Even in normal times, he ate little and reportedly only at night. It was claimed that the emperor Julian, who held Marcus Aurelius in high esteem, dismissed the cooks of his cousin Constantius as soon as he had succeeded him.

The exact opposite was Vitellius, whose gluttony was notorious. Tacitus, in his *Histories*, comments disapprovingly on his greed and his ruinously expensive tastes.

'His passion for elaborate banquets was shameful and insatiate. Dainties to tempt his palate were constantly brought from Rome and all Italy....The preparation of banquets for him ruined the leading citizens of the communities through which he passed.'

Tacitus describing Vitellius's greed

The biographer Suetonius records:

> Most notorious of all was the dinner given by his brother to celebrate the
> emperor's arrival in Rome, at which two thousand of the choicest fishes and
> seven thousand birds are said to have been served. He himself eclipsed even
> this at the dedication of a platter, which on account of its enormous size he
> called the 'Shield of Minerva, Defender of the City'.

His voracious appetite was unprecedented and even manifested itself at
religious rituals:

> He could never refrain, even when he was sacrificing or making a journey,
> from snatching bits of meat and cakes amid the altars, almost from the very
> fire, and devouring them on the spot; and in the cookshops along the road,
> viands smoking hot or even those left over from the day before.

Caligula, Nero and Commodus – all bloody tyrants – were also sybarites: Suetonius's
Lives of the Caesars tells us that Caligula gave banquets in which the annual revenue
from three provinces was eaten up and that Nero extended his lunch till the evening.
Some (such as Herodian in his *History of the Empire*) believed that Commodus was
not murdered, but died of his immoderate eating habits. Maximinus Thrax, whom
the ancient authors accused of barbarian descent, was allegedly able to devour
enormous quantities: 40 pounds of meat and 100 pints of wine in a single day. His
eating habits were truly barbarian:

'It seems sufficiently agreed, too, that he
abstained wholly from vegetables, and almost
always from anything cold, save when he had to
drink. Often, he would catch his sweat and put it in
cups or a small jar, and he could exhibit by this
means two or three pints of it.'

Suetonius describing Maximinus Thrax

Trajan and Hadrian, who were both good emperors, did not disapprove of good
food (Trajan is even said to have had oysters carried to the front during his Parthian
War) but their fondness for eating well was not uncontrolled. It is clear that the
model for the good emperor was profoundly inspired by Stoicism: abstinence
from all excesses was crucial for the life in harmony with nature that was the
aim of Stoic philosophers.

Imperial gluttony could be literally fatal. Suetonius tells us that Claudius was 'extravagantly fond' of mushrooms, and reports a rumour that the emperor's wife Agrippina poisoned his mushrooms at a family dinner:

> Many say that as soon as he swallowed the poison he became speechless, and after suffering excruciating pain all night, died just before dawn. Some say that he first fell into a stupor, then vomited up the whole contents of his overloaded stomach, and was given a second dose, perhaps in a gruel, under pretence that he must be refreshed with food after his exhaustion, or administered in a syringe, as if he were suffering from a surfeit and required relief by that form of evacuation as well.

Dinner party

If the emperor was lucky, he had a few spare moments in the afternoon. Augustus used to have a siesta, but only briefly, fully dressed and in sandals. So did Claudius, Domitian, Trajan and Severus Alexander. Others preferred some athletic activity. According to Suetonius, Vespasian took time for:

> A nap, lying with one of his concubines, of whom he had taken several after the death of Caenis. After his siesta he went to the bath and the dining-room; and it is said that at no time was he more good-natured or indulgent, so that the members of his household eagerly watched for these opportunities of making requests.

Some emperors looked after state affairs in the afternoon, received their counsellors, attended to their correspondence or went for a walk having conversations with their friends or staff. The later afternoon was then usually reserved for a second bath.

Then, before sunset, it was time for dinner (*cena*). This was normally a formal occasion. To host a dinner party (*convivium*) gave a wealthy man the opportunity to see his friends, to confirm social ties and to reciprocate favours (*beneficia*). In Roman high society, relations were extremely formalized. 'Friendship' (*amicitia*) was a bond of mutual solidarity that was regularly underpinned by the exchange of material or symbolic *beneficia*. An invitation to a dinner party could repay a *beneficium* or anticipate a future one. On the other hand, failure to invite a friend could cause serious offence.

Roman *convivia* were anything but casual. Places were assigned according to the guest's social rank, by strict protocol. For the meal, the guests reclined on couches (Latin *lectus* or Greek *kline*). Romans sat at the table only at ordinary meals: dinner party guests lay on their left side and used only their right hand for eating and drinking. The couches were lined up along three walls of the dining room (*triclinium*). The *triclinium* that Nero built in his luxurious new palace in Rome, the Domus Aurea ('Golden House'), had walls covered with gold, gemstones and mother-of-pearl. The ceiling was made of ivory and crowned by a continuously rotating dome, from which flowers and perfume rained onto the participants through little windows. This structure, described by Suetonius, has recently been unearthed by French archaeologists. Of course, not all dinner parties were held in

A dining scene, in a wall painting from Pompeii. On the right, a slave supports a drunken guest. A young slave takes off the shoes of a guest sitting on the left, and another slave hands him a drinking vessel.

Nero's rotating dining room from the Domus Aurea. The room, which has a diameter of 16 m (about 52 ft), was recently discovered by a team of French archaeologists. The room was set in motion by flowing water. According to Suetonius, there were ivory panels in the ceiling, which could be opened to let flowers rain down on the guests.

such spectacularly lavish surroundings, but for the host it was a matter of honour to entertain his guests properly. Ordinary hosts usually entertained between three and nine diners (nine was considered the ideal number), but emperors received guests by the hundreds. Claudius is said to have hosted a function for six hundred people, and Domitian may have invited even more to his parties.

The art of hospitality

The food served in the various courses had to be exquisite and as exotic as possible. It was often arranged in a rather eccentric manner. Petronius's 1st-century novel *Satyricon* describes the extravagant dinner party held by Trimalchio, a poorly educated but fabulously rich freedman, at his country estate:

> Then the preliminary course was served in very elegant style. For all were now at table except Trimalchio, for whom the first place was reserved, by a reversal of ordinary usage. Among the other hors d'oeuvres stood a little ass of Corinthian bronze with a packsaddle holding olives, white olives on one side, black on the other. The animal was flanked right and left by silver dishes, on the rim of which Trimalchio's name was engraved and the weight. On arches built up in the form of miniature bridges were dormice seasoned with honey and poppy-seed. There were sausages, too, smoking hot on a silver grill, and underneath (to imitate coals) Syrian plums and pomegranate seeds.

The *convivium* described here is fictitious, but Petronius – who was a contemporary of Nero's and his adviser in matters of taste – may have been an habitué of even more sumptuous gatherings hosted by the emperor. It is even possible to suspect that the character of Trimalchio might be a caricature of Nero.

Roman cuisine was spicy and elaborate. Meat and fish were served with sophisticated sauces, such as *garum* or *liquamen*, a seasoning dip made from

A service of silver dishes from Boscoreale (near Naples, Italy). The hoard of 109 pieces, mostly from the early imperial period, was found in 1896. Similar dishes may have been used when dozens of guests were entertained at imperial dinner parties.

fermented fish that had been exposed to the sun for months. Meat was usually boiled or marinated in honey and vinegar. The emperor's chefs used ingredients from all parts of the Roman world – oysters from Campania, cheese from Dalmatia, grapes and plums from Syria, *garum* from Spain, pork from Gaul, figs from the Aegean islands – but even private hosts could afford exotic fruit, vegetables, fish and meats. Petronius's character Trimalchio served ram from Taranto in southern Italy, honey from Attica and mushrooms from as far as India. For dessert, the guests had a variety of fruit and sweets made with honey. The *convivium* was followed by a carousal (*comissatio*), for which the women had to leave the dining room. Wines like the Falernum proffered by Trimalchio were rich and sometimes resinated. The wine was normally mixed with water – it was considered unrefined to drink pure wine. Alternatives to wine were *mulsum*, a kind of mead, and, in autumn, must (partly fermented grape juice).

Along with the food and drink came exquisite entertainment. Trimalchio laid on jugglers and acrobats, and comedians, actors, mimes and musicians performed at Augustus's parties. Particularly popular was Gabba, a court jester whose jokes were famous and who was allowed to utter even political criticism. The participants themselves engaged in hilarious or seriously academic conversation. For some, the *convivium* was a stage. Trimalchio recited his own poetry, of rather unpretentious simplicity:

A glass vessel with grapes and plums. This is a detail from a wall painting in the 'House of Julia Felix' in Pompeii, *c.* AD 70. Still life paintings were quite popular in the Roman world and many have been found in Pompeii, Herculaneum and the Villa Boscoreale.

When least we think, things go astray
Dame Fortune o'er our life holds sway
Then drink, make merry, whilst ye may!

Nero may have been one of the most eccentric hosts of imperial *convivia,* but it was Domitian who gave dinner parties with the upper crust of Rome's society a completely new meaning. Most of the previous emperors had, when dining with senators, tried to conceal the enormous gap between themselves and the old aristocracy. In order to create an intimate atmosphere, they chose a private rather than an official setting for their function. Domitian, however, had his new palace on the Palatine Hill equipped with a dining hall of unprecedented size (see pages 78–79), specifically designed to emphasize the division rather than conceal it.

A wall painting from Stabiae, showing a young female musician playing the cithara, 1st century AD.

The emperor and the Senate

A *convivium* was an appropriate occasion for the emperor and the senatorial elite to communicate with each other. Here, the role of the old ruling class within the new political order was put on display, power relations were negotiated and established and the emperor's authority was at stake, if he failed to live up to his guests' expectations. The *convivium* was also a place for political communication – albeit in a subtle and indirect manner – which had been practically banned from the traditional stage of political controversy, the Senate House. How did this method of communication work?

First and foremost, the *convivium* displayed the harmony between the emperor and his guests, mainly senators. Being invited by the emperor meant consorting with him on – in principle – equal terms. In theory, the emperor was a fellow senator, just slightly more powerful. Paradoxically, however, even while it expressed this supposed equality, the *convivium* underlined the real difference in power. By granting his senatorial guests a collective *beneficium* in return for their individual gifts to him, the emperor made clear that the relationship was asymmetric. This principle of asymmetric gift-exchange inherent in the imperial dinner party was carried to a perverted extreme by Caligula, who – financially in dire straits – sold off personal invitations to his *convivia*.

One way in which an invitee could show gratitude for his inclusion on the guest list was by making a lively contribution to the conversation. Witty statements, storytelling or philosophical and literary discourse were appreciated. Some guests flattered their hosts with lengthy eulogies, while others came up with insults of the

The Curia Julia, or Senate House, on the Roman Forum. It was renewed several times following repeated destruction by fire. The building shown here, built of brick-faced concrete, was constructed under Diocletian.

most abusive kind. What was appropriate depended on the situation and on the speaker's position in the pecking order. Decorum was a concept deeply rooted in Roman thinking. It was the benchmark for everything Romans did or liked and, as such, was a powerful instrument to reinforce social hierarchies – even when they were seemingly being ignored. A wrong word at the wrong time could cost a speaker credit with his audience; too much luxury could be inappropriate in some circumstances, but a lack of lavishness could be equally blameworthy in others. Insults, even made by social inferiors, could be tolerable as long as they served to put in perspective an influential man's liberality. Seneca reports that a man called Varus was invited to rich men's tables precisely because his wit and mockery highlighted the host's urbanity; otherwise, insulting the host would have been an act of quite inexcusable misbehaviour.

When conversing with the emperor, the senators naturally had to weigh their words carefully. However, the emperor in his turn had to take into consideration the pride and sensibility of an aristocracy which, under the auspices of monarchic government, had been transformed from a *noblesse de robe* (an elite group of elected officials) into an increasingly exclusive class, jealous of its established traditions, whose members proudly displayed their distinctive rank insignia: red shoes and the *latus clavus*, the broad purple band on the tunic.

Augustus's arrangement with this aristocratic class was based on a tacit agreement in which political reality – the emperor's omnipotence – was delicately not mentioned aloud. Augustus treated the senators like equals, but they, in return, did not question his authority. While firmly holding on to power, he was at pains not to appear too anxious for it: when the Senate proposed renewal of the *imperium proconsulare* and *tribunicia potestas*, the emperor accepted with every appearance of reluctance. He also refused several times (before accepting!) the honorific name of *pater patriae* ('father of the fatherland').

The emperor as supreme judge

In any monarchic system, the ruler should – ideally – be the ultimate source of justice. Rome was no exception. Of course, the emperor could not personally administer the law everywhere and at all times; he, the Senate and the magistrates were immediately responsible only for the city of Rome. Rome did not impose its laws on the other cities of the Roman world, which had their own jurisdiction and their own individual constitutions and legal systems. The emperor's role was limited to two main duties: first, he oversaw the implementation of law – any law – everywhere in the empire; secondly, the imperial tribunal was the highest court in the empire, with the emperor as the supreme judge who theoretically had the ultimate say in all lawsuits.

The so-called *Judgement of Solomon*, a 19th-century copy of a lost wall painting from the 'House of the Physician' in Pompeii. Here, the dispute over a baby, which originates in Egyptian rather than biblical tradition, is enacted by pygmies.

The procedure of judicial appeal emerged from the magisterial power that the emperors, from Augustus onwards, devolved to the provincial governors. This power was derived from the emperor's *imperium proconsulare*. In legal practice, the governors, as the emperor's representatives in the provinces, were able to overrule the sentences of any city's court. If a citizen was unhappy with a local tribunal's judgment, he could appeal to the governor. As the governor was the emperor's representative, it was logical that those who were discontented with his decision could, in principle, appeal to the sovereign himself.

From Claudius onwards, this system of hierarchic appeal was institutionalized. The most famous case of a Roman citizen appealing to the emperor himself is that of St Paul in the Acts of the Apostles. St Paul, accused by Jews and threatened by a Jewish mob, was taken into custody by the Roman guard. He revealed his identity – *Civis Romanus sum* ('I am a Roman citizen') – and appealed to the governor and later to the emperor. He was brought as a prisoner to Rome where he (presumably) made his appeal in the emperor's presence. Legend has it that he was beheaded in the 60s, during Nero's reign.

The emperor's court became the control centre of the empire's judicial branch. Governors and the emperor himself spent a substantial amount of time on legal matters. The ruler's court was theoretically open to any appellant, but of course time was the one practical factor that could limit access. Nevertheless, the right to appeal promoted the empire's integration: by taking every single citizen's legal concerns seriously, the emperor presented himself as a caring sovereign to whom justice and the individual's well-being mattered. Imperial sentences were, of course, the ultimate authority and had enormous scope. They had to be deliberate and incontestable.

In earlier times, the republican praetors had informal 'think tanks' with consultants who gave advice (*consilium*) in legal matters. Augustus established a similar board, backed by his own authority, so that the responses of its members to petitioners carried the same weight as if the emperor himself were judging (*ius respondendi ex auctoritate principis*). Until the 2nd century AD, this body of expert lawyers was composed exclusively of senators, who had the social standing and the professional authority to carry out its duties. A formal advisory council, the *consilium principis*, was first introduced under Hadrian. A new elite was formed consisting of professional lawyers, who were increasingly recruited from the equestrian order. One of the two praetorian prefects was an expert in law and responsible for the systematization and canonization of Roman law, which was now in essence a collection of imperial judgments.

Page of a manuscript with passages from the Codex Theodosianus, now held in the Vatican.

Quod principi placuit, legis habet vigorem – 'an emperor's decision has the quality of a law'. This was the axiom of Roman law for the centuries that followed. Over and over again, generations of lawyers produced new compilations of imperial edicts and decisions, until, in late antiquity, the imperial edicts were gathered in two major editions: the Codex Theodosianus under the emperor Theodosius II, published in AD 438; and the more comprehensive Corpus Juris Civilis, first presented to the public under Justinian in AD 529 and later amended with supplements.

Quod principi placuit, legis habet vigorem
‘**An emperor's decision has the quality of a law**’

Considering the sheer number of imperial sentences included in the late antique codices, it is hardly surprising that a substantial proportion of an emperor's working hours was consumed by judicial hearings. Normally, he would sit in judgment in the morning, but hearings could last several hours and tended to be tiresomely routine (Claudius reportedly used to fall asleep during proceedings). Hearings were held in public: under Augustus, they took place in the Temple of Apollo on the Palatine Hill, next to his home; later imperial courts convened in the palace or on the Forum.

When emperors were travelling or on campaign, they still held hearings. For this purpose, a temporary wooden structure, the tribunal, was put up, on which the emperor was seated. A vivid impression of a Roman trial is given by the 2nd-century philosopher and novelist Apuleius in his *Apologia*, a speech in which the author defends himself against the charge of witchcraft, raised by the family of a rich widow whom Apuleius had married. The hearing takes place before the governor (proconsul) of the province of Africa in AD 158 or 159 – not an imperial court, but held under very similar conditions. Particularly interesting are the arguments put forward by Apuleius, culminating in the invitation to the governor to side with the defendant. He flatters the judge, addressing Claudius Maximus, the governor, as 'a man of stern character, burdened with the business of the whole province'. He points out how much he and Maximus have in common, as fellow intellectuals:

> Shall I take what is far the best course and, relying on your learning, Maximus, and your perfect erudition, disdain to reply to the accusations of these stupid and uncultivated fellows?

The remains of the Temple of Apollo on the Palatine, where Augustus held his legal hearings. The sanctuary, standing on a terrace, was surrounded by the emperor's property. According to Suetonius, it was Apollo himself who, with a flash of lightning, drew Augustus's attention to the spot.

He then dwells on his own noble birth, impeccable moral standards and influential friends, even in Rome. What counted in the courtroom, Apuleius's speech reveals, was less the factual evidence than a party's social standing, reputation and ability to fraternize with the judge. Imperial hearings were hardly different. We do not know exactly who qualified to be heard by the emperor himself, but we can safely assume that social rank and prestige mattered. Another factor was inevitably geography: those close to the emperor's location had a better chance of being heard than those living at a distance. As well as individuals, groups (notably cities) could appeal. Sometimes, peasants sought (and received) the emperor's support against powerful landowners, *procuratores* or other adversaries. A case of particular interest is the complaint of the Goharieni, a community of Syrian peasants, brought before Caracalla in AD 216, while the emperor was in Antioch. A bilingual (Latin and Greek) inscription on the Temple of Zeus Hypsistos at Thelsea (modern Dmeir) near Damascus records their advocate's accusations against a man who:

> Enjoys immunity from taxation and exemption from liturgies [financial contributions], wears a gold crown, enjoys precedence, has taken the sceptre in his hand and has proclaimed himself the priest of Zeus.

Caracalla declares that he considers the complaint justified, and the trial proceeds.

The case is striking in several respects. First, it reveals that an emperor had to attend to justice even on the empire's remote fringes, where local law was applied and Aramaic was the language commonly spoken. However, the people concerned, the emperor included, used Greek for the interrogation and Latin for the records. Second, though people of high social standing had the best chance of appealing to the emperor, his commitment to justice made it imperative that he also hear the complaints of humble subjects like the Goharieni. Third, although the imperial court usually heard only appeals, there were exceptions: if the emperor happened to be nearby, he could also settle disputes in the first instance. Finally, the Goharieni hearing proves that the habit of recording imperial decisions in stone extended to remote areas, even in somewhat unspectacular cases.

The desire to monumentalize the emperor's word was not restricted to lawsuits in the strict sense. His rescripts (written replies) to countless petitions brought before him by individuals, cities or tribes were likewise publicly displayed in

The inscription on this bronze stela of AD 138 records a letter from the emperor Hadrian. He confirms the status of the town Naryka in Lokris, central Greece, as an autonomous *polis*.

The Roman Forum, with the
Palatine in the background.
The Temple of Saturn, of which
eight columns still stand, was
originally dedicated in 489 BC
and repeatedly rebuilt. The
sanctuary was home to the
aerarium, the Roman state
treasury. There was also a
public notice board, where
official announcements were
posted. The three columns to
the right belong to the Temple
of the deified Vespasian.

epigraphic form. Men of some standing would appear before the emperor in person
– an act often brokered by influential friends or patrons – and hand over a written
dossier (*libellus*) containing their petition; others had their *libelli* sent to him
through a third party. The emperor would then add some written lines to the
document, the *subscriptio*, in which he either granted or denied the request. In
many cases, he referred the applicant back to the governor, who then received
instructions to comply with the petition. Alongside his legal duties, replying to
petitions was one of the core responsibilities of a Roman emperor: it made manifest
the emperor's care for his subjects and allowed them to feel close to him. It was, not
least, an act of beneficence in the continuous exchange of benefaction.

The imperial treasury

Granting subjects' requests could make an emperor popular, but it was expensive.
Imperial largesse, the administration, the court, the infrastructure, the capital's
grain supply and above all the army regularly required enormous amounts of
money. In order to finance the various expenses, the imperial budget needed steady,
reliable sources of income. In order to keep track of revenue and expenditure,
the central government required a sophisticated – by ancient standards –
financial bureaucracy.

In the republic, the Roman state treasury had been the *aerarium* in the Temple
of Saturn on the Roman Forum. Here, the revenues from booty, tribute, taxes, fines,
mines and the lease of land were collected, along with documents, the legionary
standards and other valuable items. In the last two centuries of the republic, the

A detail from the Arch of
Constantine. This panel comes
from the frieze celebrating
his victory over Maxentius.
The emperor – his head is
missing – sits on a podium
in the centre. From his right
hand we see coins falling into
the toga of the man standing
beside him, probably a senator.

continuing process of expansion had largely paid for the maintenance of a growing army and the few other public liabilities. After Augustus established the principate, the government had far more financial commitments and the dividend of war was no longer a reliable source of income. For the first time in Roman history, it was now necessary to draw up a proper budget year by year.

In order to meet the various financial requirements, in addition to the *aerarium* a whole series of funds or 'chests' were introduced, the most important of which was the *fiscus Caesaris*, the 'emperor's basket'. The money in the *aerarium* was public in the sense that it belonged to and was (ideally) under the control of the people, but the *fiscus* was in the emperor's sole domain. This does not mean that it was private money for private purposes. For their personal needs, the emperors had their own funds, the *patrimonium Caesaris* and later the *res privatae*. On the contrary the *fiscus,* which was filled from real estate taxes, duties and the revenues from mines, imperial mints and manufactories, was used for the army, the bureaucracy, imperial munificence, roads and water supply systems and for feeding Rome's population and providing benefits for Italian families. The immense sums paid out by emperors on their accession in order to ensure loyalty – the *donativum* for the soldiers and the *congiarium* for the Roman populace – may have been taken from the *fiscus*, too. For the care of veterans, Augustus introduced yet another chest: the *aerarium militare*, into which the inheritance tax revenues were paid.

Even for contemporaries, it was not always easy to distinguish between the various financial pots. A confused Cassius Dio thus fails to explain where the money for road repairs carried out under Augustus came from. In 27 BC, the emperor funded street repairs on the Via Flaminia, the road connecting Rome to the north of Italy. He tried to encourage various senators to pay for the maintenance of other main roads, but they proved reluctant:

> The other roads were repaired later, at the expense either of the public…
> or of Augustus, as one chooses to put it. For I am unable to distinguish
> between the two funds, no matter how extensively Augustus coined into
> money silver statues of himself which had been set up by certain of his
> friends and by certain of the subject peoples, purposing thereby to make it
> appear that all the expenditures which he claimed to be making were from
> his own means. Therefore I have no opinion to record as to whether a
> particular emperor on a particular occasion got the money from the public
> funds or gave it himself. For both courses were frequently followed; and why
> should one enter such expenditures as loans or as gifts respectively, when
> both the people and the emperor are constantly resorting to both the one
> and the other indiscriminately?

The revenue side was equally complicated. The main source of income for the state was the tax on landed property – the crucial means of production in a largely agriculturalist economy. It was, with some exceptions, raised as a tax in money. Italy and cities that had been awarded Italian law were exempt, until Diocletian abolished

A relief depicting a notary collecting taxes.

the peninsula's traditional privileges at the end of the 3rd century AD. In order to assess those liable for taxation, a land register was established and a census held at regular intervals. This system, which largely fell apart during the crises of the 3rd century, was renewed and further rationalized by Diocletian, who introduced a poll tax and a land tax component – a provision that, for the first time in its history, secured the empire reliable tax revenues over the long term.

Other taxes included that on inheritance, which only Roman citizens had to pay (that is probably why Caracalla issued, in AD 212, the *Constitutio Antoniniana*, an edict that made all free inhabitants of the empire Roman citizens), a sales tax, a charge due on the enfranchisement of slaves, and duties payable on imperial frontiers as well as on the borders between provinces and customs districts. When a new emperor assumed power and on anniversaries it was common practice for the cities 'voluntarily' to offer him golden crowns (*aurum coronarium*). On other occasions, such as victories, cities 'volunteered' to pay contributions (*munera, collationes*). In his Res Gestae (21), Augustus proudly points out that he remitted 35,000 pounds weight of coronary gold in his fifth consulship and he refused to accept contributions from then on.

This fragmentary inscription, now in the Pergamon Museum in Berlin, shows Diocletian's price edict, which set maximum prices for a range of commodities. Similar inscriptions, in Latin and Greek, were put up throughout the empire.

> **'Whenever I was saluted as imperator, I did not accept the coronary gold, although the municipia and colonies voted it in the same kindly spirit as before.'**
>
> Augustus boasts that he did not use his imperial role to enrich himself

Such austerity was the exception rather than the rule, but it was seen as a characteristic of the 'good' emperor in later periods too. During the wars against the Marcomanni and Quadi, Marcus Aurelius had some of his personal belongings auctioned for the war chest. On the other hand, bad emperors often confiscated entire estates and had rich men executed in order to take possession of their goods and chattels.

A more reliable source of personal income for the emperor was the landed property he owned in the form of large estates (*latifundia*). Like any senator, the emperor had *latifundia* in all parts of the empire. They were large enterprises, managed with the purpose of maximizing profits. Often they

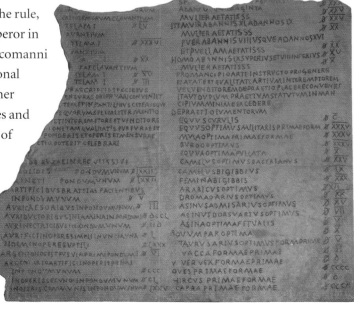

A Roman *villa rustica*, depicted in a mosaic of the 4th century AD. Country estates, using slave labour, produced vast quantities of wheat, olive oil and wine.

produced specialized, high-value crops, such as grapes or olives, for market. The actual management of the estates was farmed out to tenants (*conductores*), who themselves leased the land to peasant farmers (*coloni*). Large *latifundia* in private ownership were often run in a similar way, but in the case of the imperial estates, equestrian *procuratores* were in charge of overseeing the management and the cash flow into the imperial chest.

Managing an empire

Augustus's new empire and the many duties the emperor assumed in it required something the republic had gone without: a bureaucracy. The question was, who could fill the numerous posts in the empire's new administration? Augustus's obvious choice for the most senior positions was the senators. Although the relationship between the ruler and the Senate was precarious at times, no emperor could do without the senatorial aristocracy – at least until the late 2nd century AD. The senators were indispensable because they were the only ones qualified for the highest military commands and the higher echelons in the imperial administration: senators served

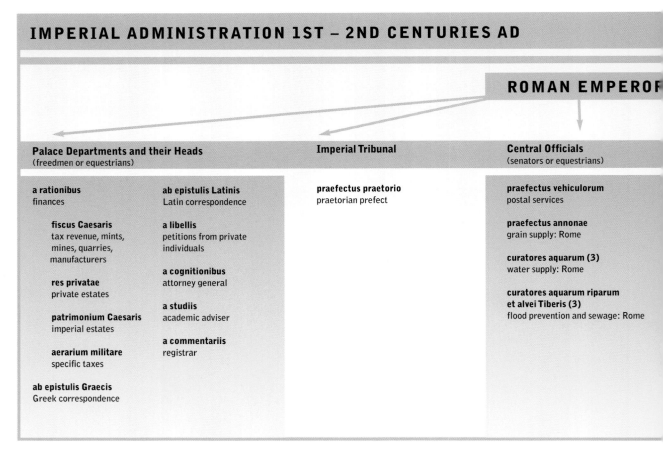

IMPERIAL ADMINISTRATION 1ST – 2ND CENTURIES AD

ROMAN EMPEROR

Palace Departments and their Heads
(freedmen or equestrians)

a rationibus
finances

fiscus Caesaris
tax revenue, mints,
mines, quarries,
manufacturers

res privatae
private estates

patrimonium Caesaris
imperial estates

aerarium militare
specific taxes

ab epistulis Graecis
Greek correspondence

ab epistulis Latinis
Latin correspondence

a libellis
petitions from private
individuals

a cognitionibus
attorney general

a studiis
academic adviser

a commentariis
registrar

Imperial Tribunal

praefectus praetorio
praetorian prefect

Central Officials
(senators or equestrians)

praefectus vehiculorum
postal services

praefectus annonae
grain supply: Rome

curatores aquarum (3)
water supply: Rome

**curatores aquarum riparum
et alvei Tiberis (3)**
flood prevention and sewage: Rome

Court

praepositus sacri cubiculi
(Head of Court Administration)

• chief steward
• quartermaster
• servants
• palace guard

as provincial governors (*legati pro praetore* and *pro consule*); as legionary commanders (*legati legionis*); as judges, priests or high officials. One such was Frontinus who, as *curator aquarum*, was in charge of Rome's water supply system under Trajan.

The best-known senatorial official is Pliny the Younger. Born in AD 61 or 62, he was the nephew and adoptive son of Pliny the Elder, the famous natural philosopher who died in the eruption of Vesuvius in 79. An inscription from Comum (Como), his birthplace, gives us the details of his career: he was *tribunus militum* in Syria (82), quaestor, plebeian tribune, praetor (93–94) and finally consul (100). In about 111, he became governor (*legatus Augusti pro praetore*) of the province of Pontus and Bithynia in northern Asia Minor. Pliny was a prolific correspondent, who exchanged dozens of letters with the emperor, mainly about the governance of his province. As a cautious man, Pliny wanted to be on the safe side: 'It is my invariable rule, Sir, to refer to you in all matters where I feel doubtful.'

One such matter was a relatively new religion, to which the people in Pliny's province flocked: Christianity. Pliny enquires of Trajan whether he should

The structure of the imperial administration in the earlier and later empire.

Consilium principis (advisory council), from Hadrian onwards

Provinces	Military Forces at Rome
proconsuls Africa and Asia	**praefecti praetorio** praetorian prefects (1–3) cohortes praetoriae (9–16) (Praetorian Guard)
propraetors	
legati Augusti pro consule	**praefectus urbi** urban prefect cohortes urbanae (3–7) (municipal police: Rome)
legati Augusti pro praetore	
praefectus Aegypti Egypt	**praefectus vigilum** cohortes vigilum (7) (fire department: Rome)
procuratores Norium, Raetia and Judaea	

Military	**Civilian**
legati legionis legionary commanders	**quaestores provinciae** provincial finance officials
	procuratores subordinate finance officials

IMPERIAL ADMINISTRATION 3RD – 4TH CENTURIES AD

ROMAN EMPEROR
Schola notariorum (imperial office)

	Central Administration		Territorial Administration	Military
quaestor sacri palatii (Minister of Justice) • sacrum consistorium (law experts)	**fiscus** • mines, mints, etc • imperial estates • private assets • tax revenue **Heads of Department** scrinium memoriae scrinium epistularum scrinium libellorum (etc)	**magister officiorum** (chief civilian official) • imperial bodyguards • secret agents (agentes in rebus) • armouries • admission to imperial audiences	**praefecti praetorio** **vicarii** (dioceses) Provincial governors (**consulares, correctores** etc)	**magister militum** (commander-in-chief) **magistri militum praesentales** Regional **magistri militum** **duces** Legionary commanders

distinguish between young ones and adults, between repentant ones and those who were stubborn, whether the profession of Christianity alone is a crime: 'on all these points I am in great doubt'. Pliny wants to make sure that his course of action meets the emperor's approval and explains his measures:

> I asked them whether they were Christians; if they admitted it, I repeated the question twice, and threatened them with punishment; if they persisted, I ordered them to be at once punished: for I was persuaded, whatever the nature of their opinions might be, a contumacious and inflexible obstinacy certainly deserved correction.

To Pliny's relief, the emperor is pleased with his governor's treatment of the Christians: 'You have adopted the right course, my dearest Secundus'. Under Trajan, there was some repression of Christianity, but the period of the great, systematic persecutions was still to come in the 3rd and early 4th centuries. Repeatedly, Pliny used his direct access to the emperor to broker benefactions for his protégés or people to whom he owed a favour.

> **'Having been attacked last year by a very severe and dangerous illness, I employed a physician, whose care and diligence, Sir, I cannot sufficiently reward, but by your gracious assistance. I entreat you therefore to make him a citizen of Rome; for as he is the freedman of a foreign lady, he is, consequently, himself also a foreigner.'**
>
> Pliny the Younger writing to Trajan

The physician who saved Pliny from serious illness is Egyptian, and first requires the citizenship of Alexandria, before he can be made a Roman citizen. Trajan grants this, too, but he replies with some irritation:

> It is my resolution, in pursuance of the maxim observed by the princes my predecessors, to be extremely cautious in granting the freedom of the city of Alexandria: however, since you have obtained of me the freedom of Rome for your physician Arpocras, I cannot refuse you this other request. You must let me know to what district he belongs, that I may give you a letter to my friend Pompeius Planta, governor of Egypt.

Senators like Pliny served as the empire's top officials, but they were by no means professional administrators. Besides, they tended to be self-reliant and could be proud and pigheaded. Regarding themselves as the emperor's partners, if not competitors, they were often unwilling to comply with his orders unconditionally. That is why emperors, for the recruitment of their civil service, increasingly relied on professionals. These could be found in the equestrian order and among the growing group of imperial freedmen.

Equestrian officials

By the late republic, Rome's 'knights', originally those who had fought on horseback, had become a wealthy class of entrepreneurs and traders. From Augustus onwards, access to the equestrian order was controlled by the emperor, who could appoint any free-born citizen worth at least 400,000 *sestertii*. Augustus filled the ranks of the imperial administration with these men. As a result, Rome's second class became a group of hand-picked administrative professionals.

The first top job reserved for an equestrian official was that of prefect of the province of Egypt. This important province had been established in 30 BC, after the victory over Mark Antony and Cleopatra, and it soon became vital for Rome's grain supply. Another position that soon became crucial for equestrians was that of *praefectus praetorio*: the prefect of the Praetorian Guard (see page 106). This office, established in 2 BC, was responsible for the emperor's safety and for the command of the urban garrison in Rome. In the republic, the capital had been demilitarized. When Augustus, in 27 BC, arranged for two cohorts to be garrisoned in Rome, it was a clear break with tradition, barely camouflaged by the civilian clothes that the soldiers were ordered to wear instead of their uniforms when they were in the city.

Soon the praetorian prefects, with the capital's soldiers rallying behind them, became key figures in government and in the making of emperors. Sejanus, Tiberius's praetorian prefect, was the grey eminence behind the emperor; when Tiberius left for Capri, Sejanus no longer bothered to conceal his power, and was finally overthrown. Macro, his successor in office, played a central role in Caligula's accession to the throne. After Caligula's assassination, the Praetorian Guard's actions were decisive once again: the soldiers granted Claudius asylum in their camp and hailed him as the next emperor. Later, some of their commanders, such as Ulpianus, who worked under Severus Alexander, and Aemilius Papinianus, praetorian prefect under Septimius Severus, were acclaimed lawyers; others, like Timesitheus, who served under the child-emperor Gordian III, were effectively regents for under-age rulers. In late antiquity, the office achieved a completely new significance: after Constantine the Great had disbanded the Praetorian Guard, the empire was divided into three, later four, prefectures and the praetorian prefects became the chief officials of this new administrative unit. This formed part of a more generic reform of the imperial government, reducing the size of the provinces and tightening central control by introducing several new tiers of regional administration.

Copper *as* minted by the praetorian prefect Sejanus in AD 31, with a portrait of Tiberius on the front (obverse). On many coins of this type the name of Sejanus was obliterated following his execution.

THE PRAETORIAN GUARD

Augustus established the Praetorian Guard in 27 BC to protect the emperor and to maintain law and order in the capital. Each of the almost 10,000 guardsmen received better pay and substantially greater privileges than the soldiers defending Rome's frontiers, but this did not completely guarantee their loyalty. Soldiers of the Guard killed Caligula and proclaimed Claudius emperor in AD 41; in 238, the Guard mutinied against the two Senate-appointed emperors, Balbinus and Pupienus, killed them and declared Gordian III Augustus.

The extent of the power that the Praetorian Guard acquired is demonstrated by the story of Pertinax. His short reign in early AD 193 was brought to an end by his plummeting popularity with the soldiers. Because they were not 'allowed to plunder any longer', according to Cassius Dio, and fearing for their privileges, soldiers of the Praetorian Guard plotted against Pertinax. Some of them entered the palace and killed the emperor. What followed was one of the most disgraceful episodes in the Guard's history. 'For, just as if it had been in some market or auction-room, both the City and its entire empire were auctioned off. The sellers were the ones who had slain their emperor, and the would-be buyers were Sulpicianus and Julianus, who vied to outbid each other,' reports Cassius Dio. Didius Julianus's bid (25,000 *denarii* for each soldier) was successful; he won the auction and bought his way into the purple, though his rule lasted only three months.

Particularly powerful were the commanders of the Guard, the praetorian prefects. After Tiberius left Rome for Capri, the praetorian prefect Sejanus began to dominate Roman politics. The ambitious equestrian was dreaded by the senators. When rumours circulated that Sejanus intended to usurp imperial power for himself and his family, Tiberius finally returned to Rome and had him executed. In 37, Sejanus's successor Macro was a key figure in the succession of Caligula. Later, praetorian prefects were often leading law experts – the office was the acme of any equestrian career. The praetorian prefect Timesitheus acted as regent for the emperor Gordian III (238–244), who was only twelve years old at his accession.

The praetorians were a powerful factor in Roman politics, but their power had its limits. They could create and destroy emperors, but if substantial parts of the regular army did not agree with their choice, they were helpless. In AD 69, the praetorians backed Otho, but he had no chance against Vitellius, whom the Rhine legions supported; and in 193 the short-lived Didius Julianus proved unable to stand up to Septimius Severus. In the 3rd century, the emperors formed new units of bodyguards and the Praetorian Guard soon became obsolete. It was finally disbanded by Constantine the Great after his victory at the Milvian Bridge (312).

Marble relief of Praetorian Guards, from Rome, *c.* AD 51–52. Their archaizing uniform and equipment distinguished the guardsmen of the Praetorian cohorts from other soldiers.

Besides the praetorian prefect, the system of government Augustus established created an immense demand for administrative professionals to whom the emperor could delegate his responsibilities. Again, these were mainly recruited from the equestrian order. After a series of food shortages, worsened by the Senate's mismanagement, Augustus personally took responsibility for the capital's grain supply: a *praefectus annonae* was put in charge of having large quantities of grain transported to, and stored in, Rome. At first, Augustus approached the Senate to have the quaestors – traditional Senatorial magistrates – deal with the grain supply.

Roman officials. A high-ranking civil servant gives instructions to notaries, in a limestone relief found at Ostia, 1st/3rd century AD.

They failed and the urban populace reacted with (perhaps not wholly spontaneous) demonstrations, forcing the Senate to appeal to Augustus to intervene. Only then did Augustus appoint an equestrian to the post. The *praefectus vehiculorum* supervised the imperial courier service (*cursus publicus*) with its infrastructure. An equestrian *praefectus vigilum* saw to Rome's public fire service, which was also a creation of the first emperor. An army of *procuratores* ('managers'), also of equestrian rank, supervised the provinces' taxation, imperial estates, mines and quarries, the water supply of Rome and many other public services.

The new equestrian officials owed their power and status entirely to the emperor: they were not rooted in any family tradition of note, and lacked the senatorial aristocracy's strong cohesion. This made them much more disciplined, loyal and acquiescent to the emperor's will. In addition – again in contrast to senatorial officials, who were essentially serving for the sake of honour – the equestrians' careers took a professional turn at a very early stage. Whereas the senator's position was, first and foremost, an expression of his status, for the equestrian official it was exactly the other way round: he defined himself and his social rank through the position he held. An impressive demonstration of where an equestrian career could lead is offered by Marcus Gnaeus Licinius Rufinus, a native of the city of Thytira in Lydia, who became one of the empire's top jurists under the Severans and advanced even further under Maximinus Thrax and Gordian III. The identity of this man, who is mentioned in the Corpus Juris Civilis, is highlighted by the recent find of an honorific inscription from his home town. The inscription sums up the various stages of Rufinus's career: the son of an *eques* became *consiliarius Augusti* ('advisor of the emperor'), and then ran through the better part of the whole imperial portfolio, as the emperor's right hand for Greek correspondence, treasurer and chief registrar. He then switched over to the senatorial *cursus honorum*, holding the praetorship. This qualified him for the office of governor of Noricum, which he held in the 220s. Around 230, Rufinus reached the consulship and sat, in 238, on a senatorial board in charge of selecting a new emperor to replace Maximinus, who had been declared a public enemy. Membership of such a committee marked the climax of any senatorial career. Rufinus, born an equestrian from a small town in Lydia, had survived numerous political upheavals and had, in the end, arrived in the inner circle of power.

Freedmen in the corridors of power

The first emperor's residence on the Palatine Hill, the Domus Augusti, by design a private house rather than a palace, became the centre from which the empire was managed. Offices were set up and administrative procedures put in place. However, what was nascent here, on the Palatine, was no government in the modern sense; it was the paternalistic regime of a Roman landlord (*pater familias*) writ large. The nucleus of Augustus's imperial control centre was the *domus* ('house') of a wealthy Roman senator, from which a large *patrimonium* ('estate') was managed.

The funerary stele of Amemptus, a freedman of the empress Livia.

Freedmen and slaves were assigned to a number of duties in the management of such estates. These men were either in the landlord's ownership (slaves) or ex-slaves who remained entirely dependent on him (freedmen). Augustus was assisted by personal secretaries, usually freedmen: Suetonius probably refers to such people, called *a manu* ('handymen'), when he reports that Augustus 'held many of his freedmen in high honour and close intimacy, such as Licinus, Celadus, and others'. A tomb inscription found in Rome was dedicated to a certain Proculus Secundus Hyblaeus, *divi Augusti a ma[nu]* ('private secretary of the deified Augustus').

Later, this rudimentary bureaucracy was further institutionalized. Under Claudius, responsibilities were divided among freedmen officials, who thus received unprecedented power.

The *a rationibus* was in charge of the *fiscus Caesaris*, the emperor's personal treasury. The *ab epistulis* was responsible for the emperor's correspondence, which made him the main interface between the ruler and the subordinate administration, city councils and client kings included. The *a libellis* dealt with petitions brought before the emperor by private citizens. Other officials included the *a cognitionibus* (in charge of the emperor's jurisdiction), the *a commentariis* (the imperial registrar) and the *a studiis* (a kind of personal research assistant).

Though the palace administration was now far larger and more sophisticated than previously, the various secretaries still reported directly to the emperor; they were not strictly state officials. If they were freedmen – and in the days of Claudius and Nero most of the secretaries were former slaves – they belonged to the imperial household. Even more than the equestrian officials, they owed their status entirely to the emperor and the posts he had assigned to them. Suetonius, himself an *a studiis* under Trajan and an *ab epistulis* under Hadrian, introduces some of Claudius's top staff to us in his biography of the emperor:

> Of his freedmen he had special regard for the eunuch Posides, whom he even presented with the headless spear at his British triumph, along with those who had served as soldiers. He was equally fond of Felix, giving him the command of cohorts and of troops of horse, as well as of the province of Judaea; and he became the husband of three queens. Also of Harpocras, to whom he granted the privilege of riding through the city in a litter and of giving public entertainments. Still higher was his regard for Polybius, his *a studiis*, who often walked between the two consuls.

‘But most of all he was devoted to his secretary (ab epistulis) Narcissus and his treasurer (a rationibus) Pallas, and he gladly allowed them to be honoured in addition by a decree of the Senate, not only with immense gifts, but even with the insignia of quaestors and praetors.’

Suetonius

> Besides this he permitted them to amass such wealth by plunder, that when he once complained of the low state of his funds, the witty answer was made that he would have enough and to spare, if he were taken into partnership by his two freedmen.

So service in the palace administration could bring considerable status and social prestige to people of humble birth. Pliny, in his *Letters*, reports that Claudius's freedman Pallas resisted the acceptance of the golden ring (the equestrians' insignia) when it was offered to him by the emperor. It is hardly surprising that many people, especially senators, disapproved of the promotion of men who had neither a noble pedigree nor the *virtus* ('virtue') of a freeborn man. Suetonius, who belonged to the equestrian order, is clearly very critical of the privileges granted by Claudius to men like Narcissus and Pallas. That is why emperors after Claudius ceased to give freedmen such prominent positions in the palace bureaucracy and replaced them with equestrian officials. The last of the all-powerful freedmen was Pallas. According to Tacitus, Nero 'removed [Pallas] from the charge to which he had been appointed by Claudius, and in which he exercised virtual control over the monarchy'. In a last demonstration of his power, the outgoing Pallas descended from the Palatine Hill surrounded by crowds of his attendants. However, freedmen continued to work for the emperor; their services had become indispensable.

Portrait of the empress Messalina, Claudius's third wife, on a Greek coin.

Imperial women

Imperial women, like other females in the Roman world, were not supposed to exercise power. Their domain was the house, the *domus*. Attempts to break the mould provoked harsh criticism; only a few First Ladies were fully approved of by Roman historians. For emperors' wives the line between decorum and transgression was particularly fine: they were permanently in the spotlight, endowed with immense personal funds and could themselves be patrons of numerous clients. Many had considerable influence over their husbands or sons and thus wielded great, if indirect, power. A few exceptional women, such as the warrior queen Zenobia, ruled in their own right. However, Roman society always retained clearly defined gender roles. Powerful though many empresses became, emancipated women they were not.

Tacitus, Suetonius and other Roman historians criticised Claudius for his slavish obedience to the women around him. Claudius had four wives in total. When he became emperor in AD 41, he was married to his third wife, Valeria Messalina, a great-niece of Augustus. The judgment of Roman historians on Messalina is unanimous: she was a ruthless hussy, a jealous, scheming nymphomaniac. Messalina is said to have been responsible in AD 42 for the execution of the distinguished senator Appius Junius Silanus, who had been very close to Claudius. Reportedly he spurned Messalina's advances. Taking advantage of Claudius's credulousness and his neurotic fear of plots, she repeatedly joined forces with Narcissus, Claudius's freedman and chief minister, to scheme against the emperor's friends. The final straw was Messalina's preparation for a marriage with another senator, the consul designate Gaius Silius, while Claudius was away from Rome performing a sacrifice at the port of Ostia. This was too much and the freedmen, led by Narcissus, acted before it was too late. They denounced Messalina and Gaius Silius to the emperor and had the Praetorian Guard put down the insurgency.

After Messalina's death, Claudius married his niece Agrippina. She was Germanicus's daughter, Caligula's sister, Nero's mother: 'a woman who to this day stands unparalleled as the daughter of an imperator and the sister, the wife, and the mother of an emperor', as Tacitus describes her.

Agrippina had a son, Nero, from her first husband, Gnaeus Domitius Ahenobarbus. After her marriage to Claudius, she thought of nothing but manoeuvring her son into the imperial purple. By pursuing this aim, she acted as a true Roman aristocrat: bringing honour and glory to her *domus* was a legitimate purpose for a senator's daughter. However, the fact that Agrippina's *domus* was the Julio-Claudian house creates a dilemma for Tacitus. Because she was a member of the ruling dynasty, her actions by definition had a political dimension, but politics is not a woman's sphere. In order to explain this paradox, Tacitus depicts Agrippina in his *Annals* as a virago, a bloody tyrant in a woman's shape. Agrippina's marriage to Claudius transforms Rome:

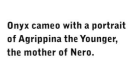

Onyx cameo with a portrait of Agrippina the Younger, the mother of Nero.

> From this moment it was a changed state, and all things moved at the fiat of a woman – but not a woman who, as Messalina, treated in wantonness the Roman empire as a toy. It was a tight-drawn, almost masculine tyranny: in public, there was austerity and not infrequently arrogance; at home, no trace of unchastity, unless it might contribute to power. A limitless passion for gold had the excuse of being designed to create a bulwark of despotism.

In a letter to Domitia Lucilla, the mother of Marcus Aurelius, the philosopher Fronto describes her as a model for the ideal imperial woman.

❛You have all the virtues and insights that befit a woman: love for your husband and your children, prudence, sincerity, truthfulness, friendliness, amenability, approachability and modesty.❜

The philosopher Fronto, writing to the mother of Marcus Aurelius

Such an exemplary First Lady was Livia, Augustus's third wife. She supported her husband, saw to the education of their children and grandchildren, and was reserved when she appeared in public. Unlike Agrippina, Livia needed neither intrigue nor murder to bring her *domus* into power. Nonetheless, everybody was aware of the 'commanding influence she had over her husband', writes Cassius Dio. When someone asked her for the secret, she replied 'that it was by being scrupulously chaste herself, doing gladly whatever pleased him, not meddling with any of his affairs, and, in particular, by pretending neither to hear nor to notice the favourites of his passion.'

Few empresses were as self-possessed as Livia. Poppaea, Nero's wife, actively sponsored the careers of many of her protégés, such as Gessius Florus, the disastrously incapable equestrian *procurator* of Judaea, whose mismanagement was partly responsible for the outbreak of the Judaean Revolt. Domitia Longina, Domitian's wife, was the daughter of Nero's most proficient general, Gnaeus Domitius Corbulo. She formed part of a network of influential aristocrats, which assisted her when Domitian discovered that she was having an affair, and repudiated her. Public demand forced him to reconcile with his wife and, later, Domitia played an active part in the plot that led to Domitian's assassination. Julia Domna, Septimius Severus's wife (see Box, opposite), was a highly visible member of the dynasty; she received numerous honorific titles and joined her son, the emperor Caracalla, when he was travelling or on campaign. Her daughter Julia Sohaemias, Elagabalus's mother, is said to have presided over a *senaculum*, a women's Senate, where idle sessions were held and irrelevant decisions made.

In some specific circumstances, the influence of imperial women could be crucial. After his disastrous campaign in Mesopotamia (AD 114–117),

LEFT **Marble bust of Pompeia Plotina, Trajan's wife. Her hairstyle is typical of the early 2nd century. The head was found in Rome's port, Ostia.**

BELOW **Life-size seated marble statue of the empress Livia, the wife of Augustus and mother of Tiberius. The statue, a Claudian replica of an early Julio-Claudian artwork, was found at Paestum.**

JULIA DOMNA, THE SYRIAN EMPRESS

The picture (right) seems to show a happy family, apart from one telling detail. It depicts Septimius Severus, a bearded man in middle age, crowned with a laurel wreath with pearls and gems; his wife Julia Domna, her roundish face surrounded by curls; and their two sons. One of them is wearing on his head a smaller copy of his father's wreath, but the other one's face is missing, deliberately scratched out.

The two boys are Bassianus, later renamed Marcus Aurelius Antoninus and, when he became emperor himself, universally known as Caracalla. The one with the erased face is Geta, the younger son, who became joint emperor with his brother on Septimius Severus's death in 211. Barely a year later, Caracalla killed Geta, reportedly in the arms of their mother, Julia Domna. The deliberate damage to the face on the Berlin Tondo bears witness to the sanctions that Caracalla imposed on his murdered brother's memory: Geta was to be forgotten for all time.

Julia Domna, the boys' mother, was a native of Emesa, in Syria. The town was home to a large temple of the local sun god Elagabalus, which attracted pilgrims from the entire Near East. For Greeks and Romans, the sanctuary was a strange place of worship: 'there was no artificially-made statue of the deity, of the kind that Greeks and Romans use; but there was a huge stone, rounded at the base and pointed at the top, and black', reports the historian Herodian. Julia belonged to the family that held the high priesthood in this temple and ruled Emesa before its absorption into the Roman empire after AD 70.

She probably met Septimius Severus when he served as governor of Syria in the early 180s. Severus was from Africa and his mother tongue was Punic, a Semitic language not too distant from Aramaic, the language spoken at Emesa. Their marriage – Julia became Severus's second wife – was typical of the period. Local aristocracies from different parts of the empire got to know each other through the transfer of men working in the higher ranks of the administration, and merged

The Berlin Tondo, a circular tempera painting on wood dating to *c.* AD 200.

into a new imperial elite. Reportedly, Severus married Julia because a horoscope had promised her a ruler as her husband.

As mother of the two princes, Julia was a key figure in the dynasty's self-representation: she was proclaimed *Augusta* in 193 and *mater castrorum* ('mother of the military camps') two years later. Her portrait appeared (with her sons) on coins issued by her husband to mark the Saecular Games in 204. Though some – anti-Severan – sources report that she enjoyed extraordinary political influence with her husband and later with Caracalla, this is hardly true: she had to look on Geta's murder helplessly and Caracalla ignored her political advice. Yet the empress certainly played an active role in the intellectual debates of her time. When Macrinus ousted Caracalla from power, he left her the title of *Augusta*, hoping – in vain – for her support. An isolated Julia, suffering from breast cancer, starved herself to death in 217. However, her sister, Julia Maesa, frantically prepared for the family's return to power, which led to the usurpation of Maesa's grandson Elagabalus in 218.

on the way back to Rome, Trajan suddenly fell ill in a small town in Cilicia. The situation was ticklish: in Mesopotamia, insurgents were trying to cast off Roman rule; on the Danube frontier tribes were tempted to incursions into Roman territory; and Trajan had failed to nominate a successor. To ensure a swift and undisputed succession, Trajan's widow Plotina and his praetorian prefect Attianus decided to spread, not quite truthfully, the news that Trajan on his deathbed had adopted Hadrian, the husband of Trajan's great-niece Sabina.

In the crisis that shook the Roman world in the 3rd century AD, some imperial women had extraordinary opportunities for action. When Aurelian fell victim to a plot, his widow Ulpia Severina may have filled the emerging interregnum for some time before the baton was passed on to Marcus Claudius Tacitus, an elderly senator. After Aurelian's death, coins with her portrait were issued, but that may only be proof of the durability of the regime created by him. In late antiquity, some imperial women were remarkable personalities. Pulcheria, Theodosius II's sister, was highly influential in the background of the Council of Chalcedon, which, in 451, banned various eastern heterodoxies. Constantine the Great's mother, Helena, is said to have found remains of the True Cross beneath the Temple of Venus built by Hadrian in Jerusalem (325). Another emperor's mother, Victoria, allegedly guaranteed the continuity of the dynasty when her son, Victorinus, was killed. He had been the emperor of the short-lived 'Gallic' empire, an autonomous power sphere in the Roman west under renegade emperors, established by Postumus in 260. Sources claim that Victoria bribed the legions to proclaim her protégé Tetricus emperor.

LEFT **A marble bust, dating to c. AD 134–147, of a Roman woman wearing the stephane, a kind of diadem. The woman is probably Vibia Sabina, the wife of Hadrian. The bust was found in Hadrian's villa at Tivoli.**

BELOW **The colonnaded main street of Palmyra, Syria. The street, which was more than a kilometre (0.6 mile) long, cut the entire city in two. The plinths fixed to the columns once held statues of distinguished Palmyrenes, to which today only numerous inscriptions bear witness.**

The Gallic empire had its counterpart in the east, where the oasis city of Palmyra, situated in the heart of the Syrian desert, rose to unprecedented power after a Roman army under Valerian was defeated by the Persians in AD 260. The man who saved Rome's eastern provinces was Septimius Odaenathus, the ruler of Palmyra, who gathered the remainders of Valerian's army and his own force of nomadic warriors and drove the Persians back. As a reward, he was bombarded with honorific titles and given a supreme command in the east, but his death in around 267 created a power vacuum. This was speedily filled by his wife, Zenobia, who assumed the regency for Vaballathus, her under-age son. Zenobia was an exceptional character by any standards, and she had soon extended her control over the provinces of Syria, Mesopotamia and Egypt. A few years later the Roman empire regained its equilibrium in the west, and Aurelian's attention turned to ridding himself of this troublesome woman. Aurelian's army entered Asia Minor and marched on Syria: Zenobia had no choice but to proclaim herself *Augusta* and Vaballathus *Augustus*. For the first time in Roman history, a woman had usurped the imperial role. Ancient sources and modern dramatizations alike have depicted Zenobia as an oriental desert queen, with a mission to overthrow the Roman empire. In fact, though Zenobia and her family were deeply rooted in the distinct local traditions of Palmyrene society, she was not motivated by anti-Roman resentment. Rather, Zenobia's move was an immediate reaction to Aurelian's aggression. In 272, she was defeated by Aurelian in a series of battles, arrested and deported to Rome.

Byzantine fresco of the empress Helena, the mother of Constantine, from the so-called Apple Church in the Göreme Valley in Cappadocia, Turkey.

Emperors on the move

The Roman empire was vast, and only a few emperors stayed at home in Rome throughout their reign. Antoninus Pius never left Italy, reportedly because a travelling emperor with his entourage unduly strained the provinces' budgets. Commodus, the rake, preferred Rome's pleasures to the discomfort of travelling. In the pre-modern world, without cars, railways or any of the infrastructure that facilitates travel today, long-distance journeys were a taxing business.

Rome had an impressive network of well-built roads, which was unprecedented in the ancient world. There were few hotels (*mansiones*) and the only means of transport overland were on foot, on horseback, in carriages drawn by horses or oxen and in palanquins, which were only used by rich people and usually carried by slaves. Even emperors travelled immense distances on foot. The 3rd-century historian Herodian tells us that Septimius Severus, on campaign against his rival Clodius Albinus, marched over high mountain passes in rain and snow, bareheaded, alongside his men. Hadrian, the touring emperor par excellence, never set 'foot in either a chariot or a four-wheeled vehicle' when he was drilling soldiers, according to Cassius Dio.

Coaches and carriages provided a less austere method of travel. Augustus toured every single province save for Sardinia and Africa in the *esseda*, originally a Celtic chariot, but by his time a rather comfortable touring coach. Marcus Aurelius also used a carriage when he travelled in Italy. His style of travelling was frugal, however: when he was still a prince, he went to the countryside once a year, where he took part in the grape harvest. In a letter to Fronto, his teacher, he writes that he spends the early morning reading and writing, before having some bread for breakfast. In the morning he works in the vineyard, in the afternoon he talks to his mother, then he has dinner with the peasants.

For Nero, on the other hand, travelling was a sumptuous undertaking. The emperor's favourite holiday destination was Greece, where he toured the festivals and competitions, travelled from theatre to theatre and collected crowns for his artistic performances. It was said that he never travelled without an entourage of at least a hundred coaches.

Travel formed part of the education of many emperors-to-be, such as the young Marcus Aurelius, or Germanicus, who toured Egypt (a classic destination of Greek intellectuals since the days of Herodotus). Cultural enthusiasm was the main driving force behind Hadrian's restless travelling. Pilgrimage was another reason for travel: emperors visited important sanctuaries to worship deities they held in personal esteem. In late antiquity, members of the ruling dynasties visited biblical places, where they often established new churches. Emperors also visited the provinces to show themselves to their subjects, thereby displaying both their accessibility and their willingness to wield personal control over provincial officials. For some, the motive for travel was simply pleasure and relaxation: the favoured summer resorts on the Gulf of Naples, where many well-to-do Romans had their villas, were often visited by emperors. What set most emperors in motion, however, was war.

ABOVE **Bronze coin with a galley, probably minted on the occasion of Hadrian's visit to Palestine (AD 132).**

BELOW **The Via Appia. Built in 312 BC by order of the consul Appius Claudius Caecus, the road connected Rome with the port of Brundisium (Brindisi) in southern Italy.**

HADRIAN'S TRAVELS

Many Roman emperors embody superlatives: Augustus, the first emperor, ruled the longest; under Trajan, the Roman empire reached its largest extent; Tacitus (ruled 275–276) was the oldest when he came to power – at the age of seventy-five; three-year-old Valentinian II was the youngest; Vespasian was arguably the most frugal; Marcus Aurelius the most learned; and Valerian, who died in Persian captivity, the unluckiest. No emperor, however, travelled the Roman empire as much and as systematically as Hadrian.

Hadrian visited Germany, the Danube provinces (AD 121), Britain and Gaul (122), which were secured with a system of fortified frontiers, the *limes*; then he journeyed on to Mauretania (123), Asia Minor, Thrace (124) and Athens (125). His second voyage led him to Lambaesis in Africa (128), Greece (129), Judaea (130), Egypt, Syria, Asia Minor and again Greece (131). Wherever the emperor turned up, he oversaw construction works, military exercises and administrative reshuffles.

Closest to Hadrian's heart was Greece, whose ancient culture he tried to revitalize. He had served as *archon* (supreme magistrate) in Athens before he became emperor. When he visited Greece in 125, he established the *Panhellenion*, a kind of parliament, into which the Greek cities of mainland Greece and Asia Minor sent their delegates. The first head of the *Panhellenion* was Hadrian's close friend Herodes Atticus, an immensely rich and cultivated Athenian, who was also the author of numerous – lost – writings. The experiment of reviving Greek identity ultimately failed: the *Panhellenion* did not survive Hadrian's death.

Hadrian's travels were not simply the product of insatiable wanderlust. He was the first Roman ruler to develop a universal conceptual design for his empire. Under him,

the imperial centre did not only react to grievances and challenges, it tried to develop coherent strategies of government. Such an approach demanded that the emperor personally knew the empire, its provinces and the variety of cultural and ethnic identities it comprised. Yet the model of the travelling emperor failed to survive into the next generation: during his entire reign, Antoninus Pius never left Italy.

Marble statue of Antinous-Osiris from Hadrian's villa at Tivoli, *c.* AD 131–138. After his death, Antinous was deified and assimilated to the Egyptian god Osiris.

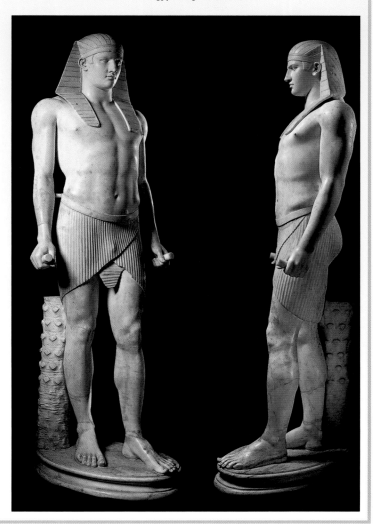

CHAPTER 5

EMPERORS ON CAMPAIGN

The Roman republic's growth from a small city-state into a great power, dominating the Mediterranean, was due to a long series of wars: in those days, a great many Romans spent more summers fighting in distant parts of the ancient world than they spent at home. Augustus's and Tiberius's reigns brought about a more peaceful era, with relatively stable, secure frontiers in the northwest, south and east. Nevertheless, war was still a constant companion in the imperial period and most emperors were, by necessity, experienced field commanders. Tiberius, Vespasian, Titus and most of the emperors of the 3rd century had commanded legions before they came to rule; Domitian, Trajan, Marcus Aurelius and Septimius Severus personally fought major campaigns on Rome's frontiers in the northwest and east; and the short-lived emperors of the crisis periods of AD 68/69 and 193 led huge armies against each other in bloody civil wars.

A new Alexander?

A particularly warlike emperor was Trajan, the son of Marcus Ulpius Trajanus, a senator from Spain who had been governor of Syria and repelled a major Parthian incursion into that province during the reign of Vespasian. The forty-four-year-old Trajan came to power after his adoptive father, Nerva, died in January 98. Nerva had adopted Trajan only in the autumn of the previous year. The aristocratic families of Gaul and Spain, in which Trajan held a strong position, had gained considerable influence since Claudius had admitted the provincial elites of Gaul to the Senate. These families had brought the elderly Nerva, whose rule was on the verge of collapse, to designate Trajan, with his undoubted military skills, as the imperial successor. This was a coup d'état in disguise, but it prevented a renewed civil war.

When Nerva died (of natural causes), Trajan was serving as governor of the relatively recently established province of Upper Germany. Instead of returning

A marble bust of Trajan, wearing the civic crown. The upper part of the emperor's body is uncovered, but he wears a shoulder strap for a sword and the aegis, a golden goatskin with the head of Gorgo and snakes, which was associated with Jupiter and symbolized universal power.

TRAJAN'S DACIAN WARS

In the spring of AD 101, a gigantic Roman army, led by the emperor Trajan in person, crossed the Danube and invaded the kingdom of Dacia, present-day Romania. The war now unfolding had a long prehistory. The Dacians, under their king Decebalus, had crossed the river in AD 85 and annihilated a Roman army, and this had provoked a counter-attack, led by Domitian, in 89. Domitian defeated Decebalus, who became a Roman client king, and received regular Roman payments to ensure his loyalty.

Now, in 101, eleven legions with about 60,000 men found little resistance when they entered the mountainous kingdom. A battle ended in a draw, and the Romans retreated to the Danube. They returned the following spring; the Dacians retreated to their mountain fortresses, which Trajan put under siege, one by one. When the fall of their capital Sarmizegetusa seemed imminent, the

Dacians sought peace. It did not last long, however: in 105, Decebalus took Longinus, the commander of the occupation army and a personal friend of Trajan, hostage. The Roman reaction was prompt and harsh (105–106): the revolt was put down, and Sarmizegetusa besieged and conquered. Decebalus, who had managed to escape, committed suicide before the Romans could capture him. Dacia, which was rich in gold and silver, was turned into a province, which Hadrian, in 118, subdivided into two: Upper and Lower Dacia. The Romans stayed until the Dacian provinces were finally evacuated by Aurelian in 271.

The spiral frieze of Trajan's Column in Rome gives an impressive visual narrative of the two wars in 114 scenes. It is a prime source for the equipment and modus operandi of the Roman army in the early 2nd century.

The capture of Decebalus: a detail from the frieze on Trajan's Column.

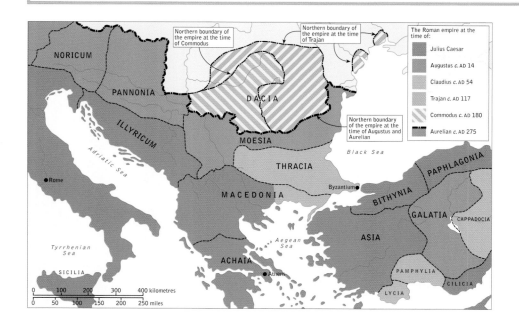

Map of Dacia and the Balkan provinces, showing the changing frontier of the empire from 44 BC to AD 275.

immediately to Rome, he continued to oversee the fortification of Rome's new possessions on the right bank of the Rhine. Quite evidently, he was keen to display his military expertise. Only a few years later (101–106), he was given the opportunity to demonstrate these skills when he subdued Dacia, the territory between the Carpathians and the Danube – roughly present-day Romania – in two bloody wars (see Box, opposite). Since AD 85 the Dacians had repeatedly challenged the Romans, but ultimately, under Domitian, they complied with a settlement that made them a Roman client state. Essentially, then, Trajan's first Dacian War was a unilateral aggression against an allied people, but it firmly established the emperor as an invincible general. The second war, in AD 105–106, was no more than a punitive expedition against the Dacians' desperate attempt to shake off the Roman yoke.

The victories over the Dacians were fundamental in establishing Trajan's official image. He styled himself *optimus princeps*, 'the best emperor', a concept based equally on his virtues and on his military achievements. Trajan was *optimus* both absolutely and in relation to the other great men of Roman history: the protagonists of the republic and (especially) his predecessors on the imperial throne. The emperor's accomplishments in battle were celebrated in the Forum of Trajan in Rome, particularly on Trajan's towering Column, with its friezes featuring scenes from his Dacian victories. The entrance to the Forum's basilica, where court sessions were held, was adorned with honorary statues of the emperor, whose plinths were inscribed *optime de re publica merito domi forisque* ('for the one with the highest merits for the state, at home and in military service').

Trajan's conquest and annexation of Dacia at least gained the country's rich silver

Trajan's Column. The spiral frieze shows scenes from the Dacian Wars: battles and sieges, marching troops, religious sacrifices, the building of encampments and bridges and, repeatedly, the emperor speaking to his soldiers. Trajan himself appears fifty-nine times.

mines for Rome, but his next victory was, in Tacitus's words, a genuine *falsus triumphus*. In AD 106, the Romans conquered the client kingdom of the Nabataeans in present-day Jordan and turned it into the province of Arabia. The Nabataean kingdom had become wealthy through its spice and incense trade with southern Arabia. It is not clear whether the decision to end local autonomy was prompted by a local succession crisis, but in the long run the provincialization of Arabia seems to have damaged regional trade and considerably reduced the wealth of the region. Moreover, Rome was now forced to deploy substantial forces in the new province and to develop its infrastructure: a new road, the Via Nova Trajana, was built between Bostra and Aqaba to increase the troops' mobility and to make the new province easier to defend.

Eight years later, Trajan fought his fourth and final war: the theatre was, once again, the Near East. In AD 113, Trajan concentrated a massive force of no less than eleven legions in the Roman province of Syria. Negotiations with the Parthians were inconclusive, and so the Roman army entered Armenia (which was duly annexed), crushed a Parthian counter-offensive and proceeded south into northern Mesopotamia. The legions wintered in Edessa (now in southern Turkey). In early 115, the Romans resumed their advance, captured the northern Mesopotamian towns of Nisibis and Singara and finally reached Babylonia, the south of the land between the rivers Euphrates and Tigris. Trajan took Ctesiphon, the residence of the Parthian (self-styled) 'King of Kings'. The mission seemed accomplished: the whole of Mesopotamia, present-day Iraq, had been conquered and turned into a new province. A thoughtful Trajan stood on the shore of the Persian Gulf, watching the vessels sailing east for India: wasn't he, almost, a new Alexander the Great, who had once and for all defeated Rome's ancient enemy in the Orient? This self-identification with Alexander was a recurrent theme in Rome: Pompey, Nero and Caracalla each played with the notion of being Alexander reborn. Trajan, at least, was wrong: in the hour of his greatest triumph, a storm was gathering further north.

Trajan at Hatra

Once the Roman legions had marched south towards Ctesiphon and the Persian Gulf, the cities, tribes and local rulers of northern Mesopotamia, who had enjoyed a considerable degree of autonomy under the Parthians, revolted against their new Roman lords.

> Trajan learned of this at Babylon; for he had gone there both because of its fame – though he saw nothing but mounds and stones and ruins to justify this – and because of Alexander, to whose spirit he offered sacrifice in the room where he had died.

The revolt was more than a small local difficulty: Trajan and his colossal army were on the verge of being cut off from their supplies. If this were not bad enough, the Mesopotamian insurgency rapidly flashed over to other provinces in the Roman Near East. At the instigation of messianic leaders, the Jews of the Diaspora – many of whom were discontented with Roman rule – went on a rampage against pagan sanctuaries and cult images, and many towns of Egypt, Cyrenaica and Cyprus were devastated in the riots. Romans and Greeks were slain by the thousands in what became known as the Babylonian Revolt or the Kitos War (AD 115–117). Meanwhile, Trajan tried to recapture the insurgent cities in northern Mesopotamia, sending his generals against the rebels. The most ferocious and successful of the generals was Lusius Quietus, of North African descent, who besieged and conquered the important cities of Edessa and Nisibis. However, Trajan himself went to deal with the place most crucial for the control of Mesopotamia, the town of Hatra, located in the midst of the desert between the Euphrates and the Tigris. Hatra was, as Cassius Dio informs us, neither big nor wealthy, but it had strong walls, determined defenders and a hinterland most hostile to the besiegers, who suffered from heat, lack of water and from ambushes by the steppe nomads.

The Bait Alaha ('House of God'), a vast sacred compound in the centre of the north Mesopotamian city of Hatra (present-day Iraq). The compound comprised various individual sanctuaries. Here, a Greek-style temple with columns (left) and a large structure with vaulted halls (*iwans*) can be seen. The city, which was under Parthian overlordship, accumulated immense wealth during the 2nd century AD. It was – unsuccessfully – besieged by the emperors Trajan and Septimius Severus.

Cassius Dio gives us a vivid, if rather melodramatic, account of the events:

Trajan sent the cavalry forward against the wall, but failed in his attempt, and the attackers were hurled back into the camp. Indeed, the emperor himself barely missed being wounded as he was riding past, in spite of the fact that he had laid aside his imperial attire to avoid being recognized; but the enemy, seeing his majestic grey head and his august countenance, suspected his identity, shot at him and killed a cavalryman in his escort. There were peals of thunder, rainbows, and lightning, rain-storms, hail and thunderbolts descended upon the Romans as often as they made assaults. And whenever they ate, flies settled on their food and drink.

The focus of attention is the emperor himself: the enemy can identify him even without his imperial rank insignia. He is a bold and courageous leader who does not shy away from taking personal risks. Still, the endeavour was doomed: circumstances were adverse, and, unlike Lusius Quietus and the other generals, Trajan failed to recapture the city by siege.

Hatra became the turning point, not just for the Parthian War, but for Trajan's entire reign: 'Trajan therefore departed thence, and a little later began to fail in health' states Cassius Dio. The ailing Trajan tried to return to Italy, but died in southern Asia Minor in August 117. The emperor's project of permanent Roman rule over Mesopotamia was abandoned by his successor Hadrian, who returned the short-lived province to the Parthians. Trajan had his triumph nonetheless: months after his death, the emperor's corpse was driven through Rome on a triumphal chariot. This eerie display paid a final tribute to the *optimus princeps*, who had sought perfection in his military ventures. It may also have been a studied attempt by Hadrian to put the blame for the ultimate failure firmly on Trajan.

Commander-in-chief

The episode at Hatra illustrates the importance of an emperor's soldierly profile, especially if he, like Trajan, had built his prestige largely on his military virtues. The great generals of the Roman republic had set the standards for a good commander: he had to be cunning and brave, a charismatic leader willing to endure hardship and danger.

'He proceeded regardless of cold or heat... he marched bareheaded through rain and snow, setting his men an example of firmness and courage.'

The historian Herodian, describing Septimius Severus on campaign

Not every emperor lived up to such expectations. Augustus was a poor general who led his armies through his proxies, men like Agrippa, Drusus and Tiberius; and it seems downright absurd to imagine rulers like Claudius or Nero leading their legions personally into battle, or exchanging their fine palaces for a general's tent (although Claudius, unlike Nero, travelled to Britain to be present for the victory over the tribes). Even for Nero it was essential to celebrate triumphs for victories won by others. Domitian, who had no military record of his own when he came to power, was a fierce campaigner. Tiberius, Vespasian and Titus, who had proved their ability to lead legions before they became emperors, could afford to have others fight for them. If an emperor's military record was overshadowed by that of other generals, this could have fatal or near-fatal consequences, as numerous 3rd-century emperors found to their cost. A good example of a successful general with ambition is Avidius Cassius. He had effectively commanded the troops in Lucius Verus's Parthian War (163–166) and, incited by the prestige of that victory, later tried unsuccessfully to depose Marcus Aurelius.

Most emperors took very seriously their duties as commander-in-chief of the Roman armies. After all, the army had played a key role in the formation of the principate, and remained its chief supporting pillar. Only after the death of Theodosius I in 395 did the emperors (with the single exception of Majorian) retreat from the battlefield and leave the business of fighting to professional generals – with disastrous consequences for imperial authority in the west (see chapter 7). To the soldiers, on the other hand, it seemed only natural that the emperor should maintain a special relationship with the legions and look after their material and emotional welfare. As with the senators, mutual friendship was best preserved through the regular exchange of 'gifts', *beneficia*. The main *beneficia* the soldiers could offer were discipline, obedience and loyalty: without them, no emperor survived for long. In return, the emperor dispensed pay, food and his own presence.

The way in which the relationship between the emperor and his legions worked is illustrated by a dossier of inscriptions from Lambaesis, a Roman garrison town in North Africa and – from the Severan period (AD 193–235) onwards – capital of the province of Numidia. In the summer of 128, Hadrian visited the garrison and reviewed a series of military exercises, in which various units were involved. Hadrian addressed these units, apparently individually: 'you have done the most difficult of all difficult things: you have thrown the javelin clad in armour. ... I applaud your spirit

An inscription from Lambaesis in the province of Numidia (Tazoult-Lambèse, Algeria) transcribing a speech given by Hadrian in praise of a unit of Pannonian cavalrymen.

also,' the emperor called out to the soldiers of a cavalry squadron from Commagene. Another unit is addressed as follows:

However, you have made criticism impossible through your ardour and zealous discharge of duty; you have gone further in that you have hurled stones with slings and have assailed the other side with missiles. Throughout you have mounted your horses briskly.

The extraordinary care of my legate Catullinus, the most honourable man, is testified by such men as you under his command.

Hadrian has warm and friendly words for his soldiers, regardless of their rank. Those who may not have excelled in the exercise he exculpates nevertheless, blaming circumstances beyond their control: 'it is hard for the horsemen of the cohorts to make a good impression even by themselves; still harder not to displease after the manoeuvre of the *alae* [the cavalry squadrons]'. Where he criticises, he does it mildly. Even more important than praise and encouragement is the familiarity with military affairs and jargon that the emperor reveals in such speeches: his comments are clearly those of a military insider. 'I am one of you, a soldier among soldiers,' is

Marble statue of a triumphant Hadrian in military dress, from Hieraptyna in Crete. The representation of this rather peaceful emperor in military gear is unusual. Hadrian wears a laurel wreath on his head and treads underfoot a subjugated barbarian. His cuirass is decorated with an image of Romulus and Remus, the legendary founders of Rome, with the she-wolf.

TRIUMPHAL PROCESSIONS

The Romans owed much of their culture, and especially many of their religious institutions, to the Etruscans. One such borrowing was the triumphal procession awarded to a general after a victorious war. Originally, the ritual procession was intended to purify the army and its general, and to bring the booty of war to Jupiter Capitolinus. The procession passed through the Campus Martius, the Circus Maximus and the Via Sacra on the Roman Forum and duly arrived at the Temple of Jupiter on the Capitoline Hill.

During the republic, the character of the triumphal procession changed. Rather than a ritual of purification, it became a display of Roman power as well as of individual glory. The procession was led by senators, magistrates and musicians, followed by visual representations of the battles, the booty, carried by soldiers, and finally the victorious general at the head of his army. He was dressed in a purple toga and an embroidered tunic; and his face was coloured with red lead, to resemble a deity. Behind him on the chariot stood a slave holding a golden wreath above his head; at regular intervals, the slave whispered in his ear: 'bear in mind that you are human'.

One of the most memorable triumphs was celebrated by Pompey on his return from the east in AD 61. It was a procession of unprecedented splendour: 'his triumph had such a magnitude that, although it was distributed over two days, still the time would not suffice, but much of what had been prepared could not find a place in the spectacle, enough to dignify and adorn another triumphal procession. Inscriptions borne in advance of the procession indicated the nations over which he triumphed', exults Plutarch in his *Life of Pompey the Great*. He is describing the spoils of a war that had left Rome in possession of the immensely rich Hellenistic east.

Later processions were not as magnificent, but no less important for the victorious generals. Titus's triumph over the Jews after his capture of Jerusalem is immortalized by the Arch of Titus on the Roman Forum. The reliefs on the arch show soldiers carrying cult utensils from the Jerusalem Temple, among them the menorah, the candelabrum holding seven candles. The arch, built under Domitian, celebrated the Flavian victory over the Jewish insurgents. The last senator who was not a member of the imperial family celebrated a triumph under Augustus. From Titus onwards, only ruling emperors were awarded triumphal processions; these were celebrated until the 4th century, when they were, under the influence of Christianity, gradually replaced by an emperor's solemn arrival, the *adventus* (see page 66).

The Triumph of Caesar by Mantegna (1486–1505) shows Caesar's victorious return from his campaigns. As well as a procession of soldiers, standard-bearers and musicians, it depicts the typical assortment of booty, exotic animals and captives that the emperor would have brought back with him.

the subtext of such exchanges. Emperors could gain substantial credit with the military, if they succeeded in presenting themselves as fellow-soldiers. Trajan provides a good example. The reliefs on Trajan's Column show him joining his soldiers in many of their daily activities during the Dacian Wars: talking to them, fighting with them, and marching with them.

The emperor haranguing his troops with a formal speech – an *adlocutio* – is a common motif in Roman art and literature. Speeches of the emperor to his troops structure the visual narrative of Trajan's Column's spiral frieze. In the frieze, *adlocutio* scenes regularly follow or precede military action, thus highlighting the speeches' role in the reciprocal exchange of *beneficia* between soldiers and emperor. Cassius Dio describes a flamboyant Caligula, who speaks to the soldiers after they have built a ship bridge across the Gulf of Misenum near Naples. The emperor praises them for their victory over the sea; but since this is a vain victory, the *beneficium* of an imperial address is utterly inappropriate. Caligula also issued coins showing him standing on a rostrum and addressing soldiers: *adlocut(io) coh(ortium)*, 'speech to the Praetorian cohorts', reads the coins' legend. By issuing such coins – which were then used to pay the soldiers' salaries – Caligula extended

An *adlocutio* scene from Trajan's Column. The emperor stands on a podium with a group of high-ranking officers, his right arm outstretched, and addresses the attentive soldiers. Legionary standards indicate the presence of several units.

the *beneficium* of an imperial address into an indefinite future. Other emperors emphasized the harmony between themselves and the military in similar ways. Among the most popular coin inscriptions were *fides exercitus* ('faithfulness of the army') and *concordia exercituum* ('unity among the armies'), especially in times of political trouble when the military's loyalty was anything but certain.

The principate's militarization

In peace, as in war, the army of which the emperor was commander-in-chief was a formidable instrument of power. When Hadrian reviewed the Lambaesis garrison's exercises, he saw a variety of highly specialized units, each designed for a specific role in battle. By the 2nd century AD, very few soldiers came from the core regions of Mediterranean civilization: Egypt, Greece and Italy. The army's main bases of recruitment were the more 'barbarian' parts on the empire's fringes: the nomadic habitats of the African and Near Eastern steppes and deserts, the Balkan provinces, Gaul and Britain. An increasing number of soldiers came from beyond the empire's frontiers: in the Augustan period, men like Arminius and his brother Flavus, recruited from non-Roman citizens, held high ranks in the Roman auxiliary forces, and later Franks, Goths and Sarmatians were much sought-after as brave and specialized warriors. Many units – like the ones Hadrian visited at Lambaesis – were at least initially recruited on an ethnic basis. Each of them had their own style of armour and fighting.

Under Augustus the number of auxiliary soldiers had matched that of the Roman citizens serving in the legions (about 125,000 men each), but under Hadrian the number of auxiliaries almost doubled (about 218,000 as compared to 155,000 legionaries). The army became even larger under Septimius Severus (AD 193–211): about 250,000 auxiliary soldiers and about 182,000 legionaries served under the command of this emperor, who changed the living conditions of the soldiery more than any of his predecessors.

Septimius Severus made the army not just larger but also more versatile, more diverse, more professional and, above all, better paid. He reportedly, on his deathbed, advised his sons Caracalla and Geta to 'be at one with each other, to make the soldiers rich and not to give a damn about anybody else' and he was the first 'soldier emperor' in the proper sense. Like Vespasian, he had risen to power through civil war. Knowing how much he

Tombstone of the standard bearer Genialis from Mainz. The inscription reads: 'Genialis, son of Clusiodus, *imaginifer* of Cohors VII Raetorum, thirty-five years of age, thirteen years of service (lies here). His heir had (this) erected.'

relied on the soldiers and how much he owed them, he did everything to keep them happy, and not only financially. It was Septimius Severus who granted soldiers – who were previously banned by law from marrying – the right to 'live with' their wives and children.

Caracalla, Septimius Severus's son and heir, took at least part of his father's advice to heart. His portraits show a grim-looking man whose rude physiognomy differs sharply from the delicately chiselled features of his predecessors. Portraits of Caracalla, head slightly inclined, emulate representations of the greatest of all ancient generals, Alexander. With the soldiers, Caracalla exhibited the friendliest of attitudes. According to Cassius Dio, he told the legionaries:

> **'I am one of you, and it is because of you alone that I care to live, in order that I may confer upon you many favours; for all the treasuries are yours.'**
>
> Caracalla, quoted by Cassius Dio

After murdering his brother Geta, he called out to them: 'Rejoice, fellow-soldiers, for now I am in a position to do you favours'. Cassius Dio goes on to explain who had to pay for this unprecedented generosity: the senators, who were stripped of their possessions; the cities, which had to contribute to the army's maintenance; and the individual inhabitants of the empire, who were overwhelmed by a rising tax burden and the services they were required to provide for the military.

In AD 215, a new crisis in Armenia gave the self-proclaimed reborn Alexander the opportunity to fulfil his dream: a major war in the east. After some diplomatic shenanigans, his troops invaded Armenia and advanced into Mesopotamia, where Caracalla set up winter quarters in Edessa (216/217). There he was murdered in 217: ironically enough, by a soldier, hired by the praetorian prefect Macrinus and some other dignitaries who feared to lose influence with Caracalla. Macrinus took the throne, but given Caracalla's dedication to the soldiers' welfare, it is no surprise that they kept him in fond memory. When, in the following year, a young priest, a distant relative of the murdered emperor, was presented to the garrison of his hometown of Emesa in Syria as Caracalla's son, the soldiers instantaneously defected from Macrinus and stirred up a revolt that brought the fourteen-year-old youth to power. His name was Avitus Bassianus, but Romans named him after the god he had worshipped in Emesa: Elagabalus.

Marble bust of the emperor Caracalla in military dress. Imitating portraits of Alexander the Great, the emperor slightly inclines his head to the left.

Soldier emperors

The reigns of Septimius Severus and Caracalla were a mere prelude to the turbulent decades to come. The Roman empire of the 1st and 2nd centuries AD had had no serious rivals. To be sure, there were enemies (the relationship with the Parthians was always difficult, though in the majority of cases Rome played the more aggressive part); lost battles (most notably the annihilation of three Roman legions under the command of Quinctilius Varus in the Teutoburg Forest in AD 9); and barbarian incursions into Roman territory; but the Romans could deal with these problems one by one. Even when battles were lost and strategic targets missed, the existence of the Roman empire itself was never at stake.

This settled climate changed in the second quarter of the 3rd century. In the east, Rome's position was challenged by the newly-formed Persian empire of the Sasanians, who repeatedly attacked the eastern provinces. Sporadic attempts to stop the incursions failed. In 254, the new emperor Valerian marched eastward at the head of a large army and launched a counter-attack that, at first, resulted only in skirmishes. Finally, in early summer 260, the two armies clashed in the vicinity of Carrhae, in Mesopotamia. Valerian was defeated, his army annihilated and the emperor himself captured by Shapur. A trilingual inscription near Persepolis, the so-called Res Gestae Divi Saporis, celebrates the unprecedented capture of a Roman emperor:

> And we took Valerian prisoner with our own hands, and the others, the praetorian prefect and the senators and the officers, whoever were the leaders of this force, were captured with our hands and deported to Persia.

The defeat at Carrhae marks the climax of Rome's military crisis in the middle of the 3rd century.

Parthian captives, in a detail from a marble relief from the Arch of Septimius Severus on the Roman Forum. The Parthians wear wide cloaks, breeches and boots. The arch, dedicated in AD 203, celebrated Septimius Severus's victory in the Parthian War (AD 193–199).

Regionalization of political control, as manifested in Postumus's Gallic empire, was, in a way, the only adequate answer to the multiple challenges of the 3rd century crisis. Substantial parts of the empire became trouble spots, but the emperor could only be on one battlefield at a time. The army was garrisoned along the frontiers, largely immobile and unable to respond promptly to sudden threats. The typical 3rd-century emperor was constantly hurrying from one end of the empire to the other at the head of hastily-deployed forces, rushing to confront his enemies on distant battlefields.

The so-called Shapur Gem, a Sasanian cameo of the 4th century AD. A Sasanian king, on horseback, seizes another mounted warrior by the wrist. The cameo is supposed to represent the capture of Valerian by the Sasanian king Shapur I in AD 260. The cameo's style reveals strong western influence.

The feverish struggle of an emperor to keep pace with simultaneous, increasingly interlaced developments in various theatres is best illustrated by the short reign of Philip the Arab (244–249), who came from the province of Arabia. He had served as a praetorian prefect under Gordian III when the Roman army was defeated by Shapur's Persians at Mesiche, in early 244. While still in enemy country, Gordian was murdered, presumably by men hired by Philip, who duly became emperor. Now it was Philip's unenviable task to make peace with the Persians, a peace that, under the circumstances, could only be unfavourable to Rome. He had to withdraw his army and to pay substantial reparations. In the summer of 244, he arrived at Rome, where he proclaimed his seven-year-old son *Caesar*. He stayed in the capital till the next year, when he had to leave for Dacia, a province recently attacked by the Carpi. He assembled an army, from units originating from various parts of the empire, and besieged a Carpi fortress, which he finally captured. We know very little about the hostilities, but he seems to have repulsed the Carpi and restored the province. Then he returned to Rome where he celebrated the capital's 1000th anniversary in 248. Still celebrating, he received the news of usurpations in a number of provinces: in Syria, a certain Jotapianus had proclaimed himself emperor; on the Danube, the officer Pacatianus had done the same. Both of these insurrections were soon put down, but in the summer of 249 Decius, the man to whom Philip had entrusted supreme command in the Balkan provinces, made his appearance as the next usurper. Philip marched against Decius's army, but was defeated, giving way to another short-lived soldier emperor.

Philip's ephemeral government illustrates the problem of interconnected external and internal crises. Weakened by a humiliating peace treaty with the Persians, which was insufficiently counterbalanced by his – perhaps not very convincing – victory over the Carpi, Philip's prestige had already suffered irreparable damage. In order to regain control of the troubled Balkans and to get rid of the usurper Pacatianus, he gave Decius a special command covering several provinces, a position that put the bulk of the Roman military under the senator's command and more or less invited him to usurp the imperial throne. Decius's usurpation was by no means exceptional: in an age when military success was the most important qualification for being emperor, any reasonably successful general could quite realistically aim for the rulership of the empire.

Faced with multiple threats, the emperors could not be present personally to deal with every one, but nor could they safely delegate the highest military commands without inviting usurpation. A practical way out of this dilemma was to appoint family members to high offices, as Philip did when he made his brother Priscus *corrector* (a kind of viceroy) of the eastern provinces, a position in which he served with exemplary loyalty. Other emperors shared power with their grown-up sons: Valerian appointed Gallienus *Augustus*, putting him on an equal footing with himself; Carus appointed his son Carinus *Caesar* and had him deal with the affairs in the west while he launched his Persian campaign in the east. However, it was Diocletian who made the division of power the primary principle of a new style of government: the Tetrarchy ended five decades of permanent military and political crisis, the age of the soldier emperors. This period had put Rome's political system under extreme stress and revealed the near-lethal weaknesses inherent in the principate. The monarchic order created by Augustus was designed for the relatively calm seas of the 1st and 2nd centuries AD. In stormier waters, a system in which the incumbent lacked any form of legitimacy, and any commander with a minimum of military merits could claim the imperial purple for himself, soon descended into anarchy. With Diocletian, a period of recovery began: we call it late antiquity.

A marble bust of Philip the Arab. The emperor is dressed in a *toga contabulata*, a civilian garment that came into use during the 2nd century AD. The toga is tied in a peculiar fashion that created a large bulge in front of the chest.

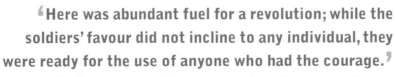

❛ Here was abundant fuel for a revolution; while the soldiers' favour did not incline to any individual, they were ready for the use of anyone who had the courage. ❜

Tacitus, on the risk of usurpations from the military

CHAPTER 6

ROME AND CONSTANTINOPLE

Augustus is said to have inherited Rome as a city built of bricks, and to have left it as one built of marble. It is true that, under the first emperor, the city utterly changed: it became an imperial capital deserving of that name, a true metropolis with impressive public buildings and works of art gathered from the entire Roman world. Yet, at the same time, Rome lost much of its former political significance. The empire was increasingly dependent on its ruler, and so the epicentre was where the emperor was – and most emperors of the 2nd and 3rd centuries constantly moved through the Roman world, travelling or on campaign. The city on the river Tiber became an ever grander, but merely ceremonial, capital. In the 4th century, the emperors left Rome, taking up residence at Constantinople, the new Christian capital. Rome, mostly vacated by the political rulers, became the centre of the western church, its bishops the Popes.

Rome before the emperors

Legend has it that Rome bears the name of its founder, Romulus, a prince from Alba Longa, a town in Latium in Central Italy. When he laid out the new city's fortifications, his brother Remus sneered at Romulus's project and jumped over the humble wall. Archaeology confirms that Rome's beginnings were modest: a few hamlets, scattered over some hills on the left bank of the river Tiber. These villages grew together to form a small town that competed with other settlements for hegemony in Latium.

    The town survived and finally defeated and destroyed its powerful neighbour, the Etruscan city of Veii. Rome's expansion did not come to a halt there: the Romans overcame the Etruscan league to the north and the tribes inhabiting the mountains of central Italy. By the beginning of the 3rd century BC, Rome was the dominant power on the Italian peninsula, and a few decades later the

confrontation with Carthage made it irrevocably a global player in the ancient
Mediterranean world.

The capital hardly reflected the growing empire's political importance.
Rome's wars and territorial gains had shifted the balance within its society:
smallholders had lost their livelihood through continuous military service and
competition from large agricultural estates. Now landless proletarians, they flooded
into the capital, which soon became an agglomeration of slums and decaying blocks
of flats, crammed with poverty-stricken immigrants. Even temples and public
buildings were mainly built from wood and thus vulnerable to the disastrous
blazes that regularly destroyed large parts of the city. The republic's capital
had grown organically for centuries, and had been largely immune to urban
planning and regulation.

This began to change when influential aristocrats accumulated enough wealth
and political credit to develop entire neighbourhoods single-handedly, thus creating
urban topographies immortalizing their own power and glory. Pompey led the way
by building a lavish theatre complex on the Campus Martius, a vast free space on the
northern outskirts of Rome, and Caesar built the Julian Basilica, a large hall housing
shops and a courtroom, on the Roman Forum and, nearby, the Forum of Caesar, a
complex of public buildings.

Spending several fortunes on the embellishment of Rome was not an act
of pure altruism. Rather, what happened here was the conversion of financial
into social capital: powerful men like Pompey and Caesar used benefaction as
a means of gaining popularity and displaying their power. This practice was
widespread in the Greek world and was now making its mark on Rome. Cicero,
the staunch advocate of the republic and its traditions, felt understandably uneasy
about so much generosity:

> 'These expenses also are more justifiable on walls,
> docks, ports, aqueducts, and all things which pertain to
> the service of the state, though what is given as it were
> into our hands is more agreeable at present, yet these
> things are more acceptable to posterity.
> Theatres, porticos, new temples, I censure with
> more reserve for Pompey's sake, but the most learned
> men disapprove of them. ... The whole plan, then,
> of such largesses is vicious in its nature.'
> Cicero

PREVIOUS PAGE **The Roman Forum, seen from the Capitol. In the centre, with columns, stands the Temple of Antoninus Pius and, in the background, the Basilica of Maxentius. The Roman Forum was the epicentre of the Roman world until, in the 3rd century, emperors began to take up residence closer to the frontiers they had to defend.**

OPPOSITE **The Forum of Julius Caesar was the first in a series of public places built by Roman rulers. The buildings, most notably a temple for Venus, were funded by the booty from Caesar's Gallic War. The compound also featured an equestrian statue of Caesar and a colonnaded plaza.**

From brick to marble

It was Augustus who profoundly changed the townscape of Rome. During his reign, many of Caesar's building projects – such as the Saepta Julia, a meeting place for the people's assembly – were finished. A new theatre on the Campus Martius, the well-preserved Theatre of Marcellus, was given the name of his nephew and son-in-law. In his Res Gestae, the emperor praises himself for having built or rebuilt numerous sanctuaries in Rome, among them the Temple of Apollo near his own house on the Palatine and the giant Temple of Jupiter Optimus Maximus on the Capitol.

Apart from the area on the northern Campus Martius where the Ara Pacis, the mausoleum of Augustus and the Egyptian obelisk used as a giant sundial were constructed (see pages 38–39), the most important single monument built under the

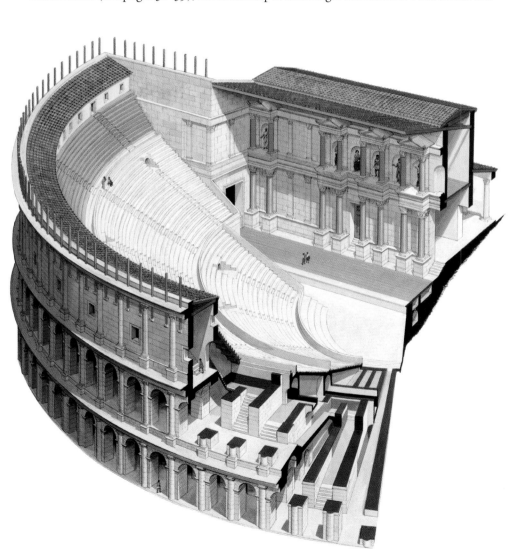

A cutaway reconstruction of the Theatre of Marcellus. The building, dedicated in 13 BC, stood 33 m (108 ft) high and was the largest theatre in Rome, accommodating 10,000 to 15,000 spectators. During the Middle Ages, the theatre was converted into a fortress by one of Rome's aristocratic families and later, in the Renaissance, became the palace of the Orsini family.

ABOVE **Part of the Roman Forum as it would have looked at the time of Augustus.**

KEY
1 The Forum of Augustus
2 The Basilica Aemilia
3 The Temple of the deified Julius Caesar
4 The Temple of Vesta
5 The Temple of Castor and Pollux
6 The Basilica Julia
7 The Temple of Saturn
8 The Temple of Concordia
9 The tabularium (state archive)
10 The Forum of Caesar
11 The Curia Julia (Senate House)

first *princeps* was the Temple of Mars Ultor on the Forum. Mars Ultor was the avenging war god, the symbol of Augustus's victories over his rivals and enemies. Augustus had vowed to build this temple before the battle of Philippi in 42 BC, but it was not completed until 2 BC, when the surrounding complex of the Forum of Augustus was inaugurated. The whole ensemble was designed as an emblem for the peace Augustus had achieved internally and externally, and it was funded from the spoils of his wars. Here, the populace of the provinces sacrificed in return for the benefits of the Roman peace that Augustus had brought them. In the colonnaded halls surrounding the temple stood statues of mythical and historical Romans: the Trojan hero Aeneas, his father Anchises and his son Ascanius with the kings of Alba Longa (the city founded by Ascanius). These were all mythical forefathers of the Julian family into which Augustus had been adopted. On the opposite side were statues of Romulus, the founder of Rome, and the great men of the Roman republic. In the centre of all this stood a statue of Augustus in a triumphal chariot. In this ensemble, Augustus's (and his family's) claim for power and the republican tradition

The Forum of Augustus with the Temple of Mars Ultor. The temple forecourt was lined by colonnades. In its centre stood a statue of Augustus in a triumphal chariot. A massive wall separated the forum from the adjacent residential neighbourhood.

of Rome were reconciled: here, the empire was presented as the republic's logical continuation and ultimate completion.

Augustus's successors followed his example and continued to adorn the capital with monumental buildings. Claudius improved the water supply system by adding two aqueducts to the network of water conduits leading to Rome. Vespasian and Titus built the Colosseum, a great public arena, where Nero's Domus Aurea had stood. Nero's palace had been highly unpopular among Romans, who felt that after the great fire of AD 64 the emperor had 'usurped' space belonging to the citizens for his own private use. On the Forum, Domitian dedicated the Arch of Titus to his brother. Nerva and Trajan added their own compounds to the growing chain of imperial fora, Trajan's being distinguished by Trajan's Column and the markets, a multi-storey labyrinth of shops, pubs and offices. Hadrian built the huge Temple of Venus and Roma at the east end of the Roman Forum, and Antoninus Pius a

Aerial photograph of the Amphitheatrum Flavium or Colosseum. Commissioned by Vespasian, it was built on the low-lying land between the Palatine and the Esquiline hills, where previously Nero's Domus Aurea had stood. The amphitheatre, which was capable of seating 50,000 spectators, was completed under Titus in AD 80 and inaugurated with lavish games.

sanctuary for his deceased wife Faustina. Marcus Aurelius twinned Trajan's Column with another pillar celebrating his victories over the Marcomanni and Quadi, and Septimius Severus put up a three-gated arch to commemorate his Parthian Wars. Under Caracalla, the huge bath complex in the southern quarter was constructed. Finally, Elagabalus had a massive temple erected on the Palatine for his ancestral god. In the troubled years of the soldier emperors, not surprisingly, construction activity slackened, but under Diocletian and his successors, the Roman townscape, though no longer the stage of major political events, was augmented with further monumental buildings.

Over the centuries, the largesse of generations of emperors transformed Rome into a spectacular and impressive city. Even the orator Aelius Aristides, a Greek from Asia Minor living in the 2nd century AD, considered his rhetorical skills insufficient to describe the capital:

BELOW LEFT **Trajan's Forum, the so-called Via Biberatica ('booze street'). The street, which formed part of the vast complex of Trajan's Markets, was paved with basalt stones and lined by shops and eateries.**

BELOW RIGHT **The Temple of Antoninus Pius and Faustina on the Roman Forum, later converted into a church.**

> "It is not only impossible to speak in a proper manner about Rome, but it is also impossible actually to see her. ... Seeing so many hills covered with buildings, so many meadows in the plains transformed into urban space, or so much land claimed by one single city, who could ever survey her accurately?"
>
> Aelius Aristides

BUILDINGS IN ROME SPONSORED BY EMPERORS

Buildings	Area	Emperor	Year
Forum of Augustus	Imperial Fora	Augustus	2 BC
Aqua Claudia, aqueduct	From northern Latium to Rome	Claudius	AD 52
Colosseum	East of the Roman Forum	Vespasian, Titus	AD 80
Arch of Titus	Roman Forum	Domitian	AD 90
Baths of Trajan	Oppius	Trajan	AD 109
Trajan's Forum and Markets	Imperial Fora	Trajan	AD 112
Pantheon, second building	Campus Martius	Hadrian	AD 118
Column of Marcus Aurelius	Campus Martius	Commodus	AD 192
Baths of Caracalla	Aventine Hill	Caracalla	AD 217
Baths of Diocletian	Esquiline Hill	Maxentius/ Diocletian	AD 306

Inside the rotunda of the Pantheon, a temple to all the gods built by Hadrian between AD 118 and 125. The span of the dome was the largest in the ancient world.

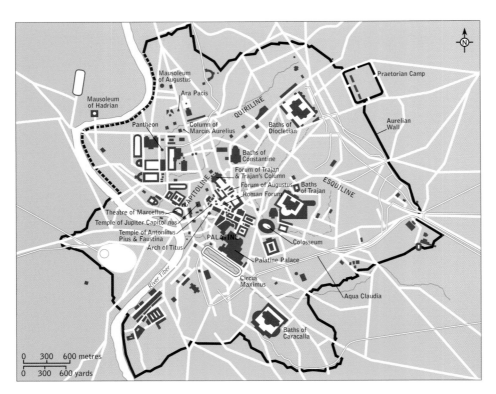

LEFT **Plan of Rome showing the major imperial buildings.**

OPPOSITE, TOP **Compital altar, c. AD 2–3. The relief features a scene of sacrifice, with four *vicimagistri* pouring libations and two sacrificial animals, a bull and a pig.**

BELOW **Rome at the time of the Severan emperors (reconstruction), with the imperial palaces (bottom left), the Fora (top left) and the Colosseum.**

Providing for the city

Aelius Aristides may have felt unable to keep track of Rome's development, but the Roman emperors certainly could. During the imperial period (in contrast to the republic) the capital had its own administration, which worked independently from that of the empire. Augustus divided the city into fourteen *regiones* (regions), each subdivided into *vici* (districts). *Vicimagistri*, who were also locally responsible for the imperial cult (see Box, page 37), presided over the *vici*. The management of the entire city was given into the hands of the *praefectus urbi*, a senior senatorial official whose immediate superior was the emperor himself. In effect, the *praefectus urbi* performed the duties of a lord mayor of Rome. When the emperor was absent from Rome, the prefect acted on his behalf. His other duties included maintaining law and order in the capital, supervising the public games, urban traffic and local markets, overseeing criminal justice and judging cases of high treason.

For the first time, the administration of Rome was uncoupled from that of the state. The city's new structure – with its *regiones* and *vici* – created a spatial framework for the organization of new public services: roads, police, fire brigades, food and water supply, sewerage and religious ceremonies. The city's infrastructure had failed to keep pace with its uncontrolled growth over the last century of the republic. Now immense investment was required. Claudius spent 445 million *sestertii* on the two aqueducts he had built, the Aqua Claudia and the Anio Novus.

(To put this amount into perspective, when Tiberius died, the entire public treasury, the *aerarium*, had a balance of 2.7 billion *sestertii*.) Claudius also financed the upgrading, maintenance and cleaning of the road network. Augustus established a new police force, the three urban cohorts, whose duty it was 'to control the slaves and those citizens whose natural boldness gives way to disorderly conduct, unless they are overawed by force' (according to Tacitus), and the *vigiles*, the public fire brigade.

The *princeps* was personally held responsible for the operation of such services. Ultimately, even the public toilets had to be the emperor's concern – and they were a source of public revenue. The biographer Suetonius reports a famous episode, in which Vespasian was criticized by his son Titus for introducing a new tax on the urine obtained from public conveniences and sold to tanneries.

Vespasian held a piece of money from the first payment to his son's nose, asking whether its odour was offensive to him. When Titus said 'No,' he replied, 'Yet it comes from urine.'

The Aqua Claudia, one of the aqueducts leading to Rome, in the countryside of the Roman Campagna.

The *annona:* bread...

The provision of the capital's growing populace with food, chiefly grain, was vitally important. In the late republic, a large part of the urban population had received subsidized grain rations, which were later dispensed free of charge. Republican Rome had repeatedly suffered from shortfalls in the food supply, which regularly resulted in famine and rioting. The transition to monarchic rule did not immediately resolve the structural problems inherent in supplying a metropolitan population with food from a distance. The emperor had to help out with the distribution of food in 28 BC, but when, in 22 BC, grain shortage struck again, he revolutionized the entire system.

The circle of recipients was, for the first time, clearly defined. Up to 200,000 citizens belonged to the *plebs frumentaria*, who were inscribed in lists and received food vouchers which could be passed on from generation to generation. The recipients received their rations from central distribution points. Under Domitian a purpose-built structure was erected on the Campus Martius: a portico with forty-five 'counters' for the dispensation of food. Grain, the Romans' staple food, was stocked in large warehouses (*horrea*) on the banks of the Tiber. It arrived there by boat from Ostia, the Roman seaport, where the cargo ships docked. The ships sailed from Egypt and North Africa, where the bulk of the Roman empire's grain surplus was produced. Originally only an unprotected bay, the harbour of Ostia was developed into a large port with offices, warehouses and docks for 250 ships under Claudius. Under Trajan and Hadrian, the port was substantially enlarged. Aelius Aristides, the Greek orator, praised it as 'an emporium common to all men and a marketplace common to the products of the entire world'.

All this was put under the supervision of an equestrian official, the *praefectus annonae*. The emperor had the ultimate responsibility for Rome's livelihood, but the prefect of the *annona* had to deal with the day-to-day problems of the grain supply: theft, corruption and problems with the infrastructure. This could be tiresome. Seneca's father-in-law Pompeius Paulinus held the office under Claudius, around the middle of the 1st century AD. In his essay *On the Shortness of Life*, Seneca advised him to give up the office and adopt the contemplative lifestyle of a philosopher. He contrasts the intellectual fulfilment of a life dedicated to study with the mundane chores of a *praefectus annonae*:

> Think you that it is just the same whether you are concerned in having corn from overseas poured into the granaries, unhurt either by the dishonesty or the neglect of those who transport it, in seeing that it does not become heated and spoiled by collecting moisture and tallies in weight and measure, or whether you enter upon these sacred and lofty studies with the purpose of discovering what substance, what pleasure, what mode of life, what shape God has…?

BELOW **A mosaic from the Aula dei Misuratori del Grano, Ostia, showing the distribution of grain.**

BOTTOM **A mosaic from the Piazzale delle Corporazioni, Ostia, with a ship and two grain measures. The inscription refers to the shipowners and merchants from Cagliari (Sardinia).**

Overseeing the *annona* might have been a potentially tedious job, but it was also a very powerful one. In AD 189, Marcus Aurelius Papyrius Dionysius, who was then *praefectus annonae*, deliberately caused a grain shortfall in the capital, exacerbating a famine that was already devastating the city. Papyrius intended to put the blame on Marcus Aurelius Cleander, the emperor Commodus's freedman, chamberlain and chief confidant, but the affair soon got out of hand. There were riots and the Praetorian Guard and the urban cohorts had to intervene. Cleander was ousted and executed, but Papyrius was also put to death; and the food crisis of 189 was the straw that broke the camel's back for Commodus's government.

...and circuses

It was not only food shortages in the capital that created potentially fatal situations for the emperor. *Panem et circenses* – 'bread and circuses' – these were the things the crowds of Rome eagerly awaited, according to the poet Juvenal who lived in the late 1st and early 2nd century. Similarly, Juvenal's younger contemporary Fronto, the orator and teacher of Marcus Aurelius, remarked that the Roman crowds were only tamed by the grain dole and spectacles.

The games – gladiatorial shows, *venationes* (animal hunts) and chariot races – formed an integral part of public life not just in the capital, but in many cities of the Roman world, particularly in the Latin west. But nowhere did the spectacles performed in circuses and amphitheatres attract crowds comparable to those in Rome. Their raison d'être went far beyond pure entertainment: the capital's *ludi* (chariot races and plays) and *munera* (gladiatorial games) were the prime occasions on which the urban populace met their emperor. Thus they were a stage for political communication.

Circuses and theatrical performances had a long tradition in Rome. Since the early days of the republic, public holidays and religious feasts had been marked by races and plays. Later, animal hunts and gladiatorial shows were added. They were intended as celebrations of Roman power: captives and exotic animals from ever more distant parts of the Roman world were put on display in circuses and amphitheatres. The older *ludi* were public performances funded by the state, but *munera* were organized privately and paid for by individuals.

For the hosts of gladiatorial games and *venationes*, the games were an excellent opportunity to accumulate prestige and to enhance their and their families' profile in the public mind. Most spectacles were staged to mark funerals and were designed to draw the public's attention to the achievements of the deceased's family. It is clear that Augustus, once he had achieved sole power, did everything to monopolize such a premium opportunity for self-representation for himself and the dynasty: he limited the number of games organized by the praetors to only two per year.

LEFT **An animal hunt in the arena, depicted on a floor mosaic of the 4th century AD, which is now in the Villa Borghese in Rome. The mosaic was purchased by Cardinal Scipione Borghese in the 17th century.**

BELOW **A gladiatorial scene, from the same floor mosaic as the animal hunt detail. The fighters' names are included; the defeated gladiator is called Mazicinus.**

A century later, Domitian made the hosting of spectacles in Rome the exclusive privilege of members of the imperial family.

The emperors contended with each other to provide the most spectacular, lavish and exotic performances. Nero had the Theatre of Pompey coated with gold and covered with awnings painted in sky blue and dotted with stars. For the racecourses he used copper green sand imported from Armenia. Titus, on the occasion of the Colosseum's inauguration, hosted animal hunts that lasted 100 days; 9,000 animals from three continents were killed. For most Roman authors, an emperor's behaviour in the circus reflected his character. An episode described by Cassius Dio highlights Domitian's megalomania and his cynicism:

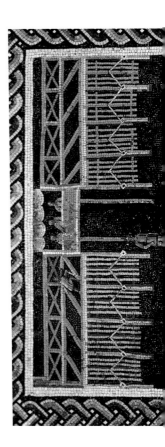

> '**In the Circus, for example, he [Domitian] exhibited battles of infantry against infantry and again battles between cavalry, and in a new place he produced a naval battle. At this last event practically all the combatants and many of the spectators as well perished. ... By way, no doubt, of consoling the people for this, he provided for them at public expense a dinner lasting all night. Often he would conduct the games also at night, and sometimes he would pit dwarfs and women against each other.**'
>
> Cassius Dio

It was essential for the emperor to behave appropriately in the circus or amphitheatre. Neither ostentatious lack of interest – as displayed by Julius Caesar, who dealt with his correspondence in his box – nor excessive enthusiasm for the games were appreciated by the crowds. Caligula was very fond of chariot races, and was a staunch supporter of the Green team; he is said to have poisoned the charioteers and horses of the other teams. In Rome the supporters of the four teams (the Greens, the Blues, the Whites and the Reds) formed factions, which tended to become violent, especially when the political climate was heated.

An emperor in the arena

Gladiatorial games and animal hunts in the arena amused bloodthirsty crowds, but they had a more profound meaning, too. In essence, the games were a religious ritual: the gladiator in the arena was *nefarius*, an outcast, stigmatized by his bloody breadwinning. Wild animals and gladiators alike represented, in the orderly universe of the Roman empire, the outlandish, savage and uncontrollable 'other'. In the arena, where the Roman people sat in the auditorium placed according to their social rank,

the representatives of civilization encountered its very nemesis. Here, the triumph of the Roman state over barbarism, of culture over the savage, of law over lawlessness, was put on stage again and again. The emperor, who held the fate of the defeated gladiator in his hands, was the supreme representative of this law, but his life-and-death decisions were not completely autonomous. If, for instance, he decided that a popular gladiator should be killed, this could cost him valuable support among the crowds; but being too velvet-gloved could provoke criticism, too.

Other requests could be raised. One circus crowd demanded that Caligula waive certain taxes; protests against war and food shortage were also frequently heard in the amphitheatre. Sometimes, tumult at the games was the prelude to an emperor's downfall: under Commodus, a horse named Pertinax ('the stubborn') won a race, cheered by a chanting crowd. Pertinax was also the name of a general who later became emperor himself, after the murder of Commodus. Once emotions in the amphitheatre ran high, a decent speech at least was needed to pour oil on the troubled waters.

Gladiators were outcasts, and yet they had the chance to acquire *virtus*, manly valour. A victorious gladiator was a hero; he could turn his back on the arena and return to civilian life as a respected man. Or he could continue his career in the

The Circus Mosaic, 2nd century AD, from Lyons (France). This restored mosaic depicts a circus with a chariot race. Chariots speed around the track barrier (*meta*), which consists of two basins filled with water. Two chariots have crashed.

arena: a gladiator who had survived and won several fights and thus conquered death had celebrity status and substantial credit with the crowds. The *virtus* that was a gladiator's prize may have induced Commodus to transgress the boundary between the auditorium and the arena and to become – in an unprecedented move – a gladiator himself.

"Commodus now gave orders for the celebration of public shows, at which he promised he would kill all the wild animals with his own hand and engage in gladiatorial combat with the stoutest of young men. As the news spread, people flocked to Rome from all over Italy and the neighbouring provinces to be spectators of something they had never seen or heard of before."

Herodian

For his contemporaries, it was sheer madness that led Commodus to appear in the arena. He perverted the idea of the amphitheatre as the interface between civilization and barbarism and, at the same time, the forum for communication between the emperor and the crowd. An emperor fighting like a gladiator was unquestionably mad – and it is as a raging lunatic that Marcus Aurelius's son is portrayed in the biographical sketches we find in the Historia Augusta, Herodian and Cassius Dio. Dio reports that, after killing an ostrich in an animal hunt, the historian himself witnessed how Commodus – imitating a victorious gladiator's pose – waved

A small bronze statue of a *secutor*, a heavily armed type of gladiator who specialized in fighting the *retiarius*, who fought with a trident and net.

the bird's head at the senators' seats with one hand, holding up his sword with the other. To avoid laughing – an insult punishable by death – Dio had to chew the laurels of his wreath and advised his neighbours to do the same.

Most modern scholars would agree that Commodus's behaviour reflects a degree of insanity, but the emperor's eccentric performances may well have had another meaning. In the later years of his reign, Commodus's entire self-representation focused on his personal *virtus*. He identified himself with the hero Hercules, who was reinvented as *Hercules Commodianus*; he awarded his name to cities, institutions, military units and the time-honoured Senate; ultimately, he even renamed Rome – the imperial capital – *Colonia Commodiana* (the 'colony of Commodus'). More than any of his predecessors, Commodus styled himself as Rome's sovereign, whose *virtus* was the sole source of his power.

Ironically, it was the emperor's desire to put himself on display in the arena that ultimately brought him down. When Commodus declared that he wanted to assume his new consulate on 1 January 193 in the circus, dressed as a gladiator, instead of in the palace and vested in the traditional purple tunic, Marcia, his lover, Eclectus, the chamberlain, and Aemilius Laetus, the praetorian prefect, decided that they had to get rid of the emperor. Commodus was killed on New Year's Eve 192. The assassination was the prelude to a new series of usurpations and civil wars from which Septimius Severus, a native of the North African city of Lepcis Magna, emerged victorious.

The emperor in the arena remained a short-lived episode in the history of both the bloody games and the principate. However, by making his own personal *virtus* the Roman empire's lynchpin, Commodus became a role model for future generations of emperors. From the late 2nd century onwards, monarchic authority rested increasingly upon the people's 'devotion to the exceptional sanctity, heroism or exemplary character' of the ruler. This is how the German sociologist Max Weber defines 'charismatic' authority, and charisma, which had always been inherent in a Roman emperor's exercise of power, became, in the disturbances of the great crisis, the crucial quality for his survival (see chapter 4).

Marble bust of Commodus as Hercules. Like the mythical hero, Commodus has his head covered with a lion's skin. In his right hand he holds a club, and in his left the apples of the Hesperides. The bust rests on a globe, the symbol of universal power, and two cornucopias. Originally, it was supported by two Amazons.

Constantine and Constantinople

During the 'long' 3rd century, it became more and more apparent that the city of Rome was no longer the epicentre of the Roman world. Rome was, as the historian Herodian put it, where the emperor was. Emperors were created far from Rome, and many of them spent their short reigns fighting on distant battlefields, without visiting Rome even once. When, in AD 248, the emperor Philip the Arab celebrated the beginning of Rome's second millennium with lavish games in the capital, it was like a farewell – at least in retrospect. Rome was good for spectacles, but it was no longer the place from which the empire was governed.

When Diocletian and Maximian and, from 293 onwards, all four Tetrarchs – Diocletian, Maximian, Galerius and Constantius I – consolidated the troubled empire, they ruled from residences which they methodically established in different

parts of the empire. Diocletian made Nicomedia in northwestern Asia Minor and Antioch in Syria his capitals; Maximian resided in the north of Italy, in Aquileia and Milan; Galerius governed from Romuliana (Gamzigrad) in present-day Serbia and from Thessalonica; and Constantius had his residence at Trier, in Upper Germany. Huge palaces were built in the new capitals, with rooms in which the emperor could live and work, but also space for offices and law courts.

Constantine the Great, who eventually succeeded the Tetrarchs, took a different path. Constantine did not settle for building another palace for himself and his administration: in the tradition of Alexander the Great, he founded a new city, which was destined to become the empire's political, economic and cultural centre for the centuries to come and its first Christian metropolis. At first, Constantinople had to compete with Antioch, but when Constantius II was sole *Augustus*, it emerged

FAR LEFT **The imperial baths in Trier (Germany). Built around AD 300 by Constantine's father Constantius I, the baths formed part of the imperial compound. The building, which was never finished, was later converted into barracks.**

LEFT **Felix Romuliana, present-day Gamzigrad (Serbia). The ruins of the palace of the Tetrarch Galerius have been excavated only partly. The complex, on which construction started in AD 298, was heavily fortified and featured mosaics and wall paintings as well as hundreds of sculptures. Nearby, the mausoleums of Galerius and his mother Romula were found.**

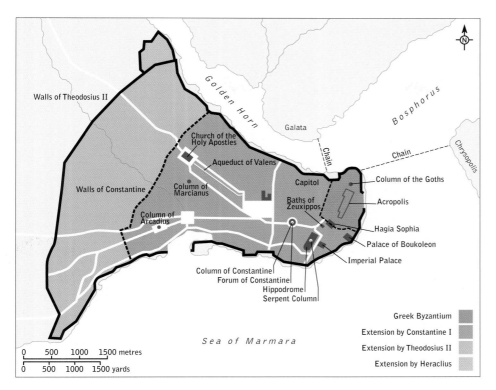

Golden Horn

Bosphorus

Walls of Theodosius II

Galata

Chrysopolis

Chain

Chain

Church of the
Holy Apostles

Aqueduct of Valens

Column of the Goths

Capitol

Walls of Constantine

Column of
Marcianus

Acropolis

Baths of
Zeuxippos

Column of
Arcadius

Hagia Sophia

Palace of Boukoleon

Imperial Palace

Column of Constantine
Forum of Constantine
Hippodrome
Serpent Column

Sea of Marmara

Greek Byzantium

Extension by Constantine I

Extension by Theodosius II

Extension by Heraclius

0   500   1000   1500 metres
0   500   1000   1500 yards

OPPOSITE **Reconstruction of the giant bronze statue of Constantine the Great in Rome. Only the stone parts – head, hands and feet – have survived. They are now on display in the courtyard of the Palazzo dei Conservatori on the Capitol in Rome.**

LEFT **Plan of Constantinople.**

BELOW **Head of the emperor Galerius, wearing a diadem.**

as the empire's unrivalled capital. The city became the capital of the eastern Roman empire after the division of AD 395; and it remained the capital of the Byzantine empire until its final downfall in 1453.

However, the road that led to Constantinople was a long one. Constantine was the illegitimate son of Constantius I, the Tetrarch who had resided in Trier. Helena, his mother, was a Christian, and Constantine may have become familiar with Christianity as an adolescent. When Constantine was approximately thirty years old, his father, who had succeeded Maximian as *Augustus* of the west in AD 305, died, after just one year in power. Constantine, who had stayed with his father in Eboracum (York) during the whole of 306, was now proclaimed emperor by the Britannic army. The Tetrarchs had attempted to establish a system of succession by resignation, co-option and marriages between *Caesares* and the daughters of *Augusti*, but dynastic loyalty was still deeply rooted in the soldiery, and when Tetrarchs such as Maximian and Constantius had sons, their claims to the empire were difficult to ignore.

Galerius, the *Augustus* of the east, did not accept the proclamation of Constantine. He appointed his friend Severus as *Augustus*, but against him the Praetorian Guard in Rome proclaimed Maxentius, Maximian's son, *Augustus*. To make the chaos perfect, Maximian, who had resigned jointly with Diocletian in AD 305, returned to active politics and forged an alliance with Constantine. In the

evolving civil war, Severus was killed and Galerius defeated. His last resort was to call on Diocletian, the retired elder statesman, who summoned a conference at Carnuntum in Pannonia (present-day Bad Deutsch-Altenburg in Lower Austria). Diocletian, Galerius and Maximian decided to make Licinius, a fellow officer and friend of Galerius, *Augustus* of the west and Constantine his *Caesar*, leaving Maximinus Daia as the *Augustus* of the east (November 308).

The compromise of Carnuntum did not last: new usurpations shook the empire. Constantine defeated Maximian in Gaul and had him executed (310), Galerius died (311), Licinius struggled with Maximinus Daia for power in the east and Constantine and Maxentius prepared for the final showdown in the west. On 28 October 312, Constantine's and Maxentius's armies clashed north of Rome, at the Milvian Bridge. The soldiers of the victorious Constantine had crosses fixed to their standards – according to his biographer Eusebius of Caesarea, the emperor had dreamed the night before the battle that he would 'conquer in this sign'.

His soldiers may have prevailed under the sign of the cross, but Constantine was not a fully Christian emperor – at least, not yet. At different times in the past, Constantine had experimented with various deities with whom he had established

ABOVE **A section from the south face of the Arch of Constantine. The frieze at the bottom commemorates the battle of the Milvian Bridge, where Constantine defeated Maxentius in AD 312. The two roundels above, both reused decorations from the period of Hadrian, show a hunting scene (left) and a sacrifice to the hunting goddess Diana (right).**

OPPOSITE ABOVE **Gold *solidus* of Constantine, minted in Ticinum in AD 316, showing Constantine (wearing a laurel wreath) alongside Sol Invictus. On the reverse is a figure of Liberalitas holding a cornucopia.**

OPPOSITE BELOW ***The Dream of Constantine*, a fresco by Piero della Francesca.**

a personal relationship: Hercules, Mars, Sol Invictus and Apollo. Even when Constantine actively promoted the God of the Christians, the language of the narratives and images used was still ambivalent enough to be read in a pagan sense as well. He clearly privileged Christianity, took a stand in inter-Christian debates and felt responsible for the Church, though he lacked a profound understanding of

the dogmatic issues dividing Christianity. Long before his baptism at the hour of his death, he gave a commitment to the new faith through substantial benefactions and promotions of fellow-Christians; but his actions could still be interpreted as religiously impartial by those who did not embrace the new religion.

Constantine embraced the Christian God and the growing Christian community in his empire because he needed both divine and human allies against his imperial rivals. In AD 311, the four emperors abandoned the policy of persecution so far pursued by the Tetrarchs and declared Christianity a *religio licita* ('permitted religion'). Two years later, Constantine and Licinius issued the Edict of Milan, which confirmed the previous declaration and guaranteed religious tolerance all over the empire: 'Christians as well as all men within the empire' were free to choose their religious affiliation. After more than sixty years of continued persecution, Christianity was finally on an equal footing with other faiths.

Constantine and Licinius ruled jointly for some years, but rivalry increasingly overshadowed their initially peaceful coexistence. In 324, Constantine defeated Licinius (who by then aggressively advocated the old pagan faith) in a series of battles in Thrace; in the following year, he had his opponent executed. Near the site of his last victory over Licinius, on the Bosphorus, where Europe meets Asia, he renamed the ancient Greek city of Byzantion (Byzantium in Latin) as Constantinople (the city of Constantine) and began to convert it into the future capital for his empire. The new residence was inaugurated on 11 May 330. It soon became the second Rome.

A Christian capital?

At first, however, Constantinople was mainly a new residence for the (now sole) ruler Constantine: more important than Trier, Milan, Serdica and the numerous other palaces, but nonetheless inferior in rank to Rome, the old capital. However, the new city's layout was grand from the outset and its position between Asia and Europe, easily defensible and commanding the straits of the Bosphorus, rapidly boosted its importance. Rome was the epicentre of Roman paganism and still home to numerous important sanctuaries, but Byzantium carried little religious baggage. Surprisingly, however, this did not mean that Constantinople was quintessentially a Christian capital from its very beginning – on the contrary.

Constantine enlarged the old town of Byzantium substantially to the west, where the *Mesê* (the 'centre'), a grand colonnaded street, divided the peninsula into two urban quarters. The new palace, built within the old town, was inspired by Diocletian's palace at Split and other Tetrarch's residences. Apart from the palace, which formed the nucleus of a continuously growing architectural ensemble, only a few buildings in Constantinople were definitely completed by Constantine. Many buildings whose origins can be traced back to Constantine were actually completed under his son Constantius II. These include the city walls; the hippodrome close to the palace; the baths of Zeuxippus and some public buildings in the centre of old Byzantium; the circular forum with a porphyry column in the centre, which was crowned by a statue of the founder; the Capitol in the west, with a temple of Jupiter Capitolinus which held a statue of Constantine as Jupiter; and finally the mausoleum of Constantine, which later became the Church of the Holy Apostles. Near the palace stood the temple of the Tyche of Constantinople, the city's divine personification. The statue on the circular forum portrayed Constantine as Sol Invictus, with a lance and globe in his hands and an aureole around his head. The founder was also present as sun god in a nearby rotunda: the statue, in the shape of a charioteer, was carried to the hippodrome in a procession once a year to celebrate the birthday of Constantinople. Finally, Constantine was buried in the mausoleum surrounded by the symbolic tombs of the twelve apostles, like Christ himself. Polytheists, however, could see in the mausoleum a place of worship for the twelve Olympian gods.

If Constantinople was dedicated to any cult, it was the worship of its founder, who was present in the shapes of Sol Invictus, Jupiter Capitolinus and Jesus Christ. This new capital marked the acme of the imperial cult, the religious veneration of the ruler. It was emblematic not so much of change, as of continuity: since Alexander the Great, the city as a monument to its founder was a recurrent motif in the self-representation of Hellenistic kings and Roman emperors, carried to the extreme by Commodus who had 'refounded' Rome as *Colonia Commodiana*. Even though Constantine in the later years of his reign clearly favoured Christianity, Constantinople was, at his death in AD 337, by no means the Christian capital of a quintessentially Christian empire.

It is hard to determine how Christian the empire actually was, when Constantine formally converted to the new faith on his deathbed. The persecutions of the 3rd and early 4th centuries had created a polarity between Christianity and paganism that had been absent before. In a way, this very opposition had transformed paganism into a coherent religious system. Paradoxically, the persecutions made Christianity more attractive: the Christian martyrs became role models for hundreds of thousands who, secretly or openly, converted to Christianity. The relatively long intervals between the various surges of persecution and the government's inability to enforce the repression effectively facilitated the establishment of a Church hierarchy.

When Constantine first took power in AD 306, Christianity was clearly a factor which had to be taken into account, and the issue of the Edict of Milan seven years later by Constantine and Licinius marked a kind of draw between the two faiths.

The wall of Constantinople, constructed under Theodosius II. The wall was approximately 20 km (12 miles) long and was built to protect the rapidly growing city.

The draw lasted for about a decade. In the final contest between the two *Augusti*, religion became a pivotal issue and each of the two had to take a firm stand: Licinius for paganism, Constantine for Christianity. After Constantine's victory, Christianity rapidly got the upper hand, but paganism was – as the religious topography of the new capital proved – far from extinguished.

The second Rome

When Constantine, at the end of his life, received his baptism, paganism was not dead, but it was dying. Constantine's sons, who succeeded him, made the rise of the new faith irreversible. The three brothers Constantine II, Constans and Constantius II reigned in harmony only for a couple of years. In 340, rivalry between Constantine and Constans (who had shared the western provinces) escalated into civil war: Constantine II was defeated and killed. Soon, the relationship between Constans and Constantius worsened, ostensibly over religious issues, but a military confrontation was avoided. However, Constans was later killed in a civil war against the usurper Magnentius. In 353, when Magnentius was defeated, Constantius became sole emperor.

Most ancient sources, which represent pagan or Nicene viewpoints, paint a dismal picture of Constantius as a ruler, but his reign was a decisive period for the empire, for Christianity and, in particular, for Constantinople. The pressure on the Roman frontiers, which had eased during the last quarter of the 3rd century, was now increasing again. The Persians had renewed their attacks on the Roman eastern provinces and the Rhine and Danube frontiers were increasingly unstable too. Usurpations and civil war were rampant once again. No less revolutionary were the changes within the empire. In AD 354, Constantius issued a law ordering the closure of pagan sanctuaries and instigating drastic measures against those who persisted in visiting them. In 357, Constantius had the altar of the goddess Victoria removed from Senate House in Rome.

Most notably, however, the old capital was now clearly eclipsed by Constantinople. Constantius continued to adorn the city on the

A detail from the Ada Cameo, a sardonyx cameo made in AD 316. It represents members of the Constantinian family, from left to right: Helena, the emperor Constantine, his baby son Constantine II, his wife Fausta and their eldest son Crispus.

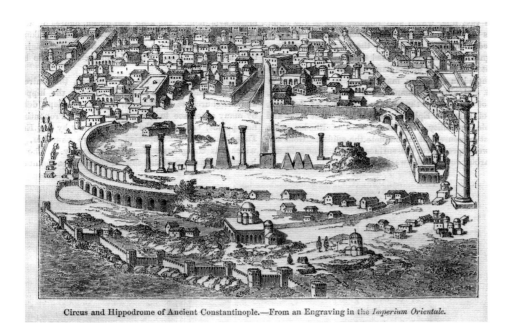

Circus and Hippodrome of Ancient Constantinople.—From an Engraving in the *Imperium Orientale.*

The Hippodrome in Constantinople, from Anselmo Maria Banduri's *Imperium Orientale*, a history of the Byzantine empire, published in 1711.

Bosphorus with grand buildings, constructing lavish new baths, the *Thermae Constantianae*. Settlers from three continents poured into Constantinople; and renowned works of art were removed from the empire's great cities to be put up in the new capital. Many buildings that had been erected by Constantine, such as the huge audience hall next to the palace, were now converted into sacred spaces: this hall became the first church of Hagia Sophia. Constantius also destroyed the statue of Constantine that had been carried through the streets to mark the city's anniversary and the procession now took on a Christian significance. The remaining pagan sanctuaries were abandoned and gradually decayed.

The palace founded by Constantine was completed and substantially enlarged. In its immediate neighbourhood was the hippodrome, the venue for chariot races. The races were a legacy of ancient Rome that the inhabitants of Constantinople cherished, but at times they could be rather risky for the emperors. In 532, a major uprising, the Nika Revolt, began in the circus and almost brought about the emperor Justinian's downfall. When Justinian attempted to restrain the behaviour of the factions and sentenced some of their leaders to death, the supporters in the hippodrome banded together against the emperor; political demands were raised and the emperor's legitimacy questioned. Finally, the government drove a wedge between the factions and suppressed the revolt, but Justinian remained unpopular with the capital's populace for many years.

When Constantius II died in 361, the new capital his father had founded was a truly Christian city. Constantinople had also received its own Senate and urban prefect, which highlighted the city's special status and its independence from the provincial administration. Its splendour and the works of art collected there from all over the empire were emblematic of the beginning of the age of late antiquity. They embodied the tradition of classical antiquity and the legacy of Rome, which had now been accepted by Constantinople; at the same time, they symbolically encapsulated the superiority of Christianity and the new empire which it had helped to transform within a few decades. Rome, after all, had become an idea, which could be transferred through space and time.

The twenty-four-year reign of Constantius II consolidated Christianity as the religion of the empire, Constantinople as its capital, the Church as its single most powerful organization and the emperor as the Church's head. The latter, in

The Greek Horses, from St Mark's Basilica in Venice. The horses are the only bronze *quadriga* surviving from antiquity. They may have been brought from Italy to Constantinople, where they were put up in the Hippodrome. Along with the porphyry group of the Tetrarchs (see page 67), the horses were looted by the Venetians in 1204.

particular, solved an age-old problem inherent in the principate: its fundamental lack of legitimacy. Now the *princeps* was a ruler by divine right, God's own agent on earth. The emperor's role had begun gradually to change as early as the 3rd century. Modesty, accessibility and the idea of the emperor as a peer of the traditional elite (the senators) had become an anachronism in a Roman state in which new, professional elites had taken the senators' place.

Some emperors had experimented with religious legitimacy before Constantine and Constantius. Elagabalus had made the ancestral god of his hometown in Syria the supreme god of the Roman pantheon; Aurelian had actively propagated the cult of the sun god Sol Invictus; the Tetrarchs had associated themselves with deities; and even Augustus had highlighted his close relationship with the god Apollo. From the 3rd century onwards, the emperors became more and more detached from ordinary life. In their lavish palaces, they became superhuman figures. Aloof, crowned with the diadem (which had been traditionally frowned upon in Rome) and wrapped in magnificent, colourful garments, the emperor's person was visibly sacred. Whoever approached him had to fall down first. 'Like the modesty affected by Augustus, the state maintained by Diocletian was a theatrical representation', comments Edward Gibbon in *The Decline and Fall of the Roman Empire,* and he adds:

> But it must be confessed that of the two comedies, the former was of a much more liberal and manly character than the latter. It was the aim of the one to disguise, and the object of the other to display, the unbounded power which the emperors possessed over the Roman world.

Emperors and bishops

This new role as the Lord's chief representative on earth made life easier for the Roman emperors in some ways, but even so, their 'unbounded power' existed only on paper. Christianity as the new state religion had severe repercussions on politics and government. Unlike the pagan religions, which thrived throughout the first three centuries of the empire, Christianity was firmly rooted in dogma. Authority was needed to decide what was the 'true' faith: orthodoxy was born. Inevitably, though, where there is orthodoxy, there is also heterodoxy, people who will not subordinate themselves to the rules established by others.

From the moment St Paul had spread the message of Christianity over the Mediterranean world, there was dispute about the true faith and the right course of action: whether to include Gentiles in the community of Christians; how to deal with those who had abandoned Christianity in the period of persecutions; whether God, the father, and Christ, the son, were 'consubstantial' manifestations of the one divine entity or, as Arius, a priest from Alexandria, preached, Christ was a mere 'creation' of

Coins issued under the emperor Elagabalus, representing the cult object (*baitylos*) from Emesa, drawn on a chariot (top) and the Elagabalium, the temple the ruler built for his ancestral god on the Palatine in Rome (middle and below).

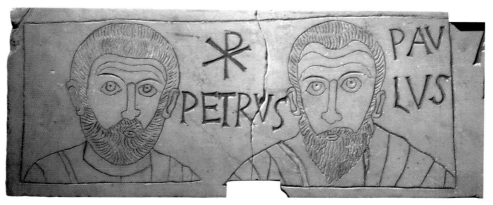

A carving from the Catacomb of St Hippolytus, Rome, depicting St Peter and St Paul. The marble board was used to close the *loculus* tomb of Asellus, who was buried in the catacomb in the 4th century AD.

God. All these issues, philosophical as they may seem to us, were of paramount importance to contemporary Christians and, accordingly, controversial.

Dogmatic dispute, which increased with the growing factionalization of Christianity, could easily get out of hand and escalate into riots involving huge crowds agitated by ever more radical preachers. A particular hotspot of religious strife was Alexandria, where Arius had preached and gathered supporters. His opponent, Bishop Alexander of Alexandria, did not hesitate to mobilize the mob against the Arians. His successor Athanasius even furnished monks with clubs and set them on his enemies.

In such a situation, the emperor had to act. As *pontifex maximus* he was the empire's highest priest and in his capacity as supreme judge it was his responsibility to settle contention. The first case in which Constantine had to mediate was the Donatist Dispute in North Africa: he was dragged into the affair by a series of petitions, first by the supporters and later by the adversaries of the controversial Bishop of Carthage, Caecilianus. Constantine, advised by independent councils, decided three times in Caecilianus's favour, thus triggering the secession of the Donatists, who had opposed his appointment. Later, in 325, Constantine summoned the bishops to a council at Nicaea, a town in Bithynia (northwest Turkey). At Nicaea, the doctrine of Arius was condemned and the Holy Trinity (God, the father, Christ, the son and the Holy Spirit) declared as orthodoxy, but the settlement lasted only for a few years. The Nicene Creed remained disputed for decades to come and some emperors – Constantius II and later Valens – openly favoured the doctrines of Arius. The schism remained unresolved.

In 381, the emperor Theodosius summoned the next ecumenical (universal) council, which he hosted in Constantinople. In fact, only the bishops of the empire's eastern half were represented. Nonetheless, it was a triumph for the Nicene Creed. At the end of the council, the 'holy synod of bishops' addressed Theodosius, 'the most religious emperor' in a letter announcing that:

We had assembled in Constantinople, according to the letter of your Piety, we first of all renewed our unity of heart each with the other, and then we pronounced some concise definitions, ratifying the Faith of the Nicene Fathers, and anathematizing the heresies which have sprung up, contrary thereto.

The council's first canon made Arianism a crime punishable by death; the period of religious freedom that had begun with Constantine's and Licinius's Edict of Milan (313) had ended for good.

No less important for Constantinople was the third canon, which ruled that the Bishop of Constantinople was, after the Bishop of Rome (later the Pope), the second patriarch of the Church: 'The Bishop of Constantinople, however, shall have the prerogative of honour after the Bishop of Rome because Constantinople is New Rome'. Fourteen years later, Theodosius, the last emperor who ruled (albeit briefly) over a united Roman empire, was dead and Constantinople the capital of an imperial half only. From 395 onwards, the Latin west and the Greek east went their increasingly separate ways in religious affairs too, which led to ever deeper schisms and finally to the establishment of two separate churches.

Emperor Theodosius I, presiding over the Council of Constantinople in AD 381. The drawing comes from a 9th-century Latin manuscript.

The Apostate

The closure of pagan sanctuaries in 354, the confirmation of the Nicene Creed at Constantinople in 381 and the complete ban on pagan sacrifice decreed by Theodosius in 392 seem inevitable stages of an irreversible historical process that had gained momentum since Constantine's conversion. The triumph of Christianity was irresistible – or was it? One man at least attempted to fight against it, more or less single-handedly: Julian, whom his numerous enemies called the Apostate. Ironically, this man was none other than Constantine's nephew, the son of the emperor's half-brother Julius Constantius.

Julian was born in Constantinople in 331. After Constantine's death in 337, Julian and his half-brother Gallus were the only survivors of a massacre that killed the entire branch of the family. Julian grew up with a distant relative, Eusebius, who was the Bishop of Nicomedia and a supporter of Arianism. Though raised in the Christian faith, young Julian began to socialize with pagan intellectuals and started reading the work of Libanius, the influential orator from Antioch. Later he went to study in Athens. Though none of this was unusual for an educated Christian, he may have turned away from the new religion as early as 350.

In 355, Constantius II made his cousin Julian *Caesar* and entrusted him with the western provinces. There, he repeatedly fought back incursions of the Alamanni, whom he defeated near Argentoratum (Strasbourg) in 357. When Constantius requested the bulk of Julian's army to be sent to the east, the soldiers revolted and proclaimed Julian *Augustus*. The coming civil war was only prevented by the sudden death of Constantius in November 361. Julian became sole emperor.

His first actions as *Augustus* reveal that Julian was obsessed by the idea of putting the wheel of history into reverse. He cut back the imperial bureaucracy, which – since Diocletian – had assumed enormous dimensions; he tried to establish a relationship of trust with the old ruling classes and the two Senates; he also addressed the local elites of the empire's many cities. The representatives of Constantius's court in Constantinople, however, were brought to trial, and many of them were executed or exiled. Julian's emperorship was intended to be one in the style of Augustus, but his subjects, above all the metropolitan populace of Constantinople, missed the grand staging of imperial power they had grown used to since the times of Constantine and Constantius, and were irritated by Julian's ascetic and conspicuously modest outer appearance.

The focus of Julian's activity, however, was not style but religion. In his zeal to roll back the influence of Christianity, he restored old temples and shrines, re-employed pagan priests, dismissed Christian officials and abolished the privileges of the Church and the clergy wherever he could. In an edict of 362, he proclaimed the freedom of religion, thus fully rehabilitating the pagan cults and leaving the Christians to their sectarian disputes, which were further fuelled by the return of heterodox exiles, who now reclaimed confiscated property from the Church and further undermined doctrinal unity. Julian himself wrote a pamphlet *Against the Galilaeans* (Christians) and attacked the dogmatic and philosophical foundations of Christianity, which he described as a renegade sect of Judaism. His famous School Edict of 362 effectively banned Christian teachers from public schools.

Gold coin (*solidus*) of Julian the Apostate.

The obvious intention of this was to deprive Christianity of its intellectual foundations. In order to foster classical erudition in his capital, Julian donated the stock of his immense private library to Constantinople's public library, which had been founded by his cousin Constantius in 356. He also funded the construction of a new building for the library.

Though he was Christianity's nemesis, Julian learned a great deal from the religion. The traditional pagan religions in the Roman world did not stand a chance against the organizational and ideological cohesion of Christianity and the hierarchic professionalism of its clergy. Julian's answer to this problem was an attempt to establish a veritable pagan 'church'. The emperor appointed high priests in the provinces in order to compete with the bishops; he established a poor relief programme run by pagan sanctuaries, modelled on Christian charity; and he tried to make Neoplatonism – a late antique school of thought, which attempted to reconcile the rationalism of classical Greek philosophy with the mysticism of some, especially eastern, religions – the dogmatic backbone of his new pagan state church.

The pamphlet against the Christians was not the only work Julian published while in Constantinople. His satire *The Caesars*, written in December 362, deals with a contest between the deceased rulers of antiquity. The Caesars are invited to a banquet at the table of the gods. The bad emperors – Caligula, Nero and the like – are sent to the underworld straight away, but a few of the remainder are singled out because they surpassed the others with their achievements: Alexander the Great, Julius Caesar, Augustus, Trajan, Marcus Aurelius and Constantine. They are given the chance to present their achievements to the audience and are then interrogated by the gods. All but Marcus Aurelius – who had not boasted about his deeds – are dismissed, because they had been motivated by nothing but lust for power. The satire is a priceless document: holding a mirror to Julian's self-conception as emperor, it reveals how a pagan intellectual of the period defined ideal government. First and foremost, however, it is Julian's merciless verdict on the reign of his uncle Constantine: Constantine, dominated by greed, had grabbed the empire's treasures to satisfy his and his friends' desires. Silenus, the wine god Dionysus's companion, comments: 'you wanted to be a banker and did not notice that you lived the life of a cook or a barber'.

Julian's conservative revolution was a failure, though a magnificent one. The emperor died, at the age of thirty-two, in the Persian War he had inherited from Constantius in 363. Was it merely the shortness of his reign that denied him success? Probably not: it is very unlikely that the pagan state church he had dreamed of would have been able to roll back Christianity. After all, the triumph of the new faith had been brought about not so much by Constantine and his sons, but by processes of the *longue durée*, which had profoundly altered the patterns of Roman society: namely the gradual decline of cultural coherence and the need for new religions with an ethical and a redemptory dimension – both developments of the 3rd century. Towards the end of his life, Julian realized that his policy met the fierce resistance not only of Christians, but even of pagans, who were alienated by the emperor's zeal. Not surprisingly, Christianity emerged stronger than ever after his death.

CHAPTER 7

DECLINE AND FALL IN THE WEST

When Julian the Apostate died in the early summer of 363, it had already become apparent that Rome was about to lose a major war. Julian's successor Jovian, whom the military in Mesopotamia appointed, had to negotiate peace with the Persians and withdraw the army from enemy territory. The empire had lost a battle, it had lost a war, but it appeared as strong as ever since the time of Diocletian. Was it really? In 378, fifteen years after Julian's death, a large Roman army was defeated by the Gothic Thervingi at Adrianople and thousands of soldiers were killed; nineteen years after his death, in 382, Theodosius was forced to strike a foedus (alliance) with the Goths; forty-seven years after his death, in 410, Alaric's Goths conquered and sacked Rome; a hundred and thirteen years after his death, in 476, the last emperor of the Roman west, Romulus Augustulus ('the little Augustus') was deposed by the Germanic leader of the foederati, Odoacer.

After the defeat at Adrianople, Germanic groups surged against the Roman frontiers with unprecedented force and began to spread throughout the empire. Did they overrun an internally stable, vigorous state at the apex of its power? Or did they, almost accidentally, finish off a dinosaur that had been in its death throes for quite some time, owing to internal strife, political and strategic shortcomings, social contradictions and cultural decline? This question has been debated ever since Montesquieu, in the early 18th century, blamed moral decadence for Rome's decline. Whatever the answer, the emperors from Valens to Romulus Augustulus rapidly lost control, isolating themselves in their palaces and becoming increasingly eclipsed by ever more powerful military men.

Valens at Adrianople

Jovian, whom the Mesopotamian army had proclaimed emperor after Julian's sudden death, ruled for less than a year. He died, against expectations, peacefully.

An ivory diptych of AD 406 depicting the western emperor Honorius (on both panels). Honorius wears military garb. The consul Probus, for whom the diptych was made, is mentioned in the inscription beneath the emperor's feet. The Probus diptych is the first of a series of surviving consular diptychs, which became fashionable in the early 5th century.

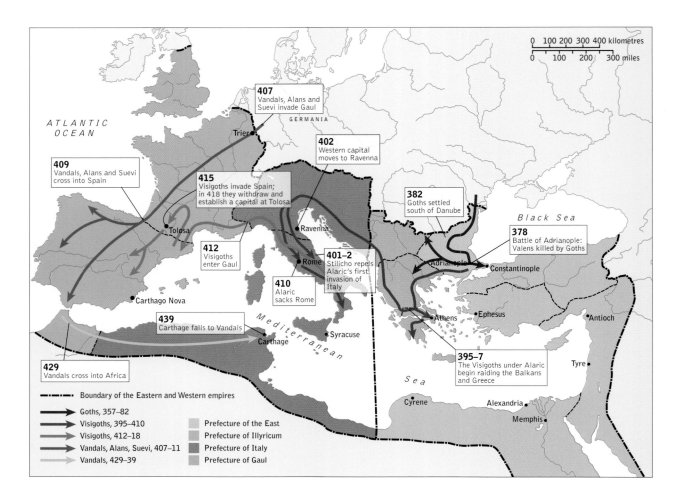

407
Vandals, Alans and Suevi invade Gaul

402
Western capital moves to Ravenna

409
Vandals, Alans and Suevi cross into Spain

415
Visigoths invade Spain; in 418 they withdraw and establish a capital at Tolosa

382
Goths settled south of Danube

378
Battle of Adrianople: Valens killed by Goths

412
Visigoths enter Gaul

401–2
Stilicho repels Alaric's first invasion of Italy

410
Alaric sacks Rome

439
Carthage falls to Vandals

429
Vandals cross into Africa

395–7
The Visigoths under Alaric begin raiding the Balkans and Greece

ATLANTIC OCEAN

GERMANIA

Trier

Tolosa

Ravenna

Rome

Carthago Nova

Mediterranean

Carthage

Syracuse

Sea

Black Sea

Adrianople

Constantinople

Athens

Ephesus

Antioch

Tyre

Cyrene

Alexandria

Memphis

0 100 200 300 400 kilometres
0 100 200 300 miles

- - - Boundary of the Eastern and Western empires
→ Goths, 357–82
→ Visigoths, 395–410
→ Visigoths, 412–18
→ Vandals, Alans, Suevi, 407–11
→ Vandals, 429–39

Prefecture of the East
Prefecture of Illyricum
Prefecture of Italy
Prefecture of Gaul

His successor, Valentinian, was a Christian officer, who on his own accession appointed his brother Valens *Augustus* for the east. In 366 Valens, after fierce fighting, defeated the usurper Procopius, who had brought Constantinople under his control.

Procopius's usurpation had added a new element to the power game in the Roman east: the Goths. In order to improve his strategic position, Procopius had called on the Goths for assistance. A large Gothic army now stood in Thrace, in the immediate hinterland of Constantinople. Valens drove out the Goths by force, crossed the Danube and devastated the land of the Gothic Thervingi, who had settled in the former Roman province of Dacia. In the end, Athanaric, the leader of the Thervingi, sought peace and a *foedus* was struck.

The greatest challenge for Valens, however, was still to come. In 376, Fritigern, a Thervingi aristocrat of Christian faith, appealed to the Romans to give asylum to the Christian members of his tribe. Following the peace with Valens, Athanaric had begun to persecute the Christians among his tribe, and in 375, the Huns began their

The later empire, now divided into eastern and western halves, was organized into four prefectures. The map shows these divisions and also the routes taken by the waves of Germanic invaders who repeatedly assailed the empire between 357 and 439.

advance into the settlement areas of the Thervingi: both factors caused the exodus of the Fritigern Goths, whom Valens, the Arian champion of Christianity, admitted to Roman territory. However, the settling of the Gothic asylum seekers went anything but smoothly. The crowd of Goths was far too large to be supplied with land, housing and food in sufficient quantities. Corrupt Roman officials exploited the newcomers' desperate situation and stripped them of their last possessions and the understandably angry refugees became increasingly rebellious.

To make matters worse, the chaos frustrated any attempt to control the borders properly. It was not only Christian Goths who crossed the frontier, but also a lot of others who were fleeing the Huns and their allies, among them many Greuthungi, members of another Gothic tribal confederation that had settled to the east of the Thervingi and had been even more affected by the advancing Huns. These men came in droves and they were all armed. Above all, the Goths' sense of tribal identity remained intact even on Roman soil. It was an unprecedented case of a tribe migrating into the empire and preserving its group identity, as well as its allegiance towards its leaders. In effect, the refugees formed a large foreign army inside Roman territory. When a local Roman commander planned to ambush Fritigern and another leader of the Goths, open hostilities broke out.

Valens was in a dilemma. He had no precise information on the enemy's strength. Though he had sent envoys to his nephew Gratian – who had been the *Augustus* of the west since Valentinian's death in 375 – asking for military backup, he was not keen on sharing with his younger relative what promised to be a most prestigious victory. Valens's government had proved inept in a critical situation: now the eastern emperor was eager to pick up the slack. The decision was made, and a strong army marched against the Goths. After all, who could rival the Roman emperor?

Gold medallion showing the emperors and brothers Valentinian and Valens, *c.* AD 375.

In fact, Valens and his officers were worse than ill-prepared for battle. One problem was numbers, which are difficult to estimate, as the data provided by the ancient sources are notoriously unreliable. The Romans certainly grossly underestimated the strength of the Goths: instead of the 10,000 men they expected, their legions encountered far more, possibly twice as many. Modern guesses assume that Valens had about 15,000 soldiers. Flaws in his own intelligence made the emperor overconfident. Besides, the Roman army, though operating on home territory, lacked supplies, which forced Valens to act precipitately. Finally, the emperor was undecided until the very last moment whether he wanted to annihilate the Goths or turn them into Roman soldiers.

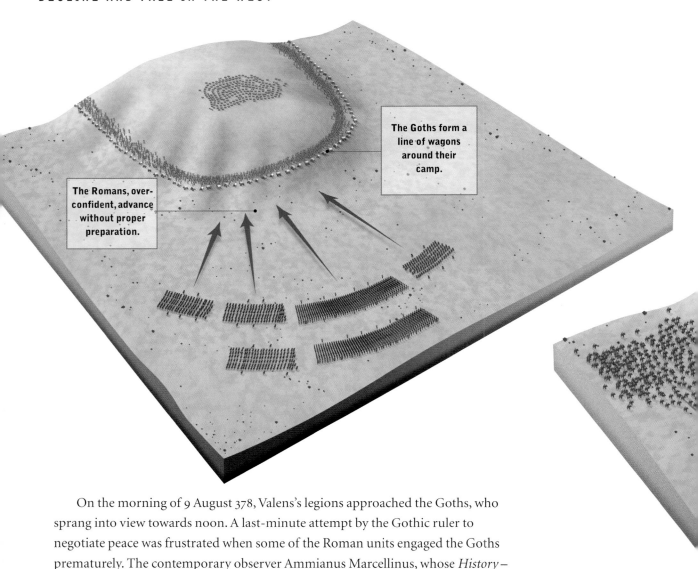

The Goths form a line of wagons around their camp.

The Romans, over-confident, advance without proper preparation.

On the morning of 9 August 378, Valens's legions approached the Goths, who sprang into view towards noon. A last-minute attempt by the Gothic ruler to negotiate peace was frustrated when some of the Roman units engaged the Goths prematurely. The contemporary observer Ammianus Marcellinus, whose *History* – our main source on the third quarter of the 4th century AD – ends with the battle of Adrianople, dramatizes the meeting of the two armies:

On every side armour and weapons clashed, and Bellona [the goddess of war], raging with more than usual madness for the destruction of the Romans, blew her lamentable war-trumpets; our soldiers who were giving way rallied, exchanging many encouraging shouts, but the battle, spreading like flames, filled their hearts with terror, as numbers of them were pierced by strokes of whirling spears and arrows. Then the lines dashed together like beaked ships, pushing each other back and forth in turn, and tossed about by alternate movements, like waves at sea.

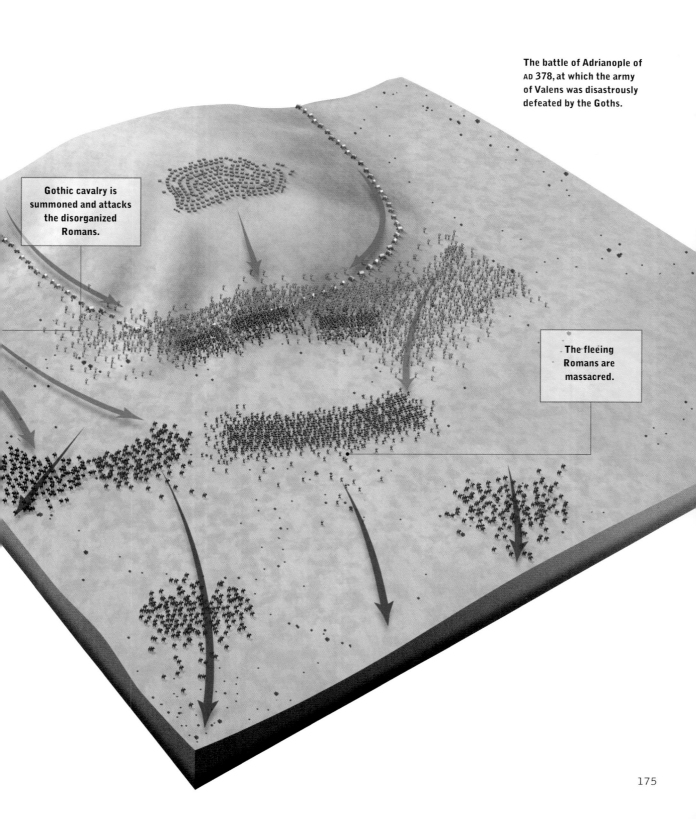

The battle of Adrianople of AD 378, at which the army of Valens was disastrously defeated by the Goths.

Gothic cavalry is summoned and attacks the disorganized Romans.

The fleeing Romans are massacred.

Valens's army suffered a devastating defeat. Two thirds of the soldiers were killed, the emperor included. 'As an effective fighting force, the eastern Roman army perished on August 9, 378', one modern scholar has commented. This view may be exaggerated, since the eastern army recovered in the 5th century, but Ammianus himself draws a line between Adrianople and the most notable defeat of a republican army: 'The annals record no such massacre of a battle except the one at Cannae'.

'The example of unprecedented piety'

The catastrophe of Adrianople and the death of Valens turned the empire, in the twinkling of an eye, into a power vacuum. The west, ruled by Gratian, the inexperienced nineteen-year-old son of Valentinian, was now the target of tribal groups, mainly Alamanni, who invaded Gaul and caused substantial damage. The Balkan peninsula was, for several months, exposed to rampaging bands of Goths, who even threatened the eastern capital, Constantinople.

The man to whom Gratian entrusted the troubled east came from Galicia, in the far northwest of Spain, and his name was Flavius Theodosius. His father, who had answered to the same name, had been a successful general under Valentinian: in the late 360s and early 370s, Theodosius the Elder had repelled various invasions in Britain and Gaul, and in 373, he had put down a dangerous usurpation in North Africa. Finally, in 376, he fell victim to an intrigue by powerful enemies and was executed. His son, the future emperor, had commanded Roman forces in the Balkans. When Theodosius the Elder was put to death, the son retired to his estates in Spain.

In the crisis following Adrianople, Gratian, for reasons we do not know, recalled Theodosius and made the thirty-one-year-old the *magister militum* of Illyricum, the western Balkans. In late antiquity, a *magister militum* ('master of the soldiers') was a senior military officer who commanded the infantry units of a defined area or theatre of war. On 19 January 379, Theodosius was proclaimed *Augustus* of the east. There, he tried to settle the conflict with the Goths. He was defeated in 380, but concluded an agreement with the tribesmen in 382. The orator Themistius describes how the leaders of the barbarians were led before Theodosius, 'like in a festive procession, treating the soil, against which they had previously raged, with reverence'.

Reality, however, was far more prosaic than Themistius would have us believe: Theodosius had struck a deal, the *foedus*, with the Germanic tribesmen from a position of weakness.

OPPOSITE ABOVE **A detail from the base of the Obelisk of Theodosius, Constantinople.** The emperor sits in his box in the Hippodrome with his family and high-ranking dignitaries. In striking contrast to early imperial reliefs, the figures are shown in full front view. This frontality became a dominant feature of such scenes from the later 3rd century.

OPPOSITE BELOW **A marble statue of the emperor Valentinian II from Aphrodisias in Asia Minor.**

BELOW **The insignia of a late Roman *magister militum*.** This is an illustration from the *Notitia Dignitatum*, a 5th-century handbook that lists thousands of offices of the imperial administration.

The Goths remained intact as a group; as *foederati*, they were settled on Roman territory, but remained under the command and jurisdiction of their own leaders; they had no *connubium* (the right to marry Roman women); finally, they were assigned tax-free land, which was taken from the local population in the Danube provinces. The *foedus* relieved the Balkan provinces of an urgent grievance, but in the long term it was a strain on peace throughout the empire.

The next challenge for Theodosius was the usurpation of a certain Magnus Maximus in the west. Maximus defeated Gratian, who was killed (383), and invaded Italy, from where Valentinian II, Gratian's younger brother, escaped to Theodosius. Theodosius defeated Maximus in a series of battles, executed him and reinstalled Valentinian as *Augustus* of the west, residing in Trier (388). There, he was found hanged in 392. Valentinian's death immediately triggered the next crisis: Arbogast, *magister militum* of the Roman west and himself of Frankish origin, proclaimed emperor the teacher of rhetoric and grammar Eugenius, who, though a Christian, nourished sympathies for polytheism. The unavoidable clash between the armies of Theodosius and Arbogast happened in northern Italy, near the Frigidus creek (5 and 6 September 394). After two days of fierce fighting, Theodosius' legions, led by the Vandal general Stilicho and reinforced by Gothic tribal warriors, got the upper hand. For the last time in history, Rome was ruled by one emperor – but only for a couple of months. On 17 January 395, the emperor, whom

LEFT **The Aula Palatina at Trier (Germany). The building was erected around AD 310 as an audience hall for Constantine's palace compound at Trier. It is the largest surviving inner room from classical antiquity.**

BELOW **A late Roman mosaic depicting St Ambrosius, the Bishop of Milan, from the Church of Sant'Ambrogio in Milan.**

Ambrosius – the church father and influential Bishop of Milan, who had once threatened to excommunicate an impenitent Theodosius – had called 'the example of unprecedented piety', died.

Shadow emperors

After the death of Theodosius the empire was, once again, divided. The deceased ruler had two sons, Arcadius, who became *Augustus* of the east, and Honorius, who received the western half. Initially, nothing indicated that the division of the year 395 was permanent. Laws issued by the two emperors continued to be valid for the entire empire, and in contemporary awareness the Roman world was still one political and cultural entity. However, the two imperial halves were slowly, but irreversibly, drifting apart.

Nothing revealed the creeping alienation better than the reaction to the challenge of the Thervingi Goths, who after the sudden death of Theodosius, lost their imperial patron. Under their new leader, Alaric, they were still trying to find a place for themselves in the Balkans, which now formed the frontier zone between the two imperial halves. In a climate of increasing rivalry between Milan and Constantinople, the two capitals, the role of Alaric's Goths oscillated between that of marauding rebels and imperial armed forces. Alaric was, depending on one's point of view, either a guerrilla leader or a Roman general.

In the midst of such turmoil Honorius, the western *Augustus*, did – nothing. He enjoyed the splendour of his palace in Milan, and later in Ravenna, to which the imperial family retreated for safety reasons. We are told (though probably unreliably) that he spent his days indulging in his favourite hobby, chicken farming, and relied, for the rest, on Stilicho, his brother-in-law and a *magister militum* of Germanic descent. Stilicho repeatedly saved Italy by deflecting the Goths towards the east and winning two major battles over Alaric at Pollentia (402) and Verona (403). The general was now far more powerful than any German in the Roman world before him, but a few years after his great victory, in 408, Stilicho fell victim to a court intrigue and was executed by command of Honorius.

Honorius was now in charge. Not surprisingly, his crisis management was woeful. When Alaric demanded provisions for his men, Honorius agreed to supply them, but repeatedly failed to carry out his promises. Understandably, this provoked anger among the Goths, and eventually resulted in the sack of Rome, probably on 24 August 410. The material impact on the old capital was moderate, but the moral shock waves went far beyond the city walls: they triggered a debate about the decline of moral standards and the role of Christianity. Many took the event for some kind of divine punishment, either for the Romans' abandonment of polytheism or for their somewhat lukewarm approach to Christianity. St Augustine's book *De Civitate Dei* ('The City of God') was inspired by the debate: he exhorted his contemporaries to fix their eyes on the heavenly New Jerusalem instead of on the old capital's splendour.

Honorius simply sat out this crisis, too. He was the prototype of a new kind of emperor, seemingly passive and in the shadow of all-powerful military men. For all emperors until Theodosius, manly valour, *virtus*, had been the elixir that guaranteed their political survival. Even rulers like Nero and Commodus had sought *virtus*, albeit in vain, in the theatre or in the arena, and the child emperor Gratian had led legions into battle. Honorius, like his brother Arcadius, owed his position to nothing but his descent and the divine right of a Christian emperor: 'the hereditary sceptre of the sons of Theodosius appeared to be the gift of nature', Edward Gibbon wrote of the two brothers. In him and his brother Arcadius, the Roman monarchy had reached its final aggregate state: divested of any political significance, the emperors were reduced to idle symbols of Rome's former glory. The historian Procopius

Marble bust of the eastern emperor Arcadius, wearing a diadem, from the Forum of Theodosius in Constantinople.

(probably maliciously) reports how, after Alaric's sack of Rome, Honorius was notified that *Roma* had fallen. The emperor was distressed, assuming that the messenger was referring to his favourite hen of the same name, and only recovered when he was told that it was just the capital that had fallen. It is simplistic, though, to blame Honorius personally. Whether the emperors were children (like Honorius and later Valentinian III during his early years and finally Romulus Augustulus) or experienced, energetic men (like Majorian) did not really matter. The imperial role was now detached from political and military action.

The last emperor

It is an irony of history that the last emperor of the western empire bore the names of the two founding fathers of Rome: Romulus Augustus. Because of his youth and his political insignificance, however, he went down as *Augustulus*, the wee little emperor. Romulus was the son of Orestes, a Roman general of Pannonian origin, who had been in the service of Attila, the Hunnic leader, and had later made a career in the western Roman army – which was, at that time, hardly Roman any more. The emperor Julius Nepos, who had been installed by the eastern emperor Leo II, appointed Orestes in 474. Instead of supporting his emperor against his numerous opponents, Orestes turned on Nepos and ousted him. While Nepos escaped to Dalmatia, Orestes invested his son Romulus with the imperial insignia (October 475).

Since Alaric's sack of Rome in 410, the west had utterly changed. Within a few decades, Spain, Britain, the Alps, the better part of Gaul and above all the rich grain-exporting provinces of North Africa had all been lost to Germanic peoples, who had established their ethnic kingdoms on Roman soil. Italy itself, largely cut off from its imperial hinterland, was fought over by various pretenders and their respective armies. Cumulatively, these armies were still the largest force in the western Mediterranean, far too large to be maintained by Italy's tax revenue alone. Underpaid, unhappy soldiers were therefore another source of trouble in those gloomy years.

Honorius's *magister militum*, Stilicho, shown on an ivory diptych of *c.* AD 396. He wears an embroidered tunic and a general's cloak. He holds a spear in his right hand and a shield with the busts of the emperors Honorius and Arcadius in his left.

In the midst of this shambles, the imperial purple fell victim to the whims of conflicting interests: an overwhelmingly Germanic soldiery; their generals, all with their own political aspirations; a squad of Germanic kings attempting to bend the empire to their own purposes; and finally the eastern emperors, imposing their will on their less powerful western brothers. Orestes and Romulus were the typical representatives of an age in which emperors were the puppets of much more powerful men. The *magister militum* and *patricius* Ricimer, who was of half-Suebic, half Visigothic origin, was the de facto ruler of the west from 457 until his death in 472. He alone made three emperors: Majorian, Libius Severus and Olybrius. Another emperor, Glycerius, was the creature of Ricimer's nephew and successor Gundobad, and two more, Anthemius and Julius Nepos, were appointed by the eastern emperor.

The last emperor of the Roman west, Romulus Augustulus, depicted on a gold coin (*tremissis*). The reverse shows a cross in a laurel wreath.

Shadow emperors these men may have been, but as long as there were Roman emperors, there was a Roman empire in the west, too: there was a court, there was, at least nominally, imperial authority, there was a system of taxation and a military hierarchy; besides, there was the notion of a state, of government, of *some* sort of 'central Romanness' as a recent study, *The Fall of the Roman Empire* by Peter Heather, calls it. All this melted into air, when, in summer 476, a revolt of Germanic soldiers in Italy washed away Orestes and brought to power one of their leaders, a Hunnic-Sciric half-breed named Odoacer. On a beautiful day in August, Odoacer, who deemed the purple of the western empire an unnecessary luxury, sent the boy Romulus Augustulus into early retirement, without appointing a successor. From that day onwards, the western empire was orphaned.

In the west, the institution of the Roman monarchy, established by Augustus in 27 BC, modified by countless of his successors and by changing circumstances, had ceased to exist, after exactly 502 years. 'Local Romanness' continued, in many parts of the former empire, and the cultural development of the Romance nations was, in many respects, a sequel to it. An attempt was made to restore (eastern) Roman sovereignty over the former western provinces, but it failed, overstretching the resources of Justinian's eastern empire. Various 'renaissances' in the – now largely Germanic – west attempted to associate themselves with the Roman empire's former glory, most notably Charlemagne's coronation as Roman emperor in the old capital in the symbolic year AD 800. By then, 'Rome' had become an idea that could be translated into a variety of historical settings. However, the emperors of the Holy Roman Empire were no true successors of Augustus and Constantine. Nor were the rulers of the Roman east, now known to history as the Byzantine emperors, whose state soon became a political and cultural entity *sui generis*. The empire of Augustus had died with the Roman world it had ruled – and one could convincingly date its demise to 31 August 476, the day Romulus Augustulus put off his purple robe and went his ways.

Augustus

Tiberius

Caligula

Claudius

THE ROMAN EMPERORS: BRIEF LIVES

Gaius Julius Caesar Octavianus **Augustus** (27 BC–AD 14) was born as Gaius Octavius in Rome on 23 September 63 BC. He entered politics at the age of eighteen, after Caesar's murder. In a coalition ('Second Triumvirate') with Mark Antony and Lepidus he defeated the assassins of Caesar (42 BC). At the naval battle of Actium, his fleet defeated Mark Antony's (31 BC). He became sole ruler (30 BC) and received the name Augustus and proconsular power (*imperium proconsulare*, including the supreme command over the army) from the Senate (27 BC). Augustus stepped down from the consulate and received the powers of a plebeian tribune (*tribunicia potestas*). The return of the legionary standards, lost by Crassus in 53 BC, was celebrated as a political triumph. Saecular Games were held in 17 BC, and the Ara Pacis consecrated in 9 BC. The annexation of Germany was prepared for (from 12 BC onwards), but ultimately failed when Varus's legions were defeated (AD 9). Augustus died in Nola (Campania) on 19 August AD 14. He was deified the following month.

THE JULIO-CLAUDIAN HOUSE (AD 14–68)

Tiberius Claudius Nero (AD 14–37), the son of Tiberius Claudius Nero and Livia (who later married Augustus), was born in Rome on 16 November 42 BC. He was joint commander-in-chief during Rome's campaign in the Alps (15 BC) and sole commander in Germany (8–7 BC and AD 4–6) and Pannonia (AD 6–9). Neglected in favour of Augustus's grandson Gaius Caesar, he retired to Rhodes (6 BC), but was called back in AD 2. His accession as emperor (AD 14) was overshadowed by a mutiny of the Rhine legions and by the Senate's reservations towards him. A frustrated

Tiberius retired to Capri (AD 27) and left his much feared praetorian prefect, Sejanus, in charge. In 31 he returned and executed Sejanus. Tiberius died in Misenum in Campania on 1 November 37.

Gaius Caesar Germanicus (**Caligula**, AD 37–41) was born in Antium in AD 12, the youngest son of Germanicus and Agrippina the Elder. He grew up in military camps; his nickname means 'little soldier's boot'. After Tiberius's death in AD 37, the praetorian prefect Macro engineered Caligula's succession. Caligula's rule had a promising start, but soon deteriorated. Caligula was murdered by the Praetorian Guard on 24 January AD 41.

Tiberius **Claudius** Drusus (AD 41–54), born on 1 August 10 BC in Lugdunum (Lyons) in Gaul, was Caligula's uncle. Ill health excluded him from public life until AD 37, when he held the consulship. After Caligula's murder, he was proclaimed emperor by the Praetorian Guard and confirmed by the Senate. He strengthened the empire's central bureaucracy; construction in Rome and the port of Ostia boomed; and members of the Gallic provincial elites were first admitted to the Senate. The south of Britain was conquered and became a Roman province. Claudius died on 13 October 54, reportedly poisoned by his fourth wife Agrippina, who wanted her son Nero to succeed. He was deified by Nero.

Lucius Domitius Ahenobarbus, known as **Nero** Claudius Caesar Drusus Germanicus (AD 54–68) after his adoption by Claudius, was born on 15 December AD 37. Nero was the son of Gnaeus Domitius Ahenobarbus, consul of AD 32, and Agrippina the Younger, a daughter of Germanicus, who

Nero

Galba

Otho

Vespasian

married her uncle Claudius in AD 49. Nero married Claudius's daughter Octavia (49) and was adopted by the emperor (50). When Claudius died in 54, Nero, instead of Claudius's son Britannicus, became emperor. He murdered Britannicus (55), Agrippina (59) and Octavia (62). At first his reign was supervised by the praetorian prefect Burrus and the philosopher Seneca; after their deaths Nero's peculiarities became clear. After the great fire, he built the Domus Aurea for himself and toured Greece competing as a musician and charioteer. Meantime, the revolt of Boudicca (61) and the plot of Piso (65) were crushed, but the Jewish Revolt in Palestine grew into a major war (66–70). Nero took his own life, after most of the army defected to the usurper Galba (9 or 11 June 68).

THE CRISIS OF AD 68–69

Servius Sulpicius **Galba** (AD 68–69) was born near Terracina in Latium on 24 December 3 BC. Galba was the son of a former consul and had a distinguished senatorial career, serving as governor of several provinces and as a high officer during Claudius's invasion of Britain. He became proconsul of Africa (44–46) and finally governor of Tarraconensis in Spain. In early April 68, he usurped power from Nero. Galba's parsimony and conservatism provoked fierce opposition: he was killed on 15 January 69.

Marcus Salvius **Otho** (AD 69) was born on 28 April 32. A friend of Nero's, he was put in charge of the province of Lusitania, present-day Portugal. He supported Galba's usurpation, then usurped power himself when Galba adopted Piso instead of him (15 January 69). Vitellius, another usurper, defeated Otho's army at Bedriacum (near Cremona in northern Italy) on 14 April 69. Otho killed himself.

Aulus **Vitellius** (AD 69), born in AD 12 or 15, was the son of a distinguished senator. He held a consulship in 48 and was proconsul of Africa in 60/61. On 1 December 68, Galba appointed him governor of the province of Lower Germany. On 2 January 69, the troops acclaimed him as emperor and his army marched to Italy. He defeated Otho at Bedriacum, then was himself defeated by Vespasian in October 69. Vitellius died in Rome, after unsuccessfully trying to negotiate his surrender (December 69).

THE FLAVIAN DYNASTY (AD 69–96)

Titus Flavius **Vespasian**us (AD 69–79), the son of an equestrian official, was born in Reate (Rieti in Latium) in AD 9. He embarked on a senatorial career, and became consul (51) and proconsul of Africa (63/64). He accompanied Nero to Greece (66) and commanded the army in the Jewish Revolt (67–69). After Vitellius's victory over Otho he was proclaimed emperor in Alexandria (1 July 69). In Egypt, he received the Senate's confirmation, after his ally Mucianus conquered Rome (21/22 December 69): the *lex de imperio Vespasiani* ('law on Vespasian's emperorship') was issued. In summer 70 Vespasian arrived in Rome. The Capitol and some adjacent areas, devastated by civil war, were rebuilt. He put the imperial treasury, ruined by Nero, back on a sound financial footing and demobilized parts of the oversized army. Nero's Domus Aurea was largely demolished to make way for the Amphitheatrum Flavium, the Colosseum. Vespasian died on 23 June 79 and was the third emperor since Augustus to be deified.

Titus Flavius Vespasianus (AD 79–81), Vespasian's elder son, was (probably) born on 30 December AD 39. He grew up at Claudius's court. Under Nero, Titus served as a military

Titus

Nerva

Trajan

Hadrian

tribune in Germany and Britain, a quaestor and finally commanded a legion in Judaea (66–69). After Vespasian's usurpation, Titus received the supreme command. He conquered Jerusalem in 70; the Temple was destroyed, and the cult utensils brought to Rome and presented in Titus's triumphal procession. Titus succeeded his father in 79. His short reign was overshadowed by the eruption of Vesuvius (24 August 79), a devastating plague and a fire in Rome (80). Titus died on 13 September 81.

Titus Flavius **Domitian**us (AD 81–96), Titus's younger brother, was born in Rome on 24 October AD 51. The brothers were appointed joint *Caesares*, but Domitian featured little in Vespasian's reign. After Titus's death, his succession was unchallenged. He defeated the Chatti and the Daci, conquered areas east of the Rhine and secured his father's conquests in southwest Germany with a series of fortifications. In Rome, some senators fiercely opposed him; a revolt in Upper Germany, led by the senator Antonius Saturninus, was put down (89). The discovery of plots made the emperor increasingly suspicious: he executed numerous dignitaries, among them many members of the Flavian family, making himself greatly hated. Domitian was murdered on 18 September 96.

THE FIVE GOOD EMPERORS AND THE ANTONINE DYNASTY (AD 96–192)

Marcus Cocceius **Nerva** (AD 96–98) came from a family of influential senators and lawyers. He was born in Narnia (Narni, Umbria) around AD 30, achieved the praetorship under Nero and held two consulships under the Flavian emperors. After Domitian's murder, the plotters engineered Nerva's proclamation, precisely because he was old,

childless and without any power base of his own. Nerva's adoption of Trajan on 27 October 97 was a clever move and consolidated his reign. He died in January 98.

Marcus Ulpius Traianus (**Trajan**, AD 98–117) was born on 18 September 53 in the Spanish veteran colony of Italica. His father, a distinguished former consul, had commanded a legion under Vespasian and Titus in Judaea (67–70) and served as governor of several provinces. Trajan himself was a military tribune in Syria (where his father was governor) around 74, held the consulship in 91 and became governor of the province of Upper Germany in 96. In October 97, Nerva adopted him. After Nerva's death, Trajan's succession was undisputed. He returned to Rome in autumn 99. There, Pliny the Younger delivered his famous panegyric on Trajan (100). Trajan fought wars in Dacia (101–102, 105–106) and against the Parthians (113–117) and conquered the Nabataean realm (106). In Rome, Trajan's Forum was laid out, and several roads were built in Italy and the provinces. *Alimenta*, a form of child benefit paid to Italian families, were established. Trajan died in August 117.

Publius Aelius **Hadrian**us (AD 117–138) was born in Italica in Spain (24 January 76). He served in Dacia (101) under Trajan, who promoted his career. He was governor of the province of Lower Pannonia (106–108), consul (108) and governor of Syria (116). When Trajan died – whether he had adopted Hadrian on his deathbed was controversial – his widow engineered Hadrian's succession. The new emperor paid out a high *donativum* to the troops, withdrew the army from Mesopotamia and negotiated peace with the Parthians. A plot by four high-ranking senators was uncovered; they were executed (118). For many years, Hadrian travelled his empire. When he stayed in Jerusalem, the city was renamed Aelia. This may have sparked the Bar Kokhba revolt (132–135), the last

Antoninus Pius

Marcus Aurelius

Lucius Verus

Pertinax

Jewish uprising in the Roman period, which led to the complete expulsion of all Jews from Judaea. In 136, he adopted Lucius Aelius Caesar, who died shortly after; on 25 February 138 he adopted Antoninus Pius, and ordered him to adopt the young Marcus Aurelius. Hadrian increasingly secluded himself in his villa in Tibur (Tivoli) and died on 10 July 138. He was buried in his own mausoleum (Castel Sant'Angelo in Rome).

Titus Aurelius Fulvus Boionius **Antoninus Pius** (AD 138–161) was born on 19 September 86. The former consul, who had been proconsul of Asia, was adopted by Hadrian in 138. On his accession, he put through Hadrian's deification, despite opposition in the Senate, and thus earned himself the epithet 'Pius'. Antoninus's administration seems to have been conservative. He was intent on a good relationship with the Senate. In Britain and southwest Germany the frontiers were expanded, and revolts in Mauretania, Egypt and Dacia were suppressed. The emperor, who never left Italy, died on 7 March 161. He was deified and buried in Hadrian's mausoleum.

Marcus Aurelius Antoninus (AD 161–180) was born on 26 April 121 and was, by order of Hadrian, adopted by Antoninus Pius in 138. Marcus received a sound education, mainly from the orator and philosopher Fronto. He married Antoninus Pius's daughter Faustina, who gave birth to (at least) fourteen children. Upon his accession, he appointed his adopted brother Lucius Verus *Augustus*; he was nominally in charge of the war against the Parthians (163–166). Legions returning to Rome from the east brought plague, of which Verus died in 169. Marcus Aurelius fought two wars against the Marcomanni and Quadi (166–175, 177–180). On campaign, he wrote, in Greek, his *Meditations*, a collection of philosophical reflections inspired by Stoicism. In 177, Marcus's son Commodus was elevated to the rank of *Augustus*. Marcus died on 17 March 180, in Vindobona

(Vienna) or Sirmium (Sremska Mitrovica, present-day Serbia). Later historians made Marcus Aurelius, who was deified shortly after his death, the archetype of the 'good' emperor.

Lucius Ceionius Commodus (**Lucius Verus**, AD 161–169) was born on 15 December 130, the son of Lucius Aelius Caesar, Hadrian's first candidate for succession. Verus served as quaestor (153) and consul (154). On Antoninus Pius's death he was proclaimed *Augustus*, but denied the office of *pontifex maximus*, which was held by Marcus Aurelius. Verus married Marcus's daughter Lucilla (163). He was nominally responsible for the Parthian War (163–166). He died, probably of plague, in 169.

Lucius Aurelius **Commodus** (AD 180–192) was the first emperor born in the purple, shortly after his father's accession, on 31 August 161. In 176 Commodus celebrated a triumph over the Germans and Sarmatians jointly with his father. In 177, he became *Augustus*. As emperor, he negotiated peace on the Danube. His turbulent reign saw the rise and sudden downfall of favourites, including the praetorian prefect Perennis (180–185) and his chamberlain, the freedman Marcus Aurelius Cleander (c. 182–190). Commodus, who performed as a gladiator in the amphitheatre, survived several plots, but was killed by the praetorian prefect Aemilius Laetus and his concubine Marcia (31 December 192).

THE CRISIS OF AD 193

Publius Helvius **Pertinax** (AD 192–193), the son of a freedman, was born on 1 August 126. He had a remarkable military career (till 167), held various equestrian offices (167–171) and was awarded praetorian rank (171). Under Marcus Aurelius, he became consul (175) and governor of various provinces. When Commodus was murdered, he was proclaimed emperor by the

Septimius Severus

Caracalla

Macrinus

Elagabalus

praetorian prefect Aemilius Laetus. His frugality, however, soon provoked fierce opposition, especially in the military. The Praetorian Guard killed Pertinax on 28 March 193.

Marcus Didius Severus Iulianus (**Didius Julianus**, AD 193), a rich former consul born on 30 January 133, 'bought' the purple in the memorable auction held by the Praetorian Guard on 28 March 193. The Senate confirmed Didius, but later declared him deposed and had him executed (2 June 193) after Septimius Severus (9 April) and Pescennius Niger (19 April) usurped power.

THE HOUSE OF SEPTIMIUS SEVERUS (AD 193–235)

Lucius **Septimius Severus** (AD 193–211) was born on 11 April 146, the son of Publius Septimius Geta, an equestrian from Lepcis Magna in North Africa. Severus embarked on a senatorial career, achieved the praetorship in 178 and then the consulship. He commanded a Syrian legion (182–183), and became governor of Gallia Lugdunensis, then Sicily, then the important province of Upper Pannonia, where he was proclaimed emperor in the succession crisis of 193. Severus proceeded to Rome, where the Senate had deposed Didius Julianus; he disbanded the Praetorian Guard and replaced it with his own soldiers. Severus defeated the army of Pescennius Niger, the third usurper of 193, at Cyzicus and Issus. In 195, he declared his adoption by Marcus Aurelius. Later, he also defeated Clodius Albinus (197), who had earlier usurped power in Britain. Severus fought the Parthians in two successful campaigns (194–195 and 197–199). In Britain, he repulsed an invasion of the Caledonians and restored Hadrian's Wall (208–211). Severus died, still on campaign, on 4 February 211, in Eboracum (York). He was deified and buried in Hadrian's mausoleum.

Caracalla (AD 211–217), originally called Lucius Septimius Bassianus, was known as Marcus Aurelius Antoninus after the declaration of his adoption into the family of Marcus Aurelius. He was born in Lugdunum on 4 April 188. He was awarded the rank of *Augustus* in 197. Shortly after the joint accession of his younger brother Geta and himself, he killed Geta and executed many alleged enemies. The *Constitutio Antoniniana*, issued in 212, awarded Roman citizenship to all free inhabitants of the empire. On the Danube, Caracalla fought successfully against the Alamanni and Carpi (213–214). His visit to Alexandria provoked an uprising, which was suppressed (215). In 216, Caracalla attacked the Parthian empire and advanced deep into Mesopotamia. Though he was popular with the soldiery, the emperor fell victim to a plot by officers, who, under Caracalla's increasingly paranoid rule, feared for their lives (8 April 217).

Marcus Opellius **Macrinus** (AD 217–218), born *c.* 165 of humble Mauretanian origin, was Caracalla's praetorian prefect when the emperor was murdered, and was probably behind the plot. The army proclaimed him emperor on 11 April 217. Macrinus was the first equestrian in the purple. He negotiated an unfavourable peace with the Parthians, which cost him prestige. This and his old-fashioned austerity upset the army. When Julia Maesa, Septimius Severus's sister-in-law, staged a usurpation for her fourteen-year-old grandson Varius Avitus (Elagabalus), substantial parts of the army in the east defected to the youth, who was believed to be the son of the still-popular Caracalla. Macrinus was defeated by Elagabalus's army on 8 June 218, and killed.

Varius Avitus (**Elagabalus**, AD 218–222) was born in the Syrian city of Emesa in 203 or 204. As a boy he served as priest in the

Severus Alexander

Maximinus Thrax

Gordian II

Balbinus

local temple of the sun god Elagabalus. In 218, his grandmother Julia Maesa engineered his usurpation in order to bring the Severan dynasty back to power. In Rome, Elagabalus erected a large temple on the Palatine Hill for his god, whom he declared the supreme deity of the Roman state pantheon. This and his eccentric style of government made him increasingly unpopular with the senators and soldiers and he was killed on 11 March 222.

Bassianus Alexianus (**Severus Alexander**, AD 222–235) was born in 208. The thirteen-year-old boy was adopted by his cousin Elagabalus and made *Caesar* in 221. Elagabalus attempted repeatedly to kill him, but he survived and was proclaimed emperor after his cousin's downfall in 222. During his rule, the Roman empire's environment changed profoundly: the Sasanian empire replaced the Parthians, and Germanic tribal confederations began to attack the Roman frontier regions. Severus Alexander fought a moderately successful war against the Persians (231–233) and celebrated a triumph; he was killed on campaign against the Alamanni, when an army in Moguntiacum (Mainz) mutinied (22 March 235).

THE SOLDIER EMPERORS (AD 235–284)

Maximinus (**Maximinus Thrax**, AD 235–238) was born in Thrace in 172 or 173. During Severus Alexander's Persian campaign (231–233), he was a high-ranking general. By 234, he was in charge of the army's instruction units (*praefectus tironibus*). He seized power in 238 and received the Senate's confirmation. The next two years he spent fighting the Alamanni on the Rhine and the Sarmatians on the Danube. In 238, after the revolt of the Gordiani in North Africa and the proclamation of Pupienus and Balbinus, Maximinus was declared enemy by the Senate and killed by his own soldiers.

Marcus Antonius Gordianus (**Gordian I**, AD 238), born around 158, followed a senatorial career. He was proconsul of the province of Africa when he was proclaimed emperor (early January 238) by local aristocrats, who had revolted against Maximinus's tax collectors. He was confirmed by the Senate, but defeated by Capellianus, the governor of the neighbouring province of Numidia, who supported Maximinus. Gordian I committed suicide, after his son had lost the decisive battle against Capellianus (*c.* 20 January 238).

Marcus Antonius Gordianus (**Gordian II**, AD 238) was the son of Gordian I, who proclaimed him *Augustus*. Gordian II was defeated by Capellianus.

Marcus Clodius **Pupienus** (AD 238), born in *c.* 164, was a distinguished senator when the revolt of the Gordiani was put down. As the Senate had already confirmed the Gordiani and declared Maximinus enemy, a new emperor was needed. The senators opted for a dual leadership and elected Pupienus and Balbinus (February 238). Pupienus successfully organized the defence of Italy against Maximinus, but the dual leadership worked only while the rulers were united by their common enemy; once Maximinus was dead, their joint government fell apart. The Praetorian Guard killed them both (May 238).

Decimus Caelius Calvinus **Balbinus** (AD 238) had a prominent senatorial career, like Pupienus, before he was elected emperor. While Pupienus fought in the north of Italy, Balbinus was in charge of affairs in Rome. Along with his co-emperor, he was killed by soldiers of the Praetorian Guard (May 238).

Marcus Antonius Gordianus (**Gordian III**, AD 238–244) was the grandson of Gordian I. When Pupienus and Balbinus were elected *Augusti*, they declared him *Caesar*. The Praetorian

Gordian III

Decius

Trebonianus Gallus

Gallienus

Guard proclaimed Gordian *Augustus* after they were killed in May 238. In 241, Gordian married the daughter of Gaius Furius Timesitheus, who became his praetorian prefect and de facto head of government. There were invasions by Goths in the Balkan Peninsula (238) and Persians in Mesopotamia and Syria (240–243). Timesitheus drove the Persians out of Roman territory, but was killed in 243. His successor as praetorian prefect, Philip, seized power after Gordian's death near the Persian capital of Ctesiphon in early 244.

Marcus Julius Philippus (**Philip the Arab**, AD 244–249) may have killed Gordian III. Philip came from the province of Arabia, where he was born in the town of Shahba around 204. He served as Gordian's praetorian prefect from 243 and was proclaimed emperor by the army. He negotiated an unfavourable peace with the Persians and fought back the invading Carpi in the Balkans (245–247), held a triumph as *Carpicus Maximus* and celebrated the 1000th anniversary of the city of Rome in April 248 with lavish games. Philip survived three attempted usurpations, before being defeated by Decius near Verona (autumn 249).

Gaius Messius Quintus **Decius** Valerinus (AD 249–251) was born in Lower Pannonia. He became consul before 232, governor of several provinces and urban prefect. By 249, he served as supreme commander of the Roman army in the Balkan provinces, where he usurped power in June 249. In late 249, he issued an edict forcing the empire's entire population to sacrifice; those who refused were severely punished. In 251, he was killed fighting the Goths in Moesia (present-day Bulgaria).

Gaius Vibius **Trebonianus Gallus** (AD 251–253), a senator and former consul, was serving as governor of the province of

Upper Moesia when Decius was killed in battle. He was proclaimed emperor by the Danube army and made peace with the Goths. In summer 253, he was challenged by the usurper Aemilius Aemilianus and killed by mutinying soldiers.

Marcus **Aemilius Aemilianus** (AD 253) succeeded Trebonianus Gallus as governor of Upper Moesia, defeated the Goths and was proclaimed emperor in summer 253. After Gallus's death he received the Senate's confirmation. His short reign saw a series of disasters: Burgundi and Carpi crossed the Danube and advanced to Asia Minor, where they plundered several cities; the Marcomanni devastated parts of Pannonia; and the Persians invaded Mesopotamia and Cappadocia. Soldiers killed Aemilianus after the army proclaimed Valerian emperor in Raetia.

Publius Licinius **Valerian**us (AD 253–260), born around 200, came from a distinguished family; he was consul before 238 and sent as an envoy to Rome by the Gordiani in 238. Valerian usurped power in Raetia in spring 253 and arrived in Rome in autumn, where he made his son Gallienus *Augustus*. In 254, he left for the east, recaptured Antioch from the Persians and took residence in the city. He drove the Persians from Cappadocia (258) and issued two edicts against the Christians (257, 258). In June 260, Valerian was captured by the Persians near Carrhae in Mesopotamia and later died in captivity.

Publius Licinius Egnatius **Gallienus** (AD 253–268), born in c. 213, was made *Augustus* by his father Valerian, with responsibility for the west. He defeated the Alamanni in south-west Germany (255) and the Carpi and Goths in Dacia (256). In 258, he put down the usurpation of Ingenuus in Pannonia. In 259, the Franks crossed the Rhine and devastated Gaul and parts of Spain. Postumus, the supreme commander on the

Claudius II Gothicus

Aurelian

Probus

Carus

lower Rhine, usurped power, but avoided a confrontation with Gallienus: the Gallic empire was established (till 274). When Valerian was captured, Gallienus became sole emperor. Odaenathus of Palmyra drove the Persians from the eastern provinces and was awarded the title of *Dux Romanorum* ('leader of the Romans') by Gallienus. In 264, Gallienus unsuccessfully attempted to recapture the Gallic empire. In 268, he fell victim to a plot by some of his senior generals.

Claudius II Gothicus (AD 268–270) belonged to the inner circle of military leadership when Gallienus was murdered. The officer, in his mid-fifties, was proclaimed emperor by the army. He defeated the Alamanni near Lake Garda (268) and the Goths near the Danube (269). He died of plague in September 270.

Claudius **Quintillus** (AD 270) was proclaimed emperor by the Senate after the death of his brother Claudius II. He was murdered by soldiers seventeen days later.

Lucius Domitius **Aurelian**us (AD 270–275), born on 9 September 214 in present-day Serbia, was, like Claudius, a member of Gallienus' military leadership. He was proclaimed emperor in Sirmium in September 270. In 271, he gained victories over the Vandals, Iuthungi and Sarmatians in Italy. The Aurelian Walls were built to protect the capital (from 271 onwards). Aurelian attacked and defeated Vaballathus of Palmyra and his mother Zenobia (272); he repulsed the Carpi, put down revolts in Palmyra and Egypt (273) and recaptured the Gallic empire (274). He was murdered by soldiers in autumn 275. His widow Ulpia Severina may have played an important role in the succession of Tacitus.

Marcus Claudius **Tacitus** (AD 275–276) was a former consul and prominent senator, who was already seventy-five years old

when he came to power. He defeated the Goths in Asia Minor, but was killed by mutinying soldiers.

Marcus Annius **Florianus** (AD 276) was Tacitus's brother and served as praetorian prefect under him. He succeeded his brother in summer 276, but was killed by soldiers a few months later.

Marcus Aurelius **Probus** (AD 276–282), who was born on 19 August 232, held a supreme command in the Near East under Tacitus. After Tacitus's death, he was proclaimed emperor. Probus campaigned against Germanic invaders in Gaul (277–278) and recruited 16,000 Alamanni for the frontier troops. In Raetia, he defeated the Burgundi and Vandals, in Illyricum the Sarmatians and in Thrace the Goths (278). Probus was slain by mutinying soldiers near Sirmium (autumn 282).

Marcus Aurelius **Carus** (AD 282–283) was born around 224 of Gallic origin and served as praetorian prefect under Probus. He was proclaimed emperor at Sirmium after Probus's death. He defeated the Sarmatians in Pannonia (282) and launched a campaign against the Persians (283). He died near Ctesiphon in the same year.

Marcus Aurelius Numerius **Numerian**us (AD 283–284) was the younger of Carus's two sons, born *c.* 253. On his father's accession, he was appointed *Caesar*; his death made him *Augustus*, along with his elder brother Carinus. Numerian, who had accompanied Carus on his Persian war, withdrew the army from enemy territory. He was murdered or died of disease in November 284.

Marcus Aurelius **Carinus** (AD 283–285), the elder son of Carus, was appointed *Caesar* when his father became emperor. Jointly

Diocletian

Maximian

Constantius I

Galerius

with his brother Numerian, he succeeded Carus in 283. Carinus, in charge of the west, put down a usurpation of the praetorian prefect Julianus Sabinus and a revolt of peasants (Bagaudae) in Gaul (284–285). In August or September 285 he defeated Diocletian's army in the battle of the Margus river (in present-day Serbia), but was killed by his own soldiers.

THE AGE OF THE TETRARCHIES (AD 284–312)

Gaius Aurelius Valerius Diocles (**Diocletian**, AD 284–305) was born in the Balkans, near Salona in Dalmatia, on 2 December, probably in 245. He was of humble origin, but rapidly climbed the army's ranks and became consul in 283 and, in 284, commander of the *protectores domestici*, an elite unit first created under Valerian. After the death of Numerian, he was proclaimed emperor by the army. He lost to Carinus in the battle of the Margus river (summer 285), but left the battlefield victorious, because Carinus was killed by his own mutinying soldiers. In 285 Diocletian made his fellow-officer Maximian *Caesar* and, in 286, elevated him to *Augustus*. Diocletian took charge of the east, residing in Nicomedia. He made peace with the Persians and campaigned in southwest Germany (288) and on the Danube frontier (289). He also repelled Arab invaders in Syria (290). In 293 each *Augustus* appointed a *Caesar* as junior emperor, thereby creating the Tetrarchy ('rule of four'). Diocletian introduced financial reforms and in 296 put down a revolt in Egypt. In 303 and 304, the emperors issued four edicts against the Christians. On 1 May 305, Diocletian and Maximian abdicated. Diocletian retired as *Senior Augustus*. In November 308, he briefly returned to active politics, when he participated in the conference of Carnuntum. The only Roman emperor ever to abdicate of his own free will, Diocletian died on 3 December 313 (?), in Spalato (Split).

Aurelius Valerius **Maximian**us (AD 286–305, 307–308 and 310), like Diocletian, came from the Balkans, was of modest descent and had a military career. In autumn 285 he was appointed *Caesar* and in early 286 *Augustus* of the west. Maximian fought Germanic tribes (286–288) and launched a disastrous maritime expedition against the Britannic empire of Carausius (289). In 291, he convened with Diocletian at Milan. On 1 May 305, Maximian abdicated with Diocletian; his son-in-law Constantius I became the new emperor of the west. In 306, Maximian was called to Rome by his son Maxentius, who had been proclaimed emperor by the Praetorian Guard and the Senate on 28 October. Maximian and Maxentius forced the newly appointed *Augustus* of the west, Severus, to surrender (307). When Maxentius claimed the title of *Augustus* for himself, Maximian fell out with his son, left Italy and went over to Constantine. He appointed Constantine *Augustus* and wedded his daughter Fausta to him. An attempt to depose Maxentius in Rome failed (April 308). Maximian participated in the Carnuntum conference and abdicated again (November 308). Soon afterwards, Maximian acted again as *Augustus* in Gaul. He revolted against Constantine in Arelate (Arles), was taken prisoner and executed (summer 310).

Julius (?) **Constantius I** (AD 305–306), born *c.* 250, came from the Balkans, like the other Tetrarchs. He served as *protector* (elite soldier) under Aurelian and was Maximian's praetorian prefect, before he was appointed *Caesar* on 1 March 293. He recaptured Britain for Maximian in 297. Later, he campaigned against Germanic tribes on the Rhine frontier (300–304). On 1 May 305, he succeeded Maximian as *Augustus* of the west. He defeated Celtic tribes on Britain's northern frontier, where he

Maxentius

Licinius

Maximinus Daia

was joined by his son, Constantine. Constantius I died in Eboracum (York) on 25 July 306.

Galerius (AD 305–311) came from a village near Serdica (present-day Sofia). He served in the army under Aurelian and Probus and perhaps as praetorian prefect under Diocletian. On 21 March 293, Diocletian appointed him *Caesar*. He married the emperor's daughter Galeria Valeria (293) and campaigned against insurgents in Egypt (295) and against the Persians, who defeated him (297). In 298, jointly with Diocletian, Galerius defeated the Persian king Narses. From 299 to 305, he campaigned on the Danube frontier against the Sarmatians and Carpi. On 1 May 305, Galerius succeeded Diocletian as emperor of the east. He appointed his nephew Maximinus Daia *Caesar* of the east. Galerius recognized Constantine as *Caesar* of the west and appointed Severus *Augustus* (306). In 307, Galerius – unsuccessfully – attacked Maxentius. Galerius participated in the Carnuntum conference (November 308). On 30 April 311, Galerius and Licinius, the *Augustus* of the west, issued the edict of Nicomedia granting all Christians in the empire freedom of worship. Galerius died of cancer in early May 311.

Severus (AD 306–307) came from the Balkan provinces and served in the military. In 305, he was appointed *Caesar* by the new *Augustus* of the west, Constantius I, whom he succeeded in August 306. In 307, he unsuccessfully attacked Maxentius in Rome and withdrew to Ravenna, where he was forced to abdicate by Maximian. He was murdered or forced to commit suicide on 16 September 307.

Marcus Valerius **Maxentius** (AD 307–312) was Maximian's son, born in the later 270s. He was proclaimed *Imperator* in Rome in 306 after the death of Constantius I. In early 307, he found

recognition as *Augustus* in Italy, Sicily, Africa, Sardinia and Corsica. He held off Galerius's attack on Italy and was recognized by Constantine in 307. In 308, his father defected to Constantine, whose relationship with Maxentius deteriorated rapidly. In 312, Constantine defeated Maxentius at the Milvian Bridge. Maxentius drowned in the Tiber (28 October 312).

Gaius Valerius Licinianus **Licinius** (AD 308–324), who was born near the Danube in the 260s, participated in Galerius's Persian war (297) and the campaign against Maxentius (307). At the Carnuntum conference, he was appointed *Augustus* of the west; Galerius was in charge of the east. Constantine became his *Caesar*. Licinius won a victory over the Sarmatians (310). After the defeat of Maxentius at the Milvian Bridge, Licinius met Constantine at Milan, where another edict of religious tolerance was issued (313). Licinius married Constantine's sister Constantia. On 30 April 313, Licinius defeated the army of Maximinus Daia and became *Augustus* of the east, including the Balkan Peninsula. In the following year, tensions between Constantine and Licinius increased; at the battle of Cibalae, Licinius was defeated and had to cede the Balkan provinces (except Thrace) to Constantine. In 315, the reconciled *Augusti* held a joint consulship. Later, Licinius adopted an increasingly hard line against the Christians. In 324, new hostilities broke out between Constantine and Licinius: Licinius was defeated in several battles, abdicated and was executed (spring 325).

Maximinus Daia (AD 310–313), Galerius's nephew and adoptive son, was of humble origins in the Balkans. He was nominated *Caesar* for the east at Nicomedia on 1 May 305. At the conference of Carnuntum in 308, he received the honorific title of a *Filius Augustorum* ('son of the *Augusti*'). Two years later, on 1 May 310, he was proclaimed *Augustus*. After the edict of Nicomedia, issued by Galerius and Constantine in 311,

Constantine I the Great

Constantine II

Constans

Constantius II

Maximinus persecuted Christians in Asia Minor and the Near East. Maximinus was defeated by Licinius near Adrianople (30 April 313) and died shortly afterwards in Tarsus.

THE HOUSE OF CONSTANTINE THE GREAT (AD 312–363)

Gaius Flavius Valerius Constantinus (**Constantine I the Great**, AD 310–337) was born on 27 February 272 or 273 in Naissus (Niš, present-day Serbia). Constantine was the son of Constantius I and his wife or concubine Helena. He served as a military tribune and joined his father's campaign against Celtic tribes in the north of Britain (306). After Constantius's death, the soldiers in Eboracum (York) proclaimed him *Augustus* (25 July 306); Galerius later recognized him as *Caesar*. He was nominated *Augustus* by Maximian (summer 307), but reduced to the rank of *Caesar* at the Carnuntum conference (November 308). From 310 onwards, he was generally accepted as *Augustus*, with his residence at Trier. Constantine fought the Franks on the Rhine (in 306–307 and summer 310) and later defeated Maximian at Massilia (Marseille). Jointly with Galerius, he issued the edict of Nicomedia, turning Christianity into a *religio licita* ('permitted religion'). On 28 October 312, he defeated Maxentius at the Milvian Bridge: he entered Rome, was appointed *Maximus Augustus* by the Senate and disbanded the Praetorian Guard. In early 313, he and Licinius met and jointly issued a second edict of religious tolerance. He fought and defeated Licinius at Cibalae, thus acquiring much of the Balkan provinces (314): he took up residence at Sirmium in Pannonia (316). In 317, he appointed his eldest sons, Crispus and Constantine (II), *Caesares*. He supported Christianity, intervened in Church disputes, and privileged the Church financially. The emperor campaigned against the Sarmatians in the Balkans (318) and against the Iazyges (322) and the Goths (323). He finally defeated Licinius at Adrianople and Chrysopolis; his eldest son Crispus won a naval victory at Gallipoli (324). In 324 the foundation stone for Constantinople was laid. In 325, Constantine, now sole ruler, nominated his mother Helena *Augusta*. He presided over the Council of Nicaea, where Arius's doctrine was condemned. He executed his son Crispus for adultery (326). On 11 May 330, Constantinople was officially inaugurated as his capital and on 25 July 335 Constantine celebrated the thirtieth anniversary of his rule there. In 337 the Persian king Shapur II invaded Mesopotamia: Constantine prepared to fight, but died on 22 May. He was deified shortly afterwards.

Flavius Claudius Constantinus (**Constantine II**, AD 337–340), the second son of Constantine the Great, was born on 7 August 316 at Arles. He was appointed *Caesar* (317), participated in the war against the Alamanni (328), won a victory over the Goths (332) and was in charge of the prefecture of Gaul (335). Only a few months after Constantine the Great's death, he assumed the title of *Augustus* (9 September 337). Constantine II, whose sphere of control included Gaul, Britain and Spain, was responsible for the massacre of numerous male members of the dynasty. In April 340, he attacked his brother Constans in Italy, but was defeated and killed.

Flavius **Constans** (v 337–350) was the youngest son of Constantine the Great. Born in 320, he was appointed *Caesar* on 25 December 333. In 335, he took charge of the prefecture of Italy, Africa and Illyricum. On Constantine the Great's death, the empire was divided and Constans received the provinces of his prefecture. Along with his brothers Constantine II and Constantius, he assumed the title of *Augustus* on 9 September 337. He defeated his brother Constantine when he invaded Italy (340): Constans became *Augustus* of the west. In 341,

Julian

Jovian

Valentinian

Valens

he issued, with his brother Constantius, an edict criminalizing sacrifice. Constans defeated the Franks on the Rhine (342) and campaigned against the Picts and Scots (343). When the general Magnus Magnentius seized power in Augustodunum (Autun), Constans was killed (January 350).

Flavius Julius Constantius (**Constantius II**, AD 337–361), born on 7 August 317, was the third son of Constantine I the Great. He was appointed *Caesar* on 8 November 324, aged seven. When Constantine the Great died in 337, Constantius received the Near East, Asia Minor, Egypt and Thrace. Elevated to the rank of *Augustus*, Constantius faced a Persian invasion in Mesopotamia (338). In 350, Constantius was forced to recognize the usurper Magnus Magnentius, who had ousted Constans in the west; he later defeated Magnentius (352). Constantius appointed his cousin Constantius Gallus *Caesar* (351), but executed him in 354 and replaced him with Julian (355). On 1 December 354, Constantius decreed the closure of all pagan sanctuaries. In 357, he visited Rome, where he celebrated a grand *adventus* (28 April). In 360, the Persians invaded Mesopotamia, but before Constantius could react to this, Julian usurped power in the west (February 360). Before his army met Julian's, Constantius died in Asia Minor (3 November 361).

Flavius Julianus (**Julian** the Apostate, AD 361–363), born *c.* 331 in Constantinople, was the son of Constantine's younger half-brother Julius Constantius. Julian was appointed *Caesar* in 355. He campaigned against the Alamanni on the Rhine and won a major battle near Strasbourg (357). In early 360, he was ordered by the emperor Constantius, who was about to launch his Persian war, to send the bulk of his army to the east. Julian was proclaimed *Augustus* by the army in Gaul. He marched eastward, but Constantius

died (3 November 361) before a battle could take place. Julian ruled as sole *Augustus*: he entered Constantinople and announced religious tolerance. He disbanded Constantius's imperial household and curtailed the privileges of the Christian Church. He supported paganism, and on 17 June 362 he issued an edict banning Christians from teaching. Julian launched his Persian campaign in spring 363; he died, wounded by a missile, on 26 June.

Flavius Claudius **Jovian**us (AD 363–364) was appointed emperor by the army, in the middle of enemy territory, after Julian's death. He was a Christian officer, thirty-two years old, born in Singidunum (Belgrade). Jovian negotiated a peace with the Persians and withdrew the army into Roman territory. He died on 17 February 364, after a reign of not even eight months.

THE HOUSES OF VALENTINIAN AND THEODOSIUS I (AD 364–455)

Flavius Valentinianus (**Valentinian I**, AD 364–375), a Christian from Pannonia, born in 321, started his career as a cavalry officer and became military tribune. He was proclaimed *Augustus* by the army after Jovian's death (25 February 364) . Valentinian took charge of the western half of the empire and appointed his younger brother Valens *Augustus* of the east (28 March). Valentinian defeated the Alamanni on the Rhine (366 and 368), insurgents in Britain (367) and the Franks and Saxons (368). The Rhine frontier was restored and fortified (369). Alamanni tribesmen were settled in Italy (370), but Valentinian fought major campaigns against the Alamanni on the Rhine (371–374) and the Quadi and Sarmatians in Pannonia, where he died (17 November 375).

Gratian

Valentinian II

Theodosius I the Great

Honorius

Flavius **Valens** (AD 364–378), born *c.* 328 in Pannonia, served as *protector* under Julian and Jovian. His brother Valentinian made him *Augustus* of the east on 28 March 364. Valens put down the usurpation of Procopius in Constantinople (366). He campaigned against the Goths under their king Athanaric (367–369); in 369, he made peace with the Goths, and the former Roman province of Dacia was assigned to them. Valens prepared for a major Persian war in 374, but was prevented by uprisings in Cilicia and Syria. When Valentinian I died in 375, Valens became *Maximus Augustus*, superior to his sixteen-year-old nephew Gratian, who ruled the west. In 376, Valens admitted the Fritigern Goths to the empire and settled them in Thrace. Hostilities broke out between the Goths and the Roman administration; the Goths defeated the Romans at Adrianople and Valens died in the battle (9 August 378).

Flavius **Gratian**us (AD 367–383), was elevated to the rank of *Augustus* at the age of eight by his father Valentinian I on 24 August 367. He married Constantia, the daughter of Constantius II (374). In 378, he won a victory over the Alamanni, but arrived too late to support his uncle Valens against the Goths. In Rome, Gratian ordered the (pagan) Altar of Victory to be removed from Senate House (382–383). In 383, Gratian campaigned successfully against the Alamanni in Raetia, but was deserted by his army when the military commander of Britain, Magnus Maximus, seized power. Gratian was taken prisoner and killed (25 August 383).

Valentinianus (**Valentinian II**, AD 375–392), born in 371, was the youngest son of Valentinian I. In November 375, following his father's death, the four-year-old boy was proclaimed *Augustus* by the Pannonian army in Aquincum (Budapest). Valentinian survived the usurpation of Magnus Maximus (283) and

escaped to Thessalonica when Maximus invaded Italy (387). After Theodosius I's victory over Maximus, Valentinian returned to Italy (388). He died on 15 May 392, possibly at the hands of the Frankish general Arbogast.

Flavius Theodosius (**Theodosius I the Great**, AD 379–395) was born on 11 January 346 or 347 in Cauca in northwest Spain. His father was a high-ranking officer, who campaigned under Valentinian I, but fell out of favour with Gratian and was executed in 376. The younger Theodosius retired to Spain, but was called back by Gratian, appointed *magister militum* (378) and *Augustus* for the east (19 January 379). Theodosius prevailed over the Goths, Alans and Huns (379). In late 380, he fell ill and received baptism, but survived. Theodosius presided over the Council of Constantinople (381). He issued various edicts against polytheists and Christian heretics and made peace with the Goths (3 October 382). He defeated the usurper Maximus in 388. On 16 June 391, Theodosius banned all pagan cults and, in 392, the worship of any pagan gods. In 392, Valentinian II died and the Frankish *magister militum* Arbogast revolted in Gaul, proclaiming the grammarian Eugenius emperor. Theodosius defeated Arbogast and Eugenius at the battle of the Frigidus river (6 September 394). Theodosius died in Milan on 17 January 395. He was buried in the mausoleum of Constantine the Great in Constantinople and deified on 8 November 395.

THE WEST
THE HOUSES OF VALENTINIAN AND THEODOSIUS I
(continued)

Flavius **Honorius** (AD 393–423), the younger son of Theodosius I, was born on 9 September 384. He was declared *Augustus* of the west on 23 January 393. After the death of his

Constantius III　　　　**Valentinian III**　　　　**Petronius Maximus**　　　　**Avitus**

father, the ten-year-old was under the influence of the *magister militum* Stilicho, who fell victim to a court intrigue in 408. Honorius's attempt to string the Goths along failed and provoked the sack of Rome (24 August 410). Honorius allied with the Visigoths (416), but Britain had already been evacuated by Roman troops (410). The Visigoths were settled in northern Spain and southern Gaul (418) and the Vandals occupied southern Spain (420). When Honorius died on 15 August 423, only Italy, the western Balkans and North Africa were still under the control of the western government.

Flavius Constantius (**Constantius III**, AD 421), who was born in Naissus (Niš, present-day Serbia), served as a high-ranking officer under Theodosius and Stilicho. Constantius defeated the usurper Constantine III (411). He then forced the Visigoths to leave Italy (412), was awarded the honorific title of *patricius* and married Honorius's half-sister Galla Placidia (417). The real power behind Honorius's regime, he settled the Visigoths in southern Gaul (418) and was proclaimed *Augustus* by Honorius (8 February 421), but died a few months afterwards.

Johannes (AD 423–425), a high court official, was appointed emperor by the Senate when Honorius died in August 423. He was not recognized by the eastern emperor Theodosius II, who in 425 engineered the proclamation of Valentinian III, the son of Constantius and Galla Placidia. Johannes was captured and executed.

Flavius Placidus Valentinianus (**Valentinian III**, AD 425–455), born on 2 July 419 at Ravenna, was the son of Constantius III and Galla Placidia, Honorius's half-sister. His accession, aged six, on 23 October brought the house of Valentinian and Theodosius back to power. Laws and edicts were issued in

Valentinian's name, but his mother, the military commander of Africa, Bonifatius and the *magister militum* Felix pulled the strings. In 433, the ambitious *magister militum* Aëtius replaced the old circle of puppet masters. Aëtius defeated the Visigoths and destroyed the realm of the Burgundi in southern Gaul (436–437); he arranged Valentinian's marriage to Licinia Eudoxia, the daughter of Theodosius II. In 451, Aëtius forged a coalition with the Visigoths and defeated the Huns at the Catalaunian Plains (northeast France). On 21 September 454, Valentinian, trying to take government into his own hands, slew the victorious general. A few months later, Aëtius' former bodyguards took revenge, killing Valentinian in Rome (16 March 455).

THE NINE SHADOW EMPERORS (AD 455–76)

Flavius **Petronius Maximus** (AD 455), born in 396 into a distinguished family of senators, served as consul twice and held high offices in the imperial administration. The assassination of Valentinian III turned Rome into a power vacuum: Maximus got control of the palace by distributing large amounts of money. He forced Valentinian's widow Eudoxia into marriage, but the eastern emperor Marcian I refused to recognize him. He was lynched by a Roman mob (31 May 455) when he attempted to escape from the Vandals who were about to capture the city.

Eparchius **Avitus** (AD 455–456), born in Gaul around 400, made a military career under Aëtius. He served as praetorian prefect of the Gallic provinces (from 439). He was later appointed supreme *magister militum* by Petronius Maximus and, on 9 July 455, proclaimed emperor with the support of the Gallic aristocracy and the Visigoths. He

Majorian

Libius Severus

Anthemius

Olybrius

marched to Rome, but was defeated by Ricimer on 17 October 456, forced to abdicate, and killed.

Flavius Julius Valerius **Majorian**us (AD 457–461) came from the Balkans. He rose through the ranks of the army under Aëtius. Under Petronius Maximus, Majorian commanded the imperial guard. The *magister militum* Ricimer made him emperor on 1 April 457, after an interregnum of several months. Relying on Aegidius, the *magister militum* in Gaul, Majorian managed to regain control in this important part of his empire. His energetic fiscal policy and legislation give proof that the western government was still capable of action. In 460, however, he was forced to make an unfavourable peace with the Vandals and was betrayed by Ricimer. He was deposed and executed (2 August 461).

Flavius **Libius Severus** (AD 461–465) was proclaimed *Augustus* in Ravenna (19 November 461) by Ricimer after Majorian's execution. He never stepped out of Ricimer's shadow and was devoted to religious rather than state affairs. In Gaul, the *magister militum* Aegidius, a former supporter of Majorian, held his ground. Libius Severus died on 14 November 465, perhaps poisoned by Ricimer.

Procopius **Anthemius** (AD 467–472), a senator, general and son-in-law of the eastern emperor Marcian, was sent to the west by Marcian's successor Leo I. Ricimer proclaimed him emperor after an interregnum of more than a year (12 April 467). Under Anthemius, a joint naval expedition with the east seized Sicily and Sardinia from the Vandals (468). The Visigoths conquered Augusta Emerita in Spain, brought the whole of western Gaul under their control (469) and defeated a Roman army near the Rhône (471). In Italy, Ricimer revolted against

Anthemius and proclaimed Olybrius *Augustus*. The powerful *magister militum* captured Rome and had Anthemius killed (11 July 472).

Anicius **Olybrius** (AD 472) was the son-in-law of the emperor Valentinian III. He was captured by the Vandals in 455, but later released. In 464, he held the consulship. Ricimer's army acclaimed him as *Augustus* in April 472. Ricimer died on 18 August 472. Olybrius fell ill and died a few months later (2 November).

Glycerius (AD 473–474) was proclaimed emperor at Ravenna (3 March 473) by Ricimer's nephew and successor Gundobad, after the sudden deaths of Ricimer and Olybrius had created a power vacuum in Italy. The east denied him recognition and sent Julius Nepos instead, with a large army. Glycerius was forced to retire. He became Bishop of Salona near Split.

Julius Nepos (AD 474–475), who had served as *magister militum* in Dalmatia (468), was proclaimed *Augustus* of the west by the eastern emperor Leo II (spring 474). He forced Glycerius to resign. Nepos made peace with the Visigoths, to whom he ceded the Auvergne (spring 475). He was expelled from Italy by the *magister militum* Flavius Orestes (August 475) and retired to Dalmatia. He was murdered in 480.

Romulus Augustus (**Romulus Augustulus**, AD 475–476) was the last western emperor. He was the son of the *magister militum* Orestes, who proclaimed the youth emperor on 31 October 475. Orestes was murdered by Odoacer, the commander of the 'allied' (barbarian) troops in Italy, on 28 August 476. A few days later (4 September), Odoacer deposed Romulus and sent him into retirement.

Julius Nepos　　**Arcadius**　　　　**Theodosius II**　　**Leo I**

THE EAST
THE HOUSES OF VALENTINIAN AND THEODOSIUS I (continued)

Flavius **Arcadius** (AD 383–408), the elder son of Theodosius the Great, was born in Spain around 377. He was declared *Augustus* (383) and succeeded his father as emperor in the east (395). Early in his reign he was, successively, influenced by his mentors Rufinus, Eutropius and the praetorian prefect Anthemius. Arcadius died, aged just over thirty, on 1 May 408.

Flavius Theodosius (**Theodosius II**, AD 408–450), the only son of Arcadius, succeeded his father at the age of seven in 408. The government was run by Anthemius, the praetorian prefect, until Theodosius's sister Pulcheria ousted him (414). Theodosius summoned the Council of Ephesus (431), which ended in the secession of the Nestorians from the orthodox Church. In 438, the Codex Theodosianus was issued. The emperor died at forty-nine, after a riding accident (28 July 450).

Flavius **Marcian**us (AD 450–457) was born in Illyricum to humble parents around 390. He rose up the military hierarchy and served under the *magister militum* Aspar, who engineered his succession in 450. The same year, he married Theodosius's sister Pulcheria to attach himself to the Theodosian dynasty. As emperor, Marcian settled the smouldering conflict with the Sasanian empire; he refused to pay tribute to the Huns. He summoned the Council of Chalcedon resulting in the condemnation of Monophysitism (451). He died suddenly in January 457.

THE HOUSE OF LEO (AD 457–518)

Flavius Valerius Leo (**Leo I**, AD 457–474), an officer from Thrace, was installed as emperor by the *magister militum*

Aspar when Marcian died. Leo I was the first emperor to be crowned by a cleric, the Patriarch of Constantinople. Leo established a new imperial bodyguard, recruited from the Isaurians, a tribe in southern Asia Minor. He married his daughter Ariadne to the Isaurian prince Zeno (468), who helped him oust Aspar (471). Under Leo's strong leadership, the eastern empire maintained peace with the Sasanians and the Goths, but his attempts to consolidate the Roman west were unsuccessful. He died on 18 January 474.

Flavius Leo (**Leo II**, AD 474) was Leo I's grandson. He became emperor at the age of seven when Leo I died in 474. His father Zeno was crowned co-emperor (29 January 474). After ten months of purely nominal rule, Leo II died (November 474).

Flavius **Zeno** (AD 474–491) was born under the name of Tarasicodissa in Isauria around 425. He was a prominent general, who married Leo I's daughter Ariadne. After Leo's death, he became *Augustus* (29 January 474) and, following the death of his son Leo II, sole emperor (November 474). A plot forced him into exile (475), but he returned to Constantinople (476). When Odoacer deposed Romulus Augustulus in the west, he did not intervene, but focused on the east, where he maintained peace with the Sasanians. Zeno died on 9 April 491.

Flavius Anastasius (**Anastasius I**, AD 491–518) was born around 430 and was a senior palace official when Zeno died. He married Zeno's widow Ariadne and was crowned emperor. His suzerainty was, in principle, accepted by the barbarian kings who had succeeded the Roman empire in the west. He made a new peace settlement with the Persians (506). Anastasius favoured the Monophysitic creed, provoking a series of clashes with the orthodox Church establishment. Having survived two dangerous usurpations (512–513), the emperor died, in old age, on 9/10 July 518.

FURTHER READING

Ancient Sources

Ammianus Marcellinus *Works* (transl. by J.C. Rolfe). 3 vols, Loeb Classical Library. Cambridge, MA: Harvard University Press, 1939–50.

Anonymous *In Praise of the Later Roman Emperors. The Panegyrici Latini* (transl. by S.E.V. Nixon and Barbara Sailor Rodgers). Berkeley, CA: University of California Press, 1994.

Apuleius *The Apologia and Florida* (transl. by H.E. Butler). Oxford: Clarendon Press, 1909.

Cassius Dio *Roman History* (transl. by Earnest Cary). 9 vols, Loeb Classical Library. Cambridge, MA: Harvard University Press, 1914–27.

Cicero *Three Books of Offices or Moral Duties* (transl. by Cyrus R. Edmonds). New York: Harper, 1860.

Flavius Josephus *Works* (transl. by William Whiston). Baltimore, MD: Armstrong and Plakitt, 1835.

Herodian *History of the Empire from the Time of Marcus Aurelius* (transl. by C.R. Whittaker). 2 vols, Loeb Classical Library. Cambridge, MA: Harvard University Press, 1969–70.

Horace *Odes and Carmen Saeculare* (transl. by John Conington). 7th edn, London: George Bell & Sons, 1877.

Marcus Aurelius *To Himself* (transl. by Gerald H. Rendall). London: Macmillan & Co., 1901.

Petronius *Satyricon* (transl. by Alfred R. Allinson). New York: The Panurge Press, 1930.

Pliny the Younger *The Letters* (transl. by William Melmoth). 2 vols, Loeb Classical Library. Cambridge, MA: Harvard University Press. Reprint 1961.

Plutarch *Plutarch's Lives* (transl. by Bernadotte Perrin). 11 vols, Loeb Classical Library. Cambridge, MA: Harvard University Press, 1914–23.

Scriptores Historiae Augustae (transl. by Susan H. Ballou and Hermann Peter). 3 vols, Loeb Classical Library. Cambridge, MA: Harvard University Press, 1921–34.

Seneca *Moral Essays* (transl. by John W. Basore). 3 vols, Loeb Classical Library. Cambridge, MA: Harvard University Press, 1928–35.

Suetonius *The Lives of the Caesars* (transl. by J.C. Rolfe). 2 vols, Loeb Classical Library. Cambridge, MA: Harvard University Press, 1913–14.

Tacitus *Works* (including *Annals* and *Histories*) (transl. by M. Hutton, W. Petersen, Clifford H. Moore and John Jackson). 5 vols, Loeb Classical Library. Cambridge, MA: Harvard University Press, 1914–37.

Velleius Paterculus *Compendium of Roman History. Res Gestae Divi August* (transl. by F.W. Shipley). Loeb Classical Library. Cambridge, MA: Harvard University Press, 1924.

The Roman Empire: History and Society

Bowman, Alan K., Averil Cameron and Peter Garnsey, eds. *The Cambridge Ancient History. Vol. 12: The Crisis of Empire. A.D. 193–337.* 2nd edn. Cambridge: Cambridge University Press, 2005.

Bowman, Alan K., Edward Champlin and Andrew Lintott, eds. *The Cambridge Ancient History. Vol. 10: The Augustan Empire, 43 B.C.–A.D. 69.* 2nd edn. Cambridge: Cambridge University Press, 1996.

Bowman, Alan K., Peter Garnsey and Dominic Rathbone, eds. *The Cambridge Ancient History. Vol. 11: The High Empire, A.D. 70–192.* 2nd edn. Cambridge: Cambridge University Press, 2000.

Brown, Peter. *Late Antiquity.* Cambridge, MA: The Belknap Press of Harvard University Press, 1998.

Cameron, Averil. *The Later Roman Empire, A.D. 284–430.* London: Fontana; Cambridge, MA: Harvard University Press, 1993.

Cameron, Averil and Peter Garnsey, eds. *The Cambridge Ancient History. Vol. 13: The Late Empire. A.D. 337–425.* 2nd edn. Cambridge: Cambridge University Press, 1997.

Cameron, Averil, Bryan Ward-Perkins and Michael Whitby, eds. *The Cambridge Ancient History. Vol. 14: Late Antiquity. Empire and Successors, A.D. 425–600.* 2nd edn. Cambridge: Cambridge University Press, 2000.

Christ, Karl. *Geschichte der Römischen Kaiserzeit. Von Augustus bis zu Konstantin.* 3rd edn. Munich: C.H. Beck Verlag, 1995.

Dahlheim, Werner. *Geschichte der römischen Kaiserzeit.* 2nd edn. Munich: R. Oldenbourg Verlag, 1989.

Garnsey, Peter D.A., and Richard Saller. *The Roman Empire: Economy, Society and Culture.* London: Duckworth; Berkeley, CA: University of California Press, 1987.

Giardina, Andrea, ed. *Società romana e impero tardoantico.* 4 vols. Bari: Laterza, 1986.

Gibbon, Edward. *The Decline and Fall of the Roman Empire.* 3 vols [1776–1788]. London: Allen Lane, 1994.

Goffart, Walter André. *Barbarian Tides: The Migration Age and the Later Roman Empire.* Philadelphia, PA: University of Pennsylvania Press, 2006.

Heather, Peter J. *The Fall of the Roman Empire: A New History*. London: Pan Books; New York: Oxford University Press, 2006.

Mazza, Mario. *Le maschere del potere: Cultura e politica nella tarda antichità*. Naples: Jovene, 1986.

Mazzarino, Santo. *La fine del mondo antico*. Milan: Garzanti, 1959.

Millar, Fergus. *The Roman Empire and Its Neighbours*. London: Duckworth; New York: Delacorte Press, 1967.

Potter, David. *The Roman Empire at Bay: A.D. 180–395*. London and New York: Routledge, 2004.

Potter, David. *Rome in the Ancient World: From Romulus to Justinian*. London and New York: Thames & Hudson, 2009. (US title: *Ancient Rome: A New History*).

Sommer, Michael. *Römische Geschichte II. Rom und sein Imperium in der Kaiserzeit*. Stuttgart: Kröner, 2009.

Wells, Colin M. *The Roman Empire*. 2nd edn. Fontana History of the Ancient World. London: Fontana; Cambridge, MA: Harvard University Press, 1992.

Winterling, Aloys. *Politics and Society in Imperial Rome*. Chichester: Wiley, 2009.

The Roman Emperor

Demandt, Alexander. *Das Privatleben der römischen Kaiser*. Munich: C.H. Beck Verlag, 2007.

Hekster, Olivier. *Romeinse keizers. De macht van het imago*. Amsterdam: Uitgeverij Prometheus, 2009.

Meijer, Fik, and S.J. Leinbach. *Emperors Don't Die in Bed*. London and New York: Routledge, 2004.

Millar, Fergus. *The Emperor in the Roman World (31 BC–AD 337)*. London: Duckworth; Ithaca, NY: Cornell University Press, 1977 (2nd edn 1992).

Millar, Fergus. 'Emperors at Work', in *Rome, the Greek World, and the East. Vol. 2: Government, Society, and Culture in the Roman Empire*, 3–22. Chapel Hill, NC: University of North Carolina Press, 2004.

Winterling, Aloys. *Aula Caesaris. Studien zur Institutionalisierung des römischen Kaiserhofes in der Zeit von Augustus bis Commodus (31 v. Chr. – 192 n. Chr.)*. Munich: R. Oldenbourg Verlag, 1999.

Individual Emperors and Dynasties

Barceló, Pedro A. *Constantius II. Und Seine Zeit: Die Anfänge Des Staatskirchentums*. Stuttgart: Klett-Cotta, 2004.

Barnes, Timothy David. *The New Empire of Diocletian and Constantine*. Cambridge, MA: Harvard University Press, 1982.

Bengtson, Hermann. *Die Flavier. Vespasian, Titus, Domitian.*

Geschichte eines römischen Kaiserhauses. Munich: C.H. Beck Verlag, 1979.

Bennett, Julian. *Trajan, Optimus Princeps: A Life and Times*. London: Routledge; Bloomington, IN: Indiana University Press, 1997.

Birley, Anthony Richard. *The African Emperor: Septimus Severus*. 2nd edn. London and New York: B.T. Batsford, 1988.

Birley, Anthony. *Hadrian: The Restless Emperor*. London and New York: Routledge, 2003.

Birley, Anthony. *Marcus Aurelius: A Biography*. 2nd edn. London: Routledge, 2004.

Blois, Lukas de. *The Policy of the Emperor Gallienus*. Leiden: Brill, 1976.

Bowersock, Glen Warren. *Julian the Apostate*. London: Duckworth; Cambridge, MA: Harvard University Press, 1978.

Clauss, Manfred, ed. *Die römischen Kaiser. 55 historische Portraits von Caesar bis Iustinian*. Munich: C.H. Beck Verlag, 1997.

Eck, Werner. *The Age of Augustus*. Oxford and Malden, MA: Blackwell Publishing, 2003.

Ferrill, Arther. *Caligula: Emperor of Rome*. London: Thames & Hudson, 1991.

Girardet, Klaus Martin. *Die konstantinische Wende: Voraussetzungen und geistige Grundlagen der Religionspolitik Konstantins des Großen*. Darmstadt: Wissenschaftliche Buchgesellschaft, 2006.

Grainger, John D. *Nerva and the Roman Succession Crisis of A.D. 96–99*. London and New York: Routledge, 2003.

Hekster, Olivier. *Commodus: An Emperor at the Crossroads*. Amsterdam: J.C. Gieben, 2002.

Hekster, Olivier. *Rome and Its Empire: A.D. 193–284*. Edinburgh: Edinburgh University Press, 2008.

Jones, Brian William. *The Emperor Domitian*. London and New York: Routledge, 1992.

Körner, Christian. *Philippus Arabs: Ein Soldatenkaiser in der Tradition des antoninisch-severischen Prinzipats*. Berlin: Walter de Gruyter, 2002.

Kolb, Frank. *Diocletian und die erste Tetrarchie: Improvisation oder Experiment in der Organisation monarchischer Herrschaft?* Berlin: Walter de Gruyter, 1987.

Kreucher, Gerald. *Der Kaiser Marcus Aurelius Probus und seine Zeit*. Stuttgart: Franz Steiner Verlag, 2003.

Lenski, Noel Emmanuel, ed. *The Cambridge Companion to the Age of Constantine*. Cambridge and New York: Cambridge University Press, 2006.

Lepper, Frank A. *Trajan's Parthian War*. London: Oxford University Press, 1948.

Leppin, Hartmut. *Theodosius der Große. Auf dem Weg zum*

christlichen Imperium. Darmstadt: Primus Verlag, 2003.

Levick, Barbara. *Tiberius the Politician.* 2nd edn. London and New York: Routledge, 1999.

Malitz, Jürgen. *Nero.* Munich: C.H. Beck Verlag, 1999.

Millar, Fergus. *A Greek Roman Empire: Power and Belief under Theodosius II (408/450).* Berkeley, CA: University of California Press, 2006.

Opper, Thorsten. *Hadrian: Empire and Conflict.* London: British Museum Press; Cambridge, MA: Harvard University Press, 2008.

Scarre, Chris. *Chronicle of the Roman Emperors: The Reign-by-Reign Record of the Rulers of Imperial Rome.* London and New York: Thames & Hudson, 1995.

Seelentag, Gunnar *Taten und Tugenden Traians: Herrschafts-darstellung im Principat.* Stuttgart: Franz Steiner, 2004.

Sommer, Michael. 'Elagabal - Wege zur Konstruktion eines "schlechten" Kaisers', *Scripta Classica Israelica* 23: 95–110 (2004).

Sommer, Michael. *Die Soldatenkaiser.* Darmstadt: Wissenschaftliche Buchgesellschaft, 2004.

Watson, Alaric. *Aurelian and the Third Century.* London and New York: Routledge, 1999.

Williams, Stephen. *Diocletian and the Roman Recovery.* London: B.T. Batsford; New York: Methuen, 1985.

Winterling, Aloys. *Caligula: A Biography.* Berkeley, CA: University of California Press, 2009.

Zanker, Paul *The Power of Images in the Age of Augustus.* Jerome Lectures. Ann Arbor, MI: University of Michigan Press, 1988.

Problems and Questions

Alexander, Paul J. 'Letters and Speeches of the Emperor Hadrian', *Harvard Studies in Classical Philology* 49: 141–77 (1938).

Ball, Larry F. *The Domus Aurea and the Roman Architectural Revolution.* Cambridge: Cambridge University Press, 2003.

Beard, Mary, John North, and Simon Price. *Religions of Rome.* 2 vols. Cambridge and New York: Cambridge University Press, 1998.

Bassett, Sarah. *The Urban Image of Late Antique Constantinople.* Cambridge and New York: Cambridge University Press, 2004.

Erdkamp, Paul. *A Companion to the Roman Army.* Oxford and Malden, MA: Blackwell, 2007.

Flaig, Egon. *Den Kaiser herausfordern: Die Usurpation im römischen Reich.* Frankfurt am Main: Campus-Verlag, 1992.

Flaig, Egon. 'Für eine Konzeptionalisierung der Usurpation im spätrömischen Reich', in François Paschoud and Joachim Szidat, eds, *Usurpationen in der Spätantike,* 15–34. Stuttgart: Franz Steiner, 1997.

Flower, Harriet I. *The Art of Forgetting: Disgrace and Oblivion in Roman Political Culture.* Chapel Hill, NC: University of North Carolina Press, 2006.

Giardina, Andrea, ed. *Roma antica.* Rome: Laterza, 2000.

Goldsworthy, Adrian, *The Complete Roman Army.* London and New York: Thames & Hudson, 2003.

Gradel, Ittai. *Emperor Worship and Roman Religion.* Oxford and New York: Clarendon Press, 2002.

Hoffmann, Adolf, and Ulrike Wulf. *Die Kaiserpaläste auf dem Palatin in Rom: Das Zentrum der römischen Welt und seine Bauten.* Mainz: Verlag Philipp von Zabern, 2004.

Kunst, Christiane, ed. *Grenzen der Macht. Zur Rolle der römischen Kaiserfrauen.* Stuttgart: Franz Steiner Verlag, 2000.

Le Bohec, Yann. *L'armée romaine sous le Haut-Empire.* Paris: Picard, 1989.

Mazza, Mario. *Lotte sociali e restaurazione autoritaria nel III secolo d. C.* Rome: Laterza, 1973.

Mazzarino, Santo. *Il pensiero storico classico.* 3 vols. Rome: Laterza, 1983.

Oliver, James H.. *The Ruling Power: A Study of the Roman Empire in the Second Century after Christ through the Roman Oration of Aelius Aristides.* Repr. edn. Vol. 43.4, *Transactions of the American Philosophical Society* New Series. Philadelphia, PA: The American Philosophical Society, 1953.

Percival, Henry R., Philip Schaff, and Henry Wace. *The Seven Ecumenical Councils of the Undivided Church. Their Canons and Dogmatic Decrees, Together with the Canons of All the Local Synods Which Have Received Ecumenical Acceptance.* Peabody, MA: Hendrickson, 2004.

Roller, Matthew B.. *Constructing Autocracy: Aristocrats and Emperors in Julio-Claudian Rome.* Princeton, NJ: Princeton University Press, 2001.

Whitby, Michael. *Rome at War. A.D. 293–696.* New York: Routledge, 2003.

Wiedemann, Thomas E.J.. *Emperors and Gladiators.* London and New York: Routledge, 1992.

Winterling, Aloys. '"Staat", "Gesellschaft" und politische Integration in der römischen Kaiserzeit', *Klio* 83: 93–112 (2001).

Zanker, Paul. 'Domitian's Palace on the Palatine and the Imperial Image', in Alan K. Bowman, Hannah Cotton, Martin Goodman and Simon Price, eds, *Representations of Empire: Rome and the Mediterranean World,* 105–30. London: Oxford University Press/British Academy, 2002.

SOURCES OF QUOTATIONS

Quotations from ancient Roman sources have been translated into English by the author, unless otherwise stated below.

Full details of published sources will be found in the Further Reading.

CHAPTER 1 THE STORY OF AN EMPIRE

PAGE 21 'The whole inhabited world like a…' Aristides, Orations 26, 100–102 (transl. by James H. Oliver).

PAGE 22 'Be at one with one another, to make the soldiers rich…' Cassius Dio, LXXVII. 15. 2 (transl. by Earnest Cary).

'Kingdom of iron and rust' and 'golden age' Cassius Dio, LXXII. 36. 4 (transl. by Earnest Cary).

CHAPTER 2 AUGUSTUS AND THE TRANSITION TO EMPIRE

PAGE 28 'After that time…' Augustus, Res Gestae (transl. by F.W. Shipley).

'As he took his seat, the conspirators…' Suetonius, Divus Iulius 82, 1 (transl. by J. C. Rolfe).

PAGE 36 'To ravage, to slaughter, to usurp under false titles…' Tacitus, Agricola I, 30 (transl. by W. S. Tyler, Project Guttenberg).

'Faith, Honour, ancient Modesty…' Horace, Carmen Saeculare 57–60 (transl. by John Conington).

PAGE 37 'That his statue in bronze should be mounted…' Cassius Dio XLIII. 14. 6 (transl. by Earnest Cary).

PAGE 43 'You will enjoy fully the reality of the kingship…' Cassius Dio LII. 40, 2 (transl. by Earnest Cary).

'You should yourself, in consultation with the best men…' Cassius Dio LII. 15, 1 (transl. by Earnest Cary).

CHAPTER 3 BECOMING EMPEROR

PAGE 48 'Death, like birth, is a revelation…' and 'Live not one's life…' Marcus Aurelius, Meditations (To Himself) (transl. by Gerald H. Rendall).

PAGE 49 'Cruel and inexorable anger is not seemly for a king…' and 'Whose care embraces all…' Seneca, De clementia ('On mercy') I. 5 (transl. by John W. Basore).

PAGE 51 'The secret of empire was now disclosed…' Tacitus, Histories I. 4 (transl. by Clifford Moore).

'Capable of ruling' Tacitus, Histories I. 49 (transl. by Clifford Moore).

PAGE 52 'Galba was weak and old…' Tacitus, Histories I. 6 (transl. by Clifford Moore).

PAGE 57 'He did not get until he had failed once…' Suetonius, Vespasian 2, 3 (transl. by J.C. Rolfe).

PAGE 60 'How glad are you…' Pliny the Younger, Panegyric on Trajan.

PAGE 61 'Though Tiberius did not hesitate at once…' Suetonius, Tiberius 24 (transl. by J.C. Rolfe).

'At last, as though on compulsion…' Suetonius, Tiberius 24 (transl. by J.C. Rolfe).

PAGES 61–62 'Only the mind of the deified Augustus…' and 'was more dignified than convincing' Tacitus Annals I. 11 (transl. by J. Jackson).

PAGE 62 'This incensed the emperor to such a degree…' (and following passages) Tacitus, Annals I. 74 (transl. by J. Jackson).

PAGE 65 'That the city had been founded a second time' Suetonius, Caligula 16, 4 (transl. by J.C. Rolfe).

PAGE 66 'All the meadows were crowded…' Panegyrici Latini XI (3), 10.

PAGE 69 'Then it was that the whole multitude…' Flavius Josephus, Wars VII. 4, 1 (transl. by William Whiston).

CHAPTER 4 BEING EMPEROR

PAGE 74 'Remarkable neither for size nor elegance…' Suetonius, Augustus 72, 1 (transl. by J.C. Rolfe).

PAGE 74 'Roofs worthy of a god' Ovid, Tristia III. 1, 34.

PAGE 77 'Do I see you reclining…?' Statius, Silvae IV. 2, 14–17.

PAGE 80 'When sleep came to him…' and 'He detested early rising…' Suetonius, Augustus 78, 2 (transl. by J.C. Rolfe).

PAGE 81 'Caligula was tormented with sleeplessness' and 'he was terrified…' Suetonius, Caligula 50, 3 (transl. by J.C. Rolfe).

'Crowded with people of almost any…' Aulus Gellius, Noctes atticae IV. 1, 1.

PAGE 82 'Then, after having himself rubbed with oil…' Historia Augusta, Severus Alexander 30, 4 (transl. by Susan H. Ballou and Hermann Peter).

'On coming out of the bath…' Historia Augusta, Severus Alexander 30, 5 (transl. by Susan H. Ballou and Hermann Peter).

'Would eat even before dinner, wherever…' and 'a light eater…' Suetonius, Augustus 76, 1 (transl. by J.C. Rolfe).

'Often served at formal dinners…' Suetonius, Tiberius 34, 1 (transl. by J.C. Rolfe).

PAGE 83 'His passion for elaborate banquets was…'
Tacitus, Histories II. 62 (transl. by Clifford Moore).

PAGE 84 'Most notorious of all…' and 'He could never
refrain…' Suetonius, Vitellius 13, 2 (transl. by J.C. Rolfe).

'It seems sufficiently agreed, too, that…' Historia Augusta,
Maximini duo 4, 2 (transl. by Susan H. Ballou and
Hermann Peter).

PAGE 85 'Many say that as soon as he swallowed the
poison…' Suetonius, Claudius 44, 3 (transl. by J.C. Rolfe).

'A nap, lying with one of his concubines…' Suetonius,
Vespasian 21, 1 (transl. by J.C. Rolfe).

PAGE 88 'Then the preliminary course was served…'
Petronius, Satyricon V. 31 (transl. by Alfred R. Allinson).

PAGE 90 'When least we think, things go astray…'
Petronius, Satyricon VIII. 54 (transl. by Alfred R. Allinson).

PAGE 95 'A man of stern character…' and 'Shall I take
what is far the best course…' Apuleius, Apologia 91
(transl. by H.E. Butler)

PAGE 96 'Enjoys immunity from taxation…' inscription on
the Temple of Zeus Hypsistos at Thelsea (modern Dmeir)
near Damascus (SEG XVII. 759).

PAGE 99 'The other roads were repaired later…' Cassius Dio,
LIII. 22, 2–4 (transl. by Earnest Cary).

PAGE 100 'Whenever I was saluted as imperator…'
Augustus, Res Gestae 21 (transl. by F.W. Shipley).

PAGES 102–104 'It is my invariable rule, Sir, to refer to
you in all matters…' and 'on all these points…' and
'I asked them whether they were Christians…' Pliny,
Epistles X. 96 (transl. by William Melmoth).

'Having been attacked last year…' Pliny, Epistles X. 5 (transl. by
William Melmoth).

'It is my resolution, in pursuance of the maxim…'
Pliny, Epistles X. 7 (transl. by William Melmoth).

PAGE 106 'Allowed to plunder any longer' Cassius Dio,
LXXIV. 8. 1 (transl. by Earnest Cary).

'For, just as if it had been in some market…' Cassius Dio,
LXXIV. 11, 3 (transl. by Earnest Cary).

PAGE 108 'Held many of his freedmen in high honour
and close intimacy…' Suetonius, Augustus 67, 1 (transl.
by J.C. Rolfe).

PAGE 109 'Of his freedmen he had special regard…'
Suetonius, Claudius 28 (transl. by J.C. Rolfe).

PAGE 110 'Removed [Pallas] from the charge to which…'
Tacitus, Annals XIII. 14 (transl. by J. Jackson).

PAGE 111 'A woman who to this day stands unparalleled…'
Tacitus, Annals XII. 42 (transl. by J. Jackson).

'From this moment it was a changed state…' Tacitus, Annals
XII. 7 (transl. by J. Jackson).

'You have all the virtues and insights that befit a woman…'
Fronto, Greek letter 2.

PAGE 112 'There was no artificially-made statue…'
Herodian, (V. 3, 4).

PAGE 113 'Commanding influence she had…' Cassius Dio,
LVIII. 2, 3 (transl. by Earnest Cary).

PAGE 116 'Foot in either a chariot or a four-wheeled vehicle'
Cassius Dio, LXIX. 9, 3 (transl. by Earnest Cary).

CHAPTER 5 **EMPERORS ON CAMPAIGN**

PAGE 121 'For the one with the highest merits for the state,
at home…' CIL VI. 959.

PAGE 122 'Trajan learned of this at Babylon…' Cassius Dio,
LXVIII. 30 (transl. by Earnest Cary).

PAGE 124 'Trajan sent the cavalry forward…' Cassius Dio,
LXVIII. 31 (transl. by Earnest Cary).

'Trajan therefore departed thence, and a little later…'
Cassius Dio, LXVIII. 31 (transl. by Earnest Cary).

'He proceeded regardless of cold or heat…' Herodian, III. 6, 10

PAGES 125–6 'You have done the most difficult of all difficult
things…' and 'however, you have made criticism
impossible…' and 'it is hard for the horsemen…'
CIL VIII. 2532. Quoted from Paul J. Alexander, 'Letters and
speeches of the emperor Hadrian', *Harvard Studies in
Classical Philology* 49 (1938), 141–77.

PAGE 127 'His triumph had such a magnitude…' Plutarch, Life of
Pompey the Great 45, 1–2 (transl. by Bernadotte Perrin).

PAGE 129 'Be at one with each other, to make the soldiers
rich…' Cassius Dio, LXXVII. 15, 2 (transl. by Earnest Cary).

PAGE 130 'I am one of you, and it is because of you…'
and 'Rejoice, fellow-soldiers…' Cassius Dio, LXXVIII. 3, 2
(transl. by Earnest Cary).

PAGE 131 'And we took Valerian prisoner with our own
hands…' Res Gestae Divi Saporis, (SKZ § 22).

PAGE 133 'Here was abundant fuel for a revolution…'
Tacitus, Histories I. 6 (transl. by Clifford Moore).

CHAPTER 6 **ROME AND CONSTANTINOPLE**

PAGE 137 'These expenses also are more justifiable…'
Cicero, Offices II. 60 (transl. by Cyrus R. Edmonds).

PAGE 142 'It is not only impossible to speak in a proper
manner…' Aelius Aristides, Orations, XXVI. 6.

PAGE 146 'Vespasian held a piece of money…'
Suetonius, Vespasian 23, 3 (transl. by J.C. Rolfe).

PAGE 147 'An emporium common to all men…'
Aelius Aristides, Orations XXVI. 6.

PAGE 147–8 'Think you that it is just the same…'
Seneca, Shortness of Life 19 (transl. by John W. Basore).

PAGE 150 'In the Circus, for example, he exhibited…' Cassius Dio, LXXVII. 8, 2–4 (transl. by Earnest Cary).

PAGE 152 'Commodus now gave orders for the celebration…' Herodian, I. 15, 1–2.

PAGE 158 'Conquer in this sign' Eusebius, Life of Constantine 1, 28.

PAGE 165 'But it must be confessed that of the two comedies …' Edward Gibbon, *The History of the Decline and Fall of the Roman Empire,* London: Allen Lane, 1994, vol.1, p. 389.

PAGE 167 'We had assembled in Constantinople…' Mansi, III. 557. Quoted from Henry Percival, *From Nicene and Post-Nicene fathers,* Second Series, vol. 14. Ed. Philip Schaff and Henry Wace. Buffalo, NY, Christian Literature Publishing Co., 1900.

PAGE 169 'You wanted to be a banker and…' Julian, Caesars 335 A/B.

CHAPTER 7 **DECLINE AND FALL IN THE WEST**

PAGE 174 'On every side armour and weapons clashed…' Ammianus Marcellinus XXXI. 13, 1-2 (transl. by J.C. Rolfe).

PAGE 176 'As an effective fighting force, the eastern Roman army…' David S. Potter, *The Roman Empire at Bay. AD 180-395,* London, Routledge 2004, p. 532.

'The annals record no such massacre…' Ammianus Marcellinus XXXI. 13, 19 (transl. by J.C. Rolfe).

'Like in a festive procession, treating the soil…' Themistius, Orations XVI. 209.

PAGE 178 'The example of unprecedented piety' Ambrosius, letter LI, 12.

PAGE 179 'The hereditary sceptre of the sons of Theodosius…' Edward Gibbon, *The History of the Decline and Fall of the Roman Empire,* London: Allen Lane, 1994, vol. II, p. 98.

SOURCES OF ILLUSTRATIONS

INDEX

Page numbers in *italics* refer to illustrations and their captions; (e) emperor, (g) god/goddess, (u) usurper

a cognitionibus 102–3, 109
a commentariis 102–3, 109
a libellis 102–3, 109
a rationibus 102–3, 109
a studiis 102–3, 109
ab epistulis 109
ab epistulis Graecis 102–3
ab epistulis Latinis 102–3
Actium, battle of (31 BC) 26, 33, 33–36, 182
adlocutio 128, *128*
adoption 16, 22, 59–60, *60*, 182, 184, 186
Adrianople, battle of (AD 378) 25, 170–76, *174–75*, 194
adventus 66–69, 127, 193
aedile 56–57
Aegean 41, 89
Aelius Aristides 21, 142, 144, 147
Aelius Caesar, Lucius 185
aerarium 97, 102–3, 145
aerarium militare 98, 102
Aëtius (*magister militum*) 195–96
Africa 12, 18–19, 22, 32, 36, 57, 95, 103, 113, 117, 123, 125, 129, 147, 153, 166, 176, 180, 183, 186–87, 191–92, 195
Agricola 36
Agrippa Postumus 40
Agrippa, Marcus 32–33, 36, 39, 40–41, *41*, 125
Agrippina the Elder 40, 182
Agrippina the Younger 11, 46, 49–50, 85, 111, *111*, 112, 182–83
Alamanni 23–24, 167, 176, 186–89, 192–94
Alaric 170, 172, 179–80
Alba Longa 134, 140
Alexander the Great 11, 32, 118, 122, 130, 155, 160, 169
Alexander (Bishop of Alexandria) 166
Alexandria 33, 53–54, 62, 104, 165–66, 183, 186
Alps 36, 40, 54, 68, 180, 182
Ambrosius (Bishop of

Milan) 178, *178*
amicitia 30, 85
Ammianus Marcellinus 174, 176
Anastasius I (e) 6, 197
Anchises 140
Anthemius (e) 196, *196*
Antioch 23, 50, 96, 155, 167, 188
Antium 182
Antonine plague 21, 185
Antonine Wall 20
Antoninus Pius (e) 16, 20–21, 37, 48, 60, 65, 83, 115, 117, 141, 185, *185*
Antonius, Lucius 32
Aphrodisias 176
Apollo (g) 94–95, 138, 159, 165
Apollonia 30
Apuleius 95–96
Aqua Claudia (aqueduct) 143, 144, *146*
Aquileia 155
Arabia, Arabs 36, 122, 190; Arabia (province) 44, 122, 132, 188
Ara Pacis 38, *38–39*, 138, 182
Arbogast (*magister militum*) 177, 194
Arcadius (e) 178–80, *179*, 197, *197*
Arch of Constantine 66, 98, *158*
Arch of Septimius Severus *131*
Arch of Titus 19, 127, 141, *143*
Ardashir (Persian king) 22
Arianism 167
Arius 165–66, 192
Arles 190, 192
Armenia 33, 122, 130, 150
Arminius 19, 129
Arpocras (physician) 104
Arsacid dynasty 23
Artabanus IV (Parthian king) 22
Ascanius 140
Asia Minor 33, 46, 102, 115, 117, 124, 142, 155, 176, 188–89, 192–93, 197
Athanaric 172, 194
Athanasius (Bishop of Alexandria) 166
Attica 89
Attila (king of the Huns) 180
Augustine (Church Father) 179
Augustus (e) 4, 6, *7*, 9, *9*, 11, 20, 26–43, *27*, *28*, *30*, *35*, 44, 46, 57, 59, 60, 61, 65, 89, 92, 101, 105–8, 112, 116, 118, 127, 144–45, 148,

165, 168–69, 180–81, 182, *182*; as army commander 125, 129; as builder 134, 138–41, 143; as supreme judge 92–95; deification of 64; domestic habits 80, 82, 85; finances 98–100; house/*domus* 70, 72, 74; principate 12, 16–17, 55, 81
Augustus (title) 6, 26, 28, 34–35, 67, 115, 133, 155, 157–58, 168, 170, 172–73, 176–79, 185–97
Aurelian (e) 24, 37, 50, 114–15, 120, 165, 189, *189*, 190–91
Aurelian Walls 189
aurum coronarium 100
Autun 50, 193
auxiliary cohorts 19, 23, 129
Avidius Cassius, Gaius (u) 50, 125
Avitus (e) 195–96, *195*

Babylonia 122
Babylonian Revolt 122–24
bad emperors 63, 100, 169
Bait Alaha (Hatra) 123
Balbinus (e) 106, 187, *187*
Balkans 46–47, 58, 67, 120, 129, 132–33, 176–79, 188–92, 195–96
Bar Kokhba, Simon 20–21, 184
barbarians, barbarism 4, 12, 17, 23–25, *27*, 84, 126, 129, 131, 151–52, 176, 196–97
barbaricum 23
Basilica of Maxentius *135*
Baths of Caracalla *9*, *10*, 143
Baths of Diocletian *10*, 143
Baths of Trajan 143
Bedriacum, first and second battles of (AD 69) 54
Bellona (g) 174
Bible 80
Bonifatius (*magister militum*) 195
Boscoreale 88–89
Boudicca 19, 183
Britain 17, 19–20, 24, 50, 57, 67, 117, 125, 129, 176, 180, 182–86, 190, 192–95
Britannicus 44, 50, 60, 183
Brundisium 32, 116
Brutus, Decimus Junius 28
Brutus, Lucius Junius 28
Brutus, Marcus Junius 29, 31–32
bureaucracy 16, 25, 70, 97–98,

101, 108, 110, 168, 182
Burrus, Sextus Afranius 49–50, 183
Byzantine empire 157, 163
Byzantium *see* Constantinople

Caecilianus (Bishop of Carthage) 166
Caenis (mistress of Vespasian) 85
Caesar, Gaius Julius 6, 18, 23, 26, 28–32, *29*, 34, 37, 40, 60, 64, 120, 127, 137–39, 150, 169, 182
Caesar (title) 34–35, 62, 67, 98, 102, 109, 132–33, 157–58, 167, 184, 187–93
Caledonians 187
Caligula (e) 4, 11, 16, 34, 42–43, 46, *64*, 70, 74, 81, 84, 91, 111, 128, 150, 169, 182, *182*; accession of 63–65, 105–6; murder of 52, 106
Calpurnia 28
Campania 30, 70, 89, 182
Campus Martius 38, 127, 137, 138, 143, 147
Cannae, battle of (216 BC) 176
Capellianus 187
Capitoline Hill 127, 137–38, 157, 183
Cappadocia (province) 115, 188
Capri 63, 72, 105–6, 182
Caracalla (e) 10–11, *11*, 22, 96, 100, 112–13, 122, 130–31, *130*, 143, 186, *186*
Carausius, Marcus Aurelius (u) 50, 67, 190
Carinus (e) 8, 153, 189–90
Carnuntum conference (AD 308) 158, 190, 191, 192
Carpathians 121
Carpi 23, 152, 186, 188–89, 191
Carrhae, battle of (AD 160) 23, 131, 188
Carthage 12, 14, 44, 47, 53, 137, 166, 172
Carus (e) 133, 189, *189*
Cassius Dio 10, 22, 37, 43, 63, 98, 106, 112, 116, 123–24, 128, 130, 150, 152
Cassius Longinus, Gaius 29–32
Catalaunian Plains, battle of (AD 451) 195
Catullinus (*legatus*) 126
Celadus (freedman) 108
Chalcedon, Council of 114, 197

charisma 6, 24, 34, 42, 124, 153
Charlemagne 181
Chatti 184
Christianity 8, 12, 24, 102, 104, 127, 157, 159, 161–62, 164–69, 173, 179, 192
Chrysopolis, battle of (AD 324) 25, 192
Church 17, 25, 134, 159, 161, 164, 167–69, 192–93, 197
Cibalae, battle of (AD 314) 191–92
Cicero, Marcus Tullius 30–31, 137
Cilicia (province) 114, 194
Cimber, Lucius Tillius 28
Circus Maximus 74–80, 127
citizenship 18, 60, 81, 93, 100, 104–5, 129, 186
civic crown 7, 119
civil wars 8, 22, 24, 32, 34–36, 46, 55, 67, 69, 118, 129, 153, 158, 162, 168, 183
Civilis, Gaius Julius 19
Claudius (e) 11, 17, 37, 42, 44, 49, 50, 57, 59–60, 70, 74, 87, 93–94, 118, 125, 141, 143–45, 147, 182–83, 182; accession of 46, 105–6; death of 85; and freedmen 108–10; and women 110–11
Claudius II Gothicus (e) 189, 189
Claudius Maximus (governor) 95
Cleander, Marcus Aurelius 148, 185
Cleopatra 32–33, 105
client kings 19–20, 78, 109, 120–22
clients, clientes see patrocinium
clipeus virtutis 35
Clodius Albinus, Decimus (u) 116, 187
Cniva (king of the Goths) 24
Codex Theodosianus 94, 94, 197
Cologne 50, 53
Colosseum 10, 70, 74, 141, 141, 143, 150, 183
Column of Marcus Aurelius 142–43
Commagene 126
Commodus (e) 8, 16, 22, 44, 46, 55, 58, 60, 84, 115, 143, 148, 151, 153, 160, 179, 185; assassination of 84, 151, 153; as gladiator 152–53
consilium principis 94, 103
Constans (e) 50, 162, 192–193, 192
Constantine I the Great (e) 8, 11, 17, 21, 24–25, 35, 46, 66–67, 70, 72, 80, 98, 105–6, 114–15, 156,

159, 162, 178, 181, 190–93, 192; and Church 165–67; and Constantinople 154–65
Constantine II (e) 35, 162, 162, 192, 192
Constantinople 10, 12, 50, 72–73, 134, 154–69, 157, 172, 176, 179, 192–94, 192, 197; Baths of Constantine 163; Forum of Constantine 157, 160; Forum of Theodosius 179; Hagia Sophia 163; Hippodrome 72, 160, 163, 164, 176; mausoleum of Constantine the Great 160, 194; Walls of Theodosius 161
Constantinople, Council of 166–67, 194
Constantius Gallus, Flavius 167, 193
Constantius I (e) 11, 34, 67, 72, 154–55, 157, 190–92, 190
Constantius II (e) 8, 35, 46, 50, 80, 83, 155, 160, 162–69, 192–94, 192
Constantius III (e) 195, 195
Constantius, Julius 167
Constitutio Antoniniana 100, 186
consul, consulship 28, 32, 35, 40–41, 54, 56–59, 100, 102, 108–10, 116, 153, 170, 182–90, 195, 196
convivium 76, 81, 85–91
Corbulo, Gnaeus Domitius 51, 112
corona civica see civic crown
Corpus Juris Civilis 94, 107
Corsica 32, 191
Crete 57
crises 12, 17, 25, 41, 64, 130, 176–79; of 3rd century 11–12, 16, 24, 67, 114, 131–33, 153; of AD 69 19, 43, 54–55, 68, 118, 183; of AD 96 20; of AD 193 22, 55, 118, 185–86
Crispus 162, 192
Ctesiphon 22, 122, 188–89
Cumae, battle of (38 BC) 32
Curia Julia see Senate House
curator aquarum 102–3
cursus honorum 40, 56–57, 108
Cyprus (province) 33, 125
Cyrenaica 123
Cyrus (Persian king) 46
Cyzicus, battle of (AD 193) 187

Dacia (kingdom) 20, 23–24, 120–21, 132, 172, 184–85, 188; (province) 194
Dacian Wars 20, 120–21, 120–21,

128, 184
Dalmatia (province) 89, 180, 190, 196
Damascus 96
Danube 21, 23, 54, 114, 117, 120–21, 132, 162, 172, 177, 185–91
Decebalus 120
Decius (e) 24, 152–153, 188, 188
Didius Julianus (e) 106, 186
dinner party see convivium
Dio Chrysostom 21
Diocletian (e) 8, 11, 16, 24–25, 24, 34, 37, 55, 68–69, 72, 91, 99–100, 133, 142–43, 154–58, 160, 165, 168, 170, 190–91, 190
Dionysius Exiguus 16
Domitia Longina 112
Domitia Lucilla 111
Domitian (e) 16, 19, 50, 85, 127, 141, 143, 146, 150, 184; dinner parties of 87, 90; murder of 20, 112; palaces of 70, 72, 75–80; and warfare 118–21, 125
Domitius Ahenobarbus, Gnaeus 111, 182
Domus Augustana 70, 72, 75–79, 76, 78–79, 80
Domus Augusti 70, 72, 74, 108
Domus Aurea 70, 72, 74–75, 74–75, 86–87, 87, 141, 183
Domus Flavia 70, 72, 75–79, 78–79
Domus Liviae 72
Donatism 166
donativum 52–53, 98, 184
Drusus the Elder 4, 36, 39–42, 125
Drusus the Younger 4
Dyrrhachium 31

Eclectus 153
Edessa 122–23, 130
Edict of Milan 159, 161, 167
education 8, 44, 46–50, 113, 116, 185
Egypt, Egyptian 33, 73, 138
Egypt, Aegyptus (province) 33, 38, 62, 103–5, 115–17, 123, 129, 147, 183, 185, 189–93
Elagabalus (e) 37, 60, 112–13, 130, 132, 165, 186–87, 186; the god 113, 130
Emesa 37, 113, 130, 165, 186
emperor worship 37
England 18–20
Ennius 48
Ephesus, Council of 197

equestrian order 31, 44, 57–58, 64, 81–82, 94, 101–3, 105–10, 112, 147, 183, 185–86
Esquiline Hill 74, 141, 143
Etruscans 28, 127, 134
Eugenius, (u) 50, 177, 194
Euphrates 18, 20, 26, 122–23
Eusebius of Caesarea 158
Eusebius (Bishop of Nicomedia) 167

Faustina the Younger 11, 142, 185
Felix (freedman) 109
Felix (magister militum) 195
finances 56, 91, 97–101, 102–3, 109, 145, 183, 190
fiscus Caesaris 98, 102–3, 109
Flavian dynasty 6, 16, 19, 21, 44, 46, 54, 59, 127, 183–84
Flavius Josephus 63, 69
Flavius Sabinus, Titus 57
Flavius Theodosius 176
Florianus (e) 189
Formiae 31
Forum of Augustus 139, 140, 140, 143
Forum of Nerva 141
Forum of Trajan 121, 143, 184
Franks 24, 129, 188, 192–93
freedmen 58, 88, 104–5, 108–11, 148, 185
Frigidus river, battle of (AD 394) 177, 194
Fritigern 172–73, 194
Fronto, Marcus Cornelius 48, 82, 111, 116, 148, 185

Gabba (court jester) 89
Gaius Caesar 39, 42, 57, 57, 59–60, 182
Galba (e) 34, 52–58, 183, 183
Galerius (e) 11, 34–35, 67, 67, 72, 154–58, 190, 191, 192
Gallaecia (province) 176
Galla Placidia 72, 195
Gallia Lugdunensis (province) 52, 186
Gallienus (e) 24, 34, 50, 133, 188–89, 188
Gallipoli, battle of (AD 324) 192
garum 88–89
Gaul 18–19, 23–24, 36, 44, 50, 52, 59, 117, 118, 129, 137, 158, 172, 176, 180, 182, 188–90, 192–96; Gallic empire 114–15, 132, 189
Genius Augusti 37

gens 60
Germanicus *4*, 17, *39*, 42, *58*, 63–64, 111, 116, 182; career of 59
Germany, Germanic peoples 12, 17, 19, 21, 23, 25, 36, 40, 50, 53, 57, 117, 170, 172, 176, 179–81, 182–85, 187–90
Germany, Lower (province) 53, 183
Germany, Upper (province) 53, 118, 155, 184
Gessius Florus 112
Geta 22, 113, *113*, 129–30, 186
Gibbon, Edward 165, 179
gladiators 8, 26, 148–53, 185
Glycerius (e) 181, 196
Goharieni 96
'good emperors' 8, 21–22, 37, 46, 48–49, 61, 63, 82, 84, 100, 184–85
Gordian I (e) 187
Gordian II (e) 187, *187*
Gordian III (e) 22, *56*, 105–7, 132, 187–88, *188*
Goths 23–25, 129, 170–79, 188–89, 192, 194–97
Gratian (e) 60, 173, 176–79, 194, *194*
Great Palace, Constantinople 70, 72, 160, 163
Greece, Greeks 12, 18–19, 21, 30–33, 36–37, 46–48, 52, 57, 72–73, 96, 100, 102, 108, 110, 113, 116–17, 123, 129, 137, 142, 147, 159, 164, 167, 169, 183, 185
Greuthungi 173
Gundobad 181, 196

Hadrian (e) 10–11, *11*, 20–21, 48, 57, 60, 65, 72–73, 81, 84, 94, 96, 103, 109, 114, 120, 141, 143, 147, 158, 184–85, *184*; and military 124–26, 129; travels of 70, 116–17
Hadrian's Villa 70, 72–73, *73*, 114, 117, 185
Hadrian's Wall 20, *20*
Harpocras (freedman) 109
Hatra 122–24, *123*
Helena 114–15, *115*, 157, *162*, 192
Heliopolis 38
Herculaneum 70, 81, 89
Hercules (hero) 37, 68, 153, 159
heterodoxy 114, 165, 168
Hittite empire 73
Holy Trinity 166
Honorius (e) 8, 50, 72, *171*, 178–80, 194–95, *194*

Horace 36, 48
House of Constantine 21, 46, 192–93
House of Leo 6, 21, 47, 197
Houses of Valentinian and Theodosius 21, 46, 194–95
Huns 172–173, 194–97

Illyricum 172, 176, 179, 192, 197
image, imperial 10–11, 68, 121
imperator 34–35, 100, 111, 191
imperium proconsulare 34, 42, 59, 92–93, 18
India 89, 122
Issus, battle of (AD 193) 187
Italian law 99
Italica 20, 44, 184
Italy 12, 24, 30–32, 37, 44, 46–47, 54, 68, 83, 89, 99, 115–17, 124, 129, 134, 152, 155, 164, 172, 177–81, 183–85, 187, 189–96

Jerusalem 19, 21, 114, 127, 179, 184
Jesus of Nazareth 160, 166
Jewish Revolt, First (AD 66–70) 8, 18, 51, 58, 68, 183
Jewish Revolt, Second (AD 132–135) 20
Johannes (e) 195
Jotapianus, (u) 132
Jovian (e) 170, 193, *193*, 194
Judaism, Jews 19, 63, 69, 93, 123, 127, 168, 185
Julia Domna 112–13, *113*
Julia Maesa 113, 186–87
Julia Sohaemias 112
Julia (daughter of Augustus) *39*, 40–41, *41*
Julian the Apostate (e) 9, 11, 17, 35, 42, 80, 83, *168*, 193, *193*; Persian war of 25, 170, 193–94; support for paganism 167–69
Julio-Claudian dynasty 4, 6, 16–17, 19, 21, 46, 50, 55, 64, 111, 112, 182–83
Julius Constantius 167
Julius Nepos (e) 180–81, 196, *197*
Jupiter (g) 35, 37, 66, 68, 118, 127, 138, 160
justice 49, 70, 93–97, 144
Justinian 72, 94, 163, 181
Juvenal 148

Kitos War *see* Babylonian Revolt

Labarum 25
Laetus, Aemilius (praetorian

prefect) 153, 185–86
Lambaesis 117, 125, 129
Lares Augusti 37
latifundia 100–101
Latin 18, 34, 44, 48, 96, 100, 102, 148, 167
Latium 31, 40, 44, 72, 134, 143, 183
law 21–22, 29, 43, 48, 64, 92–97, 103, 106, 130, 144, 151, 155, 162, 178, 195
legatus 35, 58, 102–3, 126
Leo I (e) 6, 21, 46, 197, *197*
Leo II (e) 180, 196, 197
Lepcis Magna 12, 16, 22, 153, 186
Lepidus, Marcus Aemilius 31–32, *31*, 182
Levant 21
lex de imperio Vespasiani (law on Vespasian's emperorship) 183
Libius Severus (e) 181, 196, *196*
Licinius (e) 24–25, *25*, 158–62, 167, 191–92, *191*
Licinus (freedman) 108
Livia *4*, 17, 40–42, 72, 108, 112, *112*, 182
Livilla 41
Longinus 120
Lucius Caesar 40–41, 60
Lucius Verus (e) 34, *60*, 185, *185*
Lusitania (province) 54, 183
Lusius Quietus (general) 123–24
luxury 8, 70, 86, 92, 181
Lydia 107–8
Lyons 18, 44, 50, 151, 182, 186

Macedonia (province) 31
Macrinus (e) 44, 56–57, 62, 113, 130, 186, *186*
Macro 64, 105–6, 182
Maecenas 43
magister militum 102–3, 176–77, 179–81, 194–97
magister officiorum 102–3
Magnentius (u) 50, 162, 193
Magnus Maximus (u) 177, 194
Mainz 50, 129, 187
Majorian (e) 125, 180–81, 196, *196*
Marcellus, Gaius Claudius 40, 60
Marcia (mistress of Commodus) 153, 186
Marcian (e) 195, 196, 197
Marcomanni 21, 48, 100, 142, 185, 188
Marcus Aurelius (e) 8, *8*, 16, 21–22, 34–35, 36, 44, 46, *48*, 50, 80, *80*, 82–83, 100, 111, 116–17, 118, 125, 133, 155, 142, 148, 152,

169, 185, *185*, 186; adoption 60, *60*; education of 48; asceticism 9, 82–83; 116
Margus river, battle of (AD 285) 190
Mark Antony 26, 29–34, *29*, 105, 182
Mars (g) 140, 159
Masada 19
Mauretania (province) 117, 185–86
mausoleum of Augustus 38, 40, 64, 65, 138
mausoleum of Hadrian 185, 186
Maxentius (e) 66, 98, 137, 143, 157–58, 190–92, *191*
Maximian (e) 11, *11*, 24, 34, 37, 50, 67, *67*, 68–69, 72, 154–58, 190–92, *190*
Maximinus Daia (e) 35, 67, 158, 191, *191*
Maximinus Thrax (e) 8, 55, 84, 107–8, 187, *187*
Media 33
Mediterranean 6, 12, 14, 26, 32, 47, 118, 129, 137, 165, 172, 180
Mesiche, battle of (AD 244) 132
Mesopotamia 20–21, 23, 73, 112–15, 122–24, 130–31, 170, 184, 186, 188, 192–93; province 23, 115, 131, 188, 192–93
Messalina, Valeria 110–11, *110*
Milan 66, 68–69, 72, 155, 158, 178–79, 190–91, 194
Miletus 32
military tribune 57, 58, 102, 183–84, 192–93
Milvian Bridge, battle of (AD 312) 106, 158, *158*, 191–92
Minerva (g) 84
Misenum 32, 64, 128, 182
Modena, battle of (43 BC) 31
Moesia 23, 120, 188; Lower Moesia (province) 24; Upper Moesia (province) 188
Mucianus, Marcus Nonius Arrius 183
Munacius Plancus, Lucius 34
Mycenae 73
Mylae, battle of (36 BC) 32

Nabataeans 20, 122, 184
Naples 30, 64, 88, 116, 128
Narcissus (freedman) 109–11
Naulochus, battle of (36 BC) 32
Near East 18–19, 41, 50, 51, 113, 122–23, 129, 189, 192–93

Neoplatonism 169

Nero (e) 11, 16, 42, 44, 46, *49*,
56–57, 59, 60, 70, 72, 74–75, 84,
86–90, 93, 109–11, 112, 116, 122,
125, 141, 150, 169, 179, 182–83,
183; artistic performances of 8,
52, 81; education of 48–50; fall
of 51–54

Nerva (e) 8, 16, 20–21, 56, 58,
141, 184, *184*; adoption of
Trajan 60, 118

Nicaea, Council of 166, 192

Nicomedia 72, 155, 167, 190, 191;
Edict of 192

Nika Revolt 163

Nile 18, 73

Nisibis 122–23

Noricum (province) 108

Notitia Dignitatum 176

Numerian (e) 189–90

Numidia (North African
kingdom) 36; province 125, 187

Octavia (daughter of Claudius)
50, 183

Octavia (sister of Augustus) 33

Octavian *see* Augustus

Odaenathus, Septimius
115, 189

Odoacer 170, 181, 196–97

Olybrius (e) 181, 196, *196*, *196*

Oppian Hill 74, 143

Orestes (*magister militum*)
180–81, 196

orthodoxy 12, 165–66, 197

Ostia 56, 107, 111, 113, 147, 182

Otho (e) *53*, 54, *54*, 57–58, 106,
183, *183*

Ottomans 12

Ovid 48, 73–74

Pacatianus, (u) 132

paganism 25, 37, 123, 159–69,
193–94

Palace of Constantius I, Trier
72, *154*, 155, *178*

Palace of Diocletian, Split
72, 160

Palace of Galerius, Gamzigrad
72, 155, *155*

palaces 8, 10, 34, 56, 63, 68–69,
70–80, *72*, 81–82, 90, 94, 106,
108, 125, 139, 141, 144, 153, 155,
157, 160, 163–65, 170, 178–79,
195; as organization 102–4,
109–10, 197

Palatine Hill 70, 72, 73–79, 81,

90, 94, *97*, 108, 110, 138, 141,
142, 165, 187

Palestine 19–20, 116, 183

Pallas (freedman) 109–10

Pandateria (island) 41

Pannonia 21, 40, 120, 125, 158,
180, 182, 188–89, 192, 193, 194;
Lower Pannonia (province)
184, 188; Upper Pannonia
(province) 186

Pantheon *143*

Papinianus, Aemilius 105

Papyrius Dionysius, Marcus
Aurelius (*praefectus annonae*)
148

Parthia, Parthians 20, 23, 30,
32–33, 41, 51, 84, 118, 122–25, 131,
142, 184–86; defeated by
Ardashir 22, 187

Parthian Wars: of Caesar 30; of
Nero 51; of Caracalla 186; of
Lucius Verus 125, 185; of Mark
Antony 32–33; of Septimius
Severus 131, 142, 186; of Trajan
84, 122–24, 184

pater familias 60, 108

pater patriae 26, 92

patria potestas 60

patrimonium Caesaris 98, 102–3

patrocinium, patronage 30,
81, 110

Paul (Apostle) 93, 165, 166

Pax Augusta 36

Persia, Persians 22–23, 25, 46, 115,
117, 131–33, 162, 168–69, 170,
187–89, 190–91, 192–94, 197

Persian Wars: of Carus 189; of
Galerius 191; of Gordian III
188; of Julian 168–69, 170, 193;
of Severus Alexander 187; of
Valerian 23, 50, 115, 131, 133,
188–89

Pertinax (e) 58, 106, 151,
185–86, *185*

Perugia 32

Perusian War 32

Pescennius Niger, Gaius (u)
50, 58, 186

Peter (Apostle) 166

Petronius (writer) 88–89

Petronius Maximus (e) 8,
195–96, *195*

philhellenism 11

Philip the Arab (e) 22, 44,
132–33, *133*, 154, 188

Philippi, battle of (42 BC)
31–32, 140

Phoenicia 33

Piso, Gaius Calpurnius (senator
and plotter against Nero)
51, 183

Piso, Gnaeus Calpurnius
(senator) 62

Piso, Lucius Calpurnius (heir
of Galba) 53–54, 183

plebeian tribune 35, 56–57, 59,
102, 182

plebs 44, 51, 56, 59, 64–65, 69

plebs frumentaria 146

Pliny the Younger 60, 102–4,
109, 184

Plotina, Pompeia 114

Plutarch 127

Pollentia, battle of (AD 402) 179

Polybius (freedman) 109

Pompeii 70, 86, 89, 93

Pompey, Gnaeus 32, 37, 122,
127, 137

Pompey, Sextus 32–33

pontifex maximus 34–35, 166, 185

Pontus and Bithynia (province)
102, 166

Poppaea 112

Posides (freedman) 109

Postumus 24, 50, 114, 132, 188

praefectus annonae 102–3, 107,
147–48

praefectus sacri cubiculi 102–3

praefectus urbi, urban prefect
102–3, 144, 163, 188

praefectus vehiculorum
102–3, 107

praefectus vigilum 102–3, 107

praetor 56–57, 94, 102, 108–9,
184, 186

Praetorian Guard 49, 53–54,
64–65, 105–6, *106*, 111, 128, 148,
157, 182, 186–87, 192

praetorian prefect 49, 56, 64, 94,
102–3, 105–7, 114, 130–132, 153,
182–191, 195, 197

princeps 6, 12, 35, 38, 40, 57, 121,
124, 140, 145, 165

principate 6, 8, 12, 16–17, 19, 34,
40–43, 51, 54–55, 57, 67, 80–81,
98, 125, 129, 133, 153, 165

Priscus Attalus (u) 50

Priscus (brother of Philip the
Arab) 133

Probus (consul) 170

Probus (e) 62, 189, *189*, 191

proconsul 35, 57, 59, 95, 103, 183,
185, 187

Procopius (historian) 73, 179

Procopius, (u) 50, 172, 194

procurator 96, 101, 102–3, 107, 112

propraetor 102–3

proscriptions 31

provinces 17, 24–25, 33, 35–37,
44, 59, 84, 93, 100, 102–3, 105,
107, 115–17, 118, 120, 122–23,
133, 140, 169

Ptolemaic dynasty 33

Ptolemy I 32

Pulcheria 114, 197

Punic 22, 44, 113

Punic Wars 12, 36

Pupienus (e) 106, 187

Quadi 21, 48, 100, 142, 185, 193

quaestor 56–59, 102–3, 107, 109,
184–85

quaestor sacri palatii 102–3

Quintillus (e) 189

Raetia (province) 23–24, 103,
188–89, 193

Ravenna 72, 179, 191, 195–96

recusatio imperii 61–63

religion 11, 12, 19, 25, 36–37, 39,
69, 80, 84, 102, 121, 127, 144, 148,
150, 159–69, 191–93, 196

Remus 126, 134

Res Gestae 10, 26, 28, 100, 138

Res Gestae Divi Saporis 131

res privatae 98, 102–3

Rhine 20, 23, 36, 52, 106, 121,
162, 182, 184, 187–90, 192–93

Rhodes 41, 182

Ricimer (*magister militum*)
181, 196

Roman army 25, 35, 44, 55, 60,
69, 97–98, 106; and career 8,
17, 58, 180; emperor as
commander of 11, 118–33, 182

Roman empire 6, 10, 12–25,
31–34, 111–12, 115, 117, 120,
131, 147, 150, 153, 157, 165, 167,
181, 187, 197

Roman Forum 19, 54, 76, 91,
94, 97, *97*, 127, 131, *135*, 137, *139*,
141–43

Roman republic 12, 26, 28–29,
32, 34, 36, 40, 42, 52, 56–57, 60,
81, 94, 97, 101, 105, 118, 121, 124,
127, 137, 144, 146, 148, 176

romanization 18

Rome, city of 10, 29–30, 32–33,
37–38, 41, 46–47, 51–54, 59,
63–69, 72, 81, 83–84, 86, 93, 108,
111, 114–15, 121, 124, 132, 134–53,

144, 157, 160, 167, 182–96; decline of importance 51, 68, 154; fires 51, 70; sacked by Alaric 179–80, 195; supply of 98–99, 102, 105, 107, 146–48
Romulus 126, 134, 140
Romulus Augustulus (e) 6, 8, 17, 170, 180–81, *181*, 196, 197
Rufinus, Marcus Gnaeus Licinius 107–8
Rufus, Lucius Verginius 52
Rusticus, Marcus Junius 48

Sabinus, Julianus 190
Saecular Games 36, 40, 112, 182
Sallust 48
Salona 190, 196
salutatio 76, 81–82
Sardinia et Corsica (province) 32, 116, 191, 196
Sarmatians 23, *23*, 129, 185, 187, 189, 191–93
Sarmizegetusa 120
Sasanian dynasty 22–23, 131–32, 187, 197
Saturninus, Lucius Antonius 50
School Edict 168
Scipio Aemilianus, Publius Cornelius 60
Scipio Africanus, Publius Cornelius 60
Sejanus, Lucius Aelius 105–6, *105*, 182
Senate, senators 6, 9–10, 12, 17, 19, 22, 26, 28–35, 37–38, 40, 42–43, 48–69, *56*, 81, 94, 98, 99–100, 106–11, 112, 114, 118, 124, 127, 139, 144, 153, 162–63, 165, 168, 182–90, 192, 194–96; decline 129–33; as the emperor's guests 85–92; as officials 101–5; senatorial careers 56–58
Senate House, Curia Julia 19, 91, *91*, *139*, 162, 194
Seneca, Lucius Annaeus 46–51, *51*, 82, 92, 147, 183
Septimius Geta, Publius 186
Septimius Severus (e) 8–9, 11, *13*, 16, *16*, 22, 37, 44, 50, 55, 58, 60, 70, 76, 80–81, 105–6, 112–13, 116, 118, 123–24, 129–31, 142, 153, 186, *186*
Severan dynasty 16–17, 21–22, 43, 44, 46, 58, 107, 113, 125, 144, 187
Severus (e) 67, 157–58, 191

Severus Alexander (e) 51–52, 55, 60, 105, 187, *187*
shadow emperors 8, 21, 46, 178–81, 195–96
Shapur I (Persian king) 22, 131–32, *132*
Shapur II (Persian king) 192
Sicily (province) 32, 186, 191, 196
Silius, Gaius 111
Singara 122
Sirmium 185, 189, 192
slaves 57, 61, 86, 100, 108–9, 116, 127, 145
Sodales Augustales 37
soldier emperors 8, 21, 46, 58, 131–33, 142, 187–90
Sol Invictus (g) 37, 158–60, *159*, 165
Spain 18, 24, 36, 52, 59, 118, 176, 180, 183–84, 188, 192, 194–97
Split 72, 160, 190, 196
Statius 76, 78
Stilicho (*magister militum*) 177, 179–80, *180*, 195
Stoa, Stoicism 22, 48–49, 54, 185
Strasbourg, battle of (AD 357) 167
Suetonius 28, 57, 61–63, 65, 74, 80–87, 95, 108–10, 145
Syria 23, 33, 37, 50, 58–59, 96, 102, 113, 114–15, 117, 118, 122, 130, 132, 155, 165, 184, 186, 188, 190, 194

Tacitus (e) 114, 117, 189
Tacitus (historian) 10, 36, 42, 48, 51, 52, 61–62, 63, 68, 83, 110–11, 122, 133, 145
Tarquinius Superbus 28
Tarraconensis (province) 52, 183
Tellus 39
temples: of Antoninus Pius and Faustina *135*, 142, *142*; of Apollo 94, *95*, 138; of Elagabalus 132; of Janus 36; of Jupiter Capitolinus 127, 138, 160; of Magna Mater 74; of Mars Ultor 140, *140*; of Saturn 97, *97*, *139*; of Vespasian *97*; of Zeus Hypsistos 96
Tetrarchs, Tetrarchy 8, 11, 16, 21, 24–25, 46, 60, 66, 67, *67*, 133, 154–55, 157, 159, 160, 165, 190–92
Tetricus 114
Teutoburg Forest, battle of (AD 9) 17, 28, 131
Thapsus, battle of (46 BC) 37
Theatre of Marcellus 138, *138*

Theatre of Pompey 28, 137, 150
Themistius 176
Theodosius I the Great (e) 8, 17, 21, 25, 46, 50, 60, *71*, 72, 125, 161, 166–67, *167*, 170, 176–78, 179, 193, *194*, 195, 197
Theodosius II (e) 94, 114, 197, *197*
Theodosius, Flavius the Elder 176
Thervingi 170, 172–73, 178
Thessaloniki 72, 155, 194
Thrace (province) 36, 57, 117, 159, 172, 187, 189, 191, 193, 194, 197
Tiber 134, 147, 191
Tiberius (e) 4, 11, 16–17, 34, 36, 39, 42, *42*, 57, 60–64, 70, 72, 74, 82, 105–6, 118, 125, 145, 182, *182*; as emperor-in-waiting 40–41
Tiberius Claudius Nero (first husband of Livia) 17, 40
Tiberius Gemellus 4, 64
Tigris 20, 122–23
Timesitheus, Gaius Furius 105, 106, 188
Titus (e) 9, 37, 46, 59, *59*, 70, 74, 118, 125, 141, 143, 145–46, 150, 183–84, *184*; and First Jewish Revolt 19, 127
toga virilis 41, 59
Trajan (e) 9, 20, 23, 37, 44, 49, 60, 84, 85, 102, 104, 109, 112, 117, *119*, 128, *128*, 141–42, 143, 147, 169, 184, *184*; military expertise of 58, 118–21; death of 114; wars of 120–24
Trajan's Column 23, 120, 121, *121*, 128, *128*, 141, 142
Trajanus, Marcus Ulpius 118
travel 70, 95, 112, 115–17, 134, 184
treasury *see* finances
Trebonianus Gallus (e) 188, *188*
tria nomina 60
tribunicia potestas 35, 40, 59, 92, 182
triclinium 76, 78, 86
Trier 72, 155, 157, 160, 177–78, 192
Trimalchio 88–89
triumphal procession 16, 19, 25, 35, 40, 57, 68, 109, 122, 124, 125, 127, *127*, 151, 184, 188
Triumvirate, Second 26, 31–34, 182
Tyrrhenian Sea 32

Ulpia Severina 114, 189

urban prefect *see* praefectus urbi
usurpation, usurpers 8, 12, 24, 36, 44, 50–55, 57–58, 62–63, 67, 106, 113, 115, 125, 132–33, 141, 153, 158, 162, 172, 176–77, 183–84, 186–88, 193–95

Vaballathus 115, 189
Valens (e) 25, 35, 50, 166, *173*, 193, *193*, 194; and Adrianople 170–76
Valentinian I (e) 8, 21, 35, 46, 172–73, *173*, 193–94, *193*
Valentinian II (e) 117, 176–77, *177*, 194, *194*
Valentinian III (e) 180, 195, *195*, 196
Valerian (e) 22, 24, 34, 50, 115, 117, 131, *132*, 133, 188, 189
Vandals 24, 172, 177, 189, 195, 196
Varus (dinner party guest) 92
Varus, Publius Quinctilius 17, 131, 182
Veii 134
Venice 11, 67, 164
Verona, battles of: (AD 249) 188; (AD 403) 179
Vespasian (e) 6, 8, 9, 11, *11*, 19, 37, 46, 55, 56–59, 62, 68–69, 74–75, 80–81, 85, 97, 117, 118, 125, 129, 141, 143, 145–46, 183, *183*, 184; and crisis of AD 69 43, 53–55
Vesuvius 70, 102, 184
veterans 26, 30, 32, 44, 98, 184
Via Flaminia 99
Via Sacra 127
Victoria 114
Villa Hadriana *see* Hadrian's Villa
Villa Jovis 63, *63*, 72
Vindex, Gaius Julius 52
Virgil 48
virtus 110, 151–53, 179
Visigoths 50, 181, 195–96
Vitellius (e) 53–54, *53*, 57, 58, 68, 83, *83*, 106, 183

war 9, 24, 40, 56, 70, 80, 95, 98, 112, 118–33, 137, 140, 151; *see also* civil war, Dacian Wars, Jewish Revolt, Parthian Wars, Persian Wars

Xenophon 46, 49

York 157, 186, 191–92

Zeno (e) 197
Zenobia 50, 110, 115, 189